Teaching Controversy

Teaching Controversy

Lisa Jakubowski
and Livy Visano

WITH A FOREWORD BY CLAUDIO DURAN

FERNWOOD PUBLISHING • HALIFAX

All royalties from this book shall be donated to First Nations Projects proposed by our contributors.

Editing: Robert Clarke
Cover art: Ashley Aleta Kewayosh
Design and production: Beverley Rach
Printed and bound in Canada by: Hignell Printing Limited

A publication of: Fernwood Publishing
Box 9409, Station A
Halifax, Nova Scotia, B3K 5S3
www.fernwoodbooks.ca

Fernwood Publishing Company Limited gratefully acknowledges the financial support of the Department of Canadian Heritage, the Nova Scotia Department of Tourism and Culture and the Canada Council for the Arts for our publishing program.

Le Conseil des Arts | The Canada Council
du Canada | for the Arts

NOVA SCOTIA
Tourism and Culture

National Library of Canada Cataloguing in Publication Data

Jakubowski, Lisa Marie, 1965-
    Teaching controversy

ISBN 1-55266-074-5

1. Critical pedagogy. 2. Discrimination in education.
3. Teaching—Social aspects. I. Visano, L. A. II. Title.

LC191.J34 2002   370.11'5   C2001-904025-3

Contents

For our parents,
Anne and Stefan Jakubowski
and
Maria and Gino Visano
whose "teachings" continue to guide and inspire us

Foreword
Critical Pedagogy as Commitment

by Claudio Duran

Education, thus, becomes a practice of freedom rather than domination.... Teachers committed to critical pedagogy recognize the importance of a continuing consultation with all those engaged in the learning process throughout all of its phases. This practice includes a recognition, on the part of educators, that the subjectivity of the student, articulated through experience, is an equally essential component of learning. —from *Teaching Controversy*

In an important way this book is written as the beginning of a long pedagogical controversy. Lisa Jakubowski and Livy Visano delve deeply into the nature of teaching as an inherent aspect of "emancipatory pedagogy," and the very reading of the book will itself necessarily lead to protracted controversy in many and varied respects—particularly because the authors are proposing to us that first of all we become teachers of controversial topics and related methodologies. Their fundamental message is that teaching cannot be separated from the profound concerns of present-day society, deeply fraught as it is by hierarchies and structures of domination of all kinds.

Inevitably, in reading the book readers will be confronted with their own conceptions and perspectives on teaching, and their perspectives especially will not always coincide with those of the authors—an aspect of the experience that needs to be appreciated as an essential issue. *Teaching Controversy* will no doubt become a source of profound and potent ideas that readers will be left to grapple with for a long time.

In the following pages the authors (and their collaborators) move freely from exploring experiential situations and ideas into theorizing about teaching and pedagogy, including especially the many features that they consider essential to a critical pedagogy. Of particular significance is the dialogue between the authors included in chapter 1. The book then goes through a number of critical and crucial cases drawn from controversial issues in society, as well as discussions of more specific academic topics such as approaches to, and methodologies and contents of, teaching. After examining pedagogical matters as related to study in academic institutions, Jakubowski and Visano end by proposing an approach for radical institutional changes in universities. Some of the controversies they deal with involve racial and cultural dominations. Chapter 3 in particular includes a moving study of First Nations peoples' experiences and their potential contributions to academic settings: three First Nations members, Ursula Elijah, John Elijah and Julie George, provide extensive elaborations of their experiences.

Critical pedagogy, as described here, is essentially controversial, because it attempts to critically examine and challenge—indeed, change—traditional ways of being and thinking that have become ossified in academic institutions. These institutions are governed by an inertia that works to legitimize hierarchies and dominations of many kinds. There seems to be a profound need in many human societies to establish dominant groups that are related to a dominant social class or race, to a specific gender, or to sexual orientation, body ability, and psychological disposition—and so on. Yet another element is the domination of human beings over nature, which the examination of First Nations peoples' cosmology in chapter 3 makes clear.

The general sense of hierarchical determinations relates to the traditional pedagogical conception according to which teachers are dominant over students. Therefore, one of the first elements of critical pedagogy is a sort of Copernican revolution by way of which students are invested with a sense of equality with the teacher, which leads to a sharing of pedagogical power. This power is related to learning, because teaching is about learning. Both teacher and students are related to each other for they are both learning together. This is why the relation can be described in terms of friendship—not the kind that takes place in "buddy" relations, but the kind that Socrates talks about in Plato's dialogues: learning is a process that happens when people are engaged both in understanding issues and in an exchange in which they feel close to each other. Furthermore, friendship involves trust and the negotiation of a "safe zone" that allows learning to develop. Critical pedagogy is necessarily participatory. All of this is a practice that implies considerable emotional as well as intellectual involvement and time. The issues to be examined, after all, concern controversial social situations that are most probably going to make students and teacher feel uncomfortable. Critical pedagogues challenge the ossified and deeply entrenched dominant ideas and practices, and these challenges necessarily involve a high level of risk-taking. Thus, trust becomes a necessity. Furthermore, an inherent aspect of change is involved, and not only in the classroom setting: critical pedagogues also connect themselves to community settings. Thus the important element of social and political activism needs also to be considered. Critical pedagogy, then, deals with a profound complexity that requires a sense of balance between all the pressures coming from the relations between teachers and students in their social and psychological realities, and also from the relations between learners and the academic institutional settings. One of these relations pertains to the important issue of grading. No matter how successful the pedagogical interactions become, in the last analysis the teacher retains a significant amount of power in the inevitable process of grading.

The sense of critical pedagogy related here contains a new and far-reaching idea stemming from the authors' experience in working with First Nations people. In chapter 3, Julie George explains that one aspect of First Nations peoples' way of interacting with each other is what she calls the principle or ethic of "non-interference." This principle relates to several key challenges in human interaction, including, first of all, no power differentials, no reference to titles or positions, and respect for all voices in an interaction. Moreover, no member of the group is to expect that his or her version of events is superior to that of another. The principle means also that there ought to be no interferences in the business of another and, finally, that each and every individual takes part in the decision-making process and no opinion is ignored. The principle or ethic of non-interference can make a significant contribution to the pedagogical process, and the adaptation of this principle to the university setting is a fundamental challenge. Taking a non-interference approach implies at least two difficulties. One is that academic practices inevitably involve controversy and argumentation, and the other relates to the grading process: in both cases evaluative judgements seem to be unavoidable.

In what follows I will "react" to the book as a teacher: that is, I will refer particularly to those topics and issues I can relate to, within my pedagogical experience in the classroom and other academic forums. Indeed, reading the book has given me an occasion to reflect upon my teaching at a time when I find myself closer to retirement and in need of reassessing the meaning of teaching, especially in view of the challenges facing universities today. Two of those challenges are increased class sizes and technologically enhanced learning.

The first thing I should mention here is that I would not define myself as a critical pedagogue in a strict sense. However, when I read about critical pedagogy or interact with practitioners in the field, I recognize a number of important common factors. My teaching has developed out of the influences of the Socratic dialogue, John Dewey, Herbert Read, A.S. Neill and psychoanalysis. I cannot reconstitute here thirty-four years of university teaching, since I began as a teaching assistant in the Department of Philosophy at Universidad de Chile in 1964. In retrospect I see it as a long, difficult and rewarding process. Now, reading about the committed approaches to teaching taken by Lisa Jakubowski and Livy Visano reminds me of my most cherished value: "to work with the students and for the students" has been my motto of university teaching. This commitment is crossed by many, varied and also contradictory elements that become the medium in which the pedagogical processes develop. These are open-ended, unpredictable and in permanent flux. Sometimes they become fascinating, but they could have a tendency as well to be depressive and shocking, especially when we realize that our levels of awareness sometimes fail us when we try to understand the depth of students' responses in the different settings. A teacher is just an ordinary human being trying to do a job that involves learning. In a true pedagogical process the teacher is also learning alongside the students. At the same time a teacher is somebody with a personal history, gender, social class, race, culture, sexual orientation, psychological and temperamental dispositions, physical structure and ideology. And of course the teacher has a specific area of expertise. For some, it may be possible to conceive of teaching as merely a job. Nevertheless, this would not be in line with the factor of commitment: committed teaching is an existential position in life, for learning is at the very basis of life. But the many and varied positions of a teacher will definitely influence her or his learning and teaching. The same is the case for students. Therefore, in the pedagogical setting we can appreciate encounters of immense complexity, in which many and different ways of being interact with and influence each other. In this sense learning becomes an issue that cannot follow a predictable path: it is the expression of all those individuals in their multiple interactions. As the authors point out in chapter 4, "Teaching is a set of negotiated interpretations."

Thus it should be clear as to why I was interested in writing a foreword for a book on teaching controversy. I believe that controversy is the essence of teaching because it is the essence of life. It is possible to define controversy in specific ways, as indeed Livy Visano and Lisa Jakubowski do in this book. Clearly they want to refer to a commitment to deal with specified structures of domination, as they appear in class, race and cultural domination. The authors project as well a larger perspective to include most structures of domination, as they can be perceived at the beginning of the twenty-first century. In their view teaching should address all of these structures. Still, since human beings cannot know and do everything, a teacher might be aware of the issues in general but would necessarily have to select one or possibly two areas in which to build expertise. In any case, as the book demonstrates (particularly in chapter 3), involvement in only one of these areas can become a life-long process.

At times it seems to me that the authors almost try to go beyond the boundaries of what is humanly possible. Perhaps, this is explained by their deep and passionate involvement with controversy, in the way they understand it. Like them, I also believe that controversy is inherent in nearly everything we human beings do. It may be the case that specific controversial subjects are especially difficult to deal with in the pedagogical setting, but in my experience almost every subject that I have dealt with since I started teaching has been controversial. Some of my students have told me that I make anything that I teach controversial, and this goes back to the Socratic dialogue that becomes very soon the site not only of profound controversy but also of enormous political risk. Socrates starts, for example, by posing a question about justice and finds out at some stage that he is at risk of being killed precisely for entering the domain of trying to define the way of a just life.

I believe that controversy should not only take place in the area of teaching the social sciences and similar subjects, but also should pertain to mathematics and the natural sciences. These other disciplines may seem subjects of less controversy than the social sciences, but inherently they involve all sorts of issues, epistemological as well as socio-political and cultural. The authors refer in the last chapter to European logocentrism, and, in all fairness to learning, how European culture has defined science should become a potent area for profound debate. I am not advocating the demise of logic and European understandings of knowledge, but just that their assumptions should be the subject of controversy. In this sense reading chapter 3 of the book, about First Nations peoples' cosmology, is a humbling experience in learning.

Chapter 5 presents several significant, creative and potentially groundbreaking ideas for a deep and systematic change in how a university deals with structures of domination. The authors move from the experiential discussion of cases characteristic of earlier chapters to the elaboration of abstract theory on teaching controversy. This elaboration, though important, has the potential risk of moving away from actual teaching conditions and also of becoming overly idealistic. I believe that, although a certain degree of theorizing is important, teaching must always remain close to pedagogical experiences. Given the authors' ideas on teaching, however, the issue is to be prepared for controversy. The ideas presented in chapter 5 are themselves a subject of difficult controversy, particularly in the teaching situation, in which teachers must be prepared for intense discussion with students. Jakubowski and Visano are aware of this difficulty and most certainly would welcome such discussion. A likely scenario is one in which students will argue against a number of ideas. Also, in the event that such ideas were put into practice by a university or faculty or college, the teachers involved should expect a good deal of debate. In essence, we must be prepared for a high degree of argumentative interaction in any theorizing about teaching.

A final caution has to do with the risk of idealism. I believe that any major proposal for deep change requires passion, commitment and a significant degree of idealism. But the risk is to carry out this proposal in such a way that we lose sight of the everydayness of students (and people in general). Take, for instance, the criticisms found in the book that centre on the current concern that students have about getting jobs in a "market" economy. An excessive amount of idealism can lead teachers to forget that "a job" is a most important element in life—and critically involved teachers must also be concerned with jobs, because, after all, if they do not have a job they cannot become engaged in critical pedagogy. Finding an academic position today is extremely difficult, and this is especially the case in areas that seem closer to critical pedagogy. Even in Marxist theory, the "socialist society stage" is still a "market" society. Then, too, a significant number of students will probably not have a negative perception of liberal democratic capitalism, and most likely they will have a very negative perception of Soviet-style socialism (although not so much of Marxist theory itself). All this, if I am right, indicates the reality of a complex pedagogical situation.

The complexity is made considerably more difficult if we try to trace the potential relations that can be found in the pedagogical experience with regards to structures of domination. Who is the teacher and who are the students? Teachers and students are members of different groups across structures of domination—structures including class, gender, race, body ability and sexual orientation and, I would like to stress as well, human domination over nature and logical domination over intuition, emotion and physicality. Potentially a great number of combinations exist. Sensitive teachers will need to assess this complexity as much as possible in order to be fair to all students in their classes, and to themselves—all of which may seem a titanic task. And yet they must also try to be open to learn more about these elements. In my own case, I was originally a South American academic, and for many years after I started teaching in Canada some students would overtly or covertly criticize my English when I engaged them in discussions of controversial issues. I believe that a committed teacher must always keep in mind that students are also ordinary human beings. This implies that teachers should deal fairly with students, including cases in which the teachers themselves might feel hurt, many times rightly so.

I would add to these thoughts one further note, on psychoanalytic influences on teaching. The authors discuss this aspect of the pedagogical experience in depth when they examine "reaching in" or the "intrapsychic" in chapter 4. This is certainly a difficult and challenging area, and I will only touch on one of the main issues involved. In the same sense in which the analyst relates to the analysand as somebody who must be deeply "heard" without interference from the analyst's own dispositions, in that same sense the teacher must "hear" the students and guide them in doing the same with other participants in the pedagogical process. Many times, of course, the students help the teacher do so. In this sense, a fine connection can be made with the First Nations peoples' principle or ethic of non-interference as presented by Julie George in Lisa Jakubowski and Livy Visano's thought-provoking book on teaching controversy.

Claudio Duran
Canadian Professor of the Year, 1993
Atkinson College, York University

Acknowledgements

Teaching Controversy represents part of a wider pedagogical vision that we have shared for many years. For us, the journey to this point has been long, exciting and often challenging. During these years we have grappled to better understand the dynamics of teacher-student relationships and how these relationships impact on the effectiveness of teaching and learning; and our own "teacher-student" relationship has evolved into a close collegial friendship. It is the depth and strength of this treasured friendship, along with our respect and support for one another, that sustained this project during moments of struggle.

To begin, we want to thank Errol Sharpe, Beverley Rach, Brenda Conroy and the rest of the Fernwood "family" for so enthusiastically endorsing this project. We truly appreciate Fernwood's professionalism and courageous commitment to critical inquiry. Additionally, we want to express our gratitude to our editor, Robert Clarke, for the exceptional care and concern he has shown while editing *Teaching Controversy*. Robert's methodical and painstaking attention to detail challenged us to make this "final product" stronger.

Many people have supported and facilitated the advancement of this project throughout its various phases. We are especially grateful to our contributors, Claudio Duran, Ursula Elijah, John Elijah, Julie George and Ashley Aleta Kewayosh, who were all extremely generous in sharing their thoughtful and sensitive portrayals of controversy.

We also want to acknowledge the many students we have taught over the years. Their enthusiasm and intellectual curiosity continue to inspire us to strive towards new and more progressive pedagogical plateaus. These students, while far too many to list individually, have been particularly instrumental in helping us to unravel the strengths and weaknesses of the various teaching techniques and strategies discussed herein. Thank you for your patience, commitment and participation in our various projects.

To the faculty, staff and Ursuline Sisters of Brescia University College, and to our York University colleagues, we express our sincere appreciation for fostering healthy and supportive intellectual environments in which we could pursue our vision. Finally, we are grateful to Brescia University College for providing the administrative resources necessary to complete much of our work on this manuscript.

On a more personal note, I (Lisa) want to acknowledge the immeasurable support that only true friends and family can provide. I am especially grateful to Patrick and Terri Burman, Vita Rosa Calogero, Jason Clairmonte, Carol Duncan, Vanessa Eneas, Dominique Lepicq, Theresa Mahoney, Mary-Jo Nadeau, Tahirih Naylor, Dorothy Neilsen, Dwaine Plaza, Susan and Basil Stefura and Jumana Zabian: all of them, in their own unique ways, embody friendship in its most genuine sense. These individuals served as constant sources of encouragement and strength, both intellectually and emotionally. To my family I remain eternally indebted, for always "being there," patiently and lovingly whenever I need you. I would not be where I am today without you. It is your shared wisdom and the love and support you so selflessly give that sustains me. Finally, an extra-special thank you to Stefanie Christine and Duncan Josef—my precious niece and nephew. You are growing up so quickly and learning so much!!! As you each embark on your own educational journey, you inspire me to strive to be the very best teacher I can be.

From beginning to end, this lengthy but never solitary project would never have been possible without the assistance of many people to whom I (Livy) remain deeply indebted. I am grateful to Lisa Jakubowski for her commitment to this collaborative project, always giving so generously of her time and energy; her dedication ensured its fruition. My appreciation of controversy owes much to those courageous many who have, by personal example or in their writings, guided my thoughts into necessary but uncomfortable inquiries. These teachers include Jere Bosna, Dick Butcher, Wesley Crichlow, John Elijah, Eilert Frerichs, Harry Glasbeek, Vern Harper, Wilson Head, John Lee, Dennis Magill, Ruth Morris, Mat Petranovich, Raghu Raman, Charlie Roach, Pedro Sanchez, Dorothy Smith, Ron Trojcak, John Visano and Mary Whalen. A special thank you to Brenda for her judgement, inspiration, insights and encouragement; her faith has always been a constant source of strength. To Anthony for his patience and challenging spirit, I extend my gratitude and love.

1

Teaching Controversy
A Challenge to Cultural Hegemony

The first problem for all of us is not to learn but to unlearn.
—Gloria Steinem, 1971

As professors of sociology, we are constantly challenged to devise inclusive and creative pedagogical strategies for addressing controversy in our classrooms. Because the subject matter itself consists of exploring a range of social relationships and interactions and tends, almost by necessity, to generate a clash of viewpoints, the discussions that arise can become heated and contentious, and the learning environments divisive and uncomfortable. To avoid this discomfort students often tend to "resist" or withdraw from controversial course content. For instance, because of the power differentials that traditionally exist between student and teacher, students often assume that they will suffer negative repercussions if their remarks publicly challenge the teacher's opinion or information (Lusk and Weinberg 1994: 301–302). Or, after many long years of contact with traditional forms of schooling, students may well find it difficult to give voice to their different experiences and participate fully in the exploration of the subject under discussion.

In this context, to effectively manage classroom dynamics and maximize learning, teachers must be able both to anticipate which subject matter will be controversial and to be open to unconventional methods of integrating controversy into teaching and learning. But while teachers may be committed to creative pedagogical approaches, we often hesitate to put theory into practice because of the associated cultural and political risks. For one thing, we risk being characterized as incompetent if our teaching strategies are unsuccessful. We also risk being marginalized by a more traditional academic culture that views a "critically responsive" approach as "subversive" (Brookfield 1995: 232–35).

Our aim in the following pages is to present a broad alternative, action-oriented pedagogical approach to teaching controversy. In the tradition of the renowned critical pedagogue Paulo Freire, we contend that education is a lifelong process for both teacher and student. Education involves a constant unveiling of reality that, wherever possible, links classroom to community. In our pedagogical philosophy we stress that there is no one method that is consistently successful in the teaching of controversial material. The approach adopted will vary according to the subject matter, the context, and the level and composition of the class. However, certain concepts can be used to create a conceptual framework in which virtually any method or approach might be grounded: specifically, collective responsibility, dialogue and intersubjectivity, the Gramscian (1971) "intellectual" and the dialectic. Crucial to the success of this strategy is a reduction of the power differential between teacher and student and a recognition that all those involved in teaching and learning are equal participants with different roles to play. To make our pedagogical strategy or framework concrete, we draw our examples of teaching and learning about "difference" from both classroom and community settings.

THE CHALLENGE OF CONTROVERSY

In taking up our approach, we realize that readers themselves may well find at least two things to be controversial: our pedagogical philosophy and its associated methods; and the course content cited, which, in a general sense, explores the power and politics of various types of difference and marginality.

Teaching itself invites the process of experiencing the connections between oneself and the "other." Typically, all teaching is a challenge, but teaching controversy involves a greater degree of challenge. It represents, first of all, a commitment to critical pedagogy. For us, the term "teaching controversy" signifies a method of teaching and learning that involves both content and process, in which the process embodies pedagogical philosophies and methods that interact with course content. It means getting students to look at what assumptions they are bringing to a discussion, and at where these seemingly fixed assumptions are coming from—leading them to recognize their own biases and, possibly, the origins of those biases. Ideally, it means encouraging them to get out of the frames they have been using and perhaps thinking more unconventional thoughts.

Teaching controversy is also about expressions of power and cultural control. Teachers run the risk of being set apart and relegated to the "margins" whenever they question specific canons of the discipline. While certain types of differences are permitted, more radical or critical pedagogies are devalued because they are not easily linked to the social organization of conformity—control. Control represents the institutional or patterned responses to the "differences" that are designated as threatening.

Why are controversial forms of teaching characterized as threatening?

Perhaps because, unlike many conventional strategies, these approaches are designed to question, rather than reinforce, the moral, political, social, economic and intellectual organization (or regulation) of society. Thus for teachers striving to put critical pedagogical strategies into action, the task of providing students with an inclusive curriculum in an open and critically responsive pedagogical environment can become quite overwhelming.

Customarily, institutions of learning—and in particular those in charge—produce courses designed to protect and promote particular perspectives, and the meanings of these courses are negotiated among relatively powerful participants. Courses that refuse to grapple with controversial topics affirm a certain privilege to particular cultural interpretations by supplying experiences from which inferences are quickly drawn. For example, traditional pedagogic canons reflect the primacy of a binary code. These canons present identities, relations and activities strictly as a matter of "either/or" dichotomies: right or wrong, teacher or student, black or white, guilty or innocent, moral or immoral, good or bad, sinner or saint, ugly or beautiful, sane or mad, sacred or secular, cerebral or visceral. This bifurcation misrepresents multilayered identities and phenomena.

Throughout the process of teaching and learning, all teachers and students need to be appreciated as both **acting subjects** and **subjected actors**. Both groups must be understood as active agents situated within wider, more complex and often overlooked social, political and cultural contexts. Both teachers and students are cultural subjects within discourses of power, and they are engaged in micropolitical (local) struggles shaped by more macrocultural influences (global).

From a methodological standpoint, teaching is a social enterprise that tells us just as much about the individual or organization engaged in the pedagogical process as it does about what is being taught. There is no one "true" picture of teaching. For its part, traditional teaching consists of a series of snapshots and captured moments that reflect the preferences of the photographer and the subject under focus. Some images will remain overexposed or underexposed; others are frequently blurred, discarded or never even developed because of the associated costs. Traditional models of teaching and learning continue to judge differences, colonize compliance and shackle the imagination. What is required is a more emancipatory and transformative pedagogy, grounded in struggle. Through a more critical education, we will uncover our assumptions, learn more about our own learning, self-consciously challenge the dominant ethos and develop oppositional currents.

Teaching Controversy offers an alternative to traditional pedagogical approaches. Resistance and struggle are central features in challenging the culture of domination. Accordingly, cultural criticism is essential in locating the marginalized "other" and in developing a liberating pedagogy. As bell hooks (1990: 8) elaborates: "Critical pedagogy (expressed in writing, teaching, and habits of being) is fundamentally linked to a concern with creating strategies that will enable colonized folks to decolonize their minds and actions, thereby promoting the insurrection of subjugated knowledge."

TEACHING CONTROVERSY IS THE CHALLENGE OF CRITICAL INQUIRIES

No one book can hope to do justice to the enormous breadth and depth of teaching. Here we advise readers to engage in an active reading, to take an interrogative stance and to be informed by history and political economy in looking afresh at the familiar. We ask readers to develop a "sociological imagination" (Mills 1978) that links personal troubles with public and social issues; to connect patterns in their lives with the events of society; to appreciate the intersection of biography and history when approaching phenomena deemed to be "controversial"; to delve into social sources, meanings and implications from various vantage points, using different analytic lenses; and to demystify, become more tentative in, their traditional appraisals of controversial or social issues. In other words, we invite students to partake more fully in their own learning.

What we want to encourage is a move beyond a rudimentary exposition of basic concepts to a formulation of fundamental questions about the nature of our own learning. This involves raising questions about relationships as well as bringing to the forefront questions that have long been too conveniently ignored. We ask readers to be courageous in deconstructing traditional texts by concentrating on the contradictions and closures inherent in conventional commentaries on teaching and learning. We encourage readers to document their experiences, consciousness, intentions and relational contexts, especially when examining the teaching and learning process. We further invite readers to situate themselves in the debates and struggles that characterize the study of pedagogy, to ground their perceptions, to avoid self-incarceration, to empower themselves conceptually and to engage in open debate.

Teaching Controversy is a political project that invites readers to position themselves ideologically and historically. It is but a modest attempt, a tentative guideline that seeks to introduce readers to the world of teaching controversy by providing an accessible, progressive and alternative framework.

TEACHING CONTROVERSY AS ACTION–ORIENTED

The pedagogical framework we detail in the following pages is "action-oriented." Action-oriented approaches abandon the practice of predefining or predetermining trends. The approaches replace assumptions of the self as a passive object determined by external forces with arguments about the active, subjective, and dialectical nature of teaching and learning. Teaching shapes and is shaped by the nature of learning.

An interpretive perspective views the process of teaching and learning as a **social accomplishment**, constructed and negotiated in ongoing interactions with various social agents. This perspective challenges the normative characterization of teaching as given and static. In brief, normative approaches consistently argue that social reality is constructed by external forces (beyond the control of the individual) that propel behaviour. Fixed sets of norms and values provide the boundaries by which teaching is defined. The interpretive model presents actors as creators of their environments. In this context, actors engage in a continual process of meaning construction in relation to their social realities. As agents, they actively and reflectively shape their experiences and the experiences of those with whom they routinely interact. Through interaction, individuals collectively define situations. Participants, therefore, negotiate and reconstitute meanings.

For the interpretive perspective, providing a definition of teaching is problematic because of the emergent character of teaching. Knowledge, existing in the interaction of subject and object, is equally tentative. The interpretive process examines how people control their own behaviour and that of others through the social construction of meaning and its application in interaction (Ericson 1975). This paradigm calls for a sociology characterized by what Weber (1969) called *verstehen*: an empathic and interpretive understanding of the subjective meanings that actors attach to social action. The only way to contextualize social action is to know the subjective meanings of actors. For their part, actors take into account the actions of others and are guided by these subjective meanings. Action incorporates all human behaviour to which the acting individuals attach subjective meanings. The individual actor, therefore, becomes the basic unit of analysis, and the process by which meanings are assigned becomes a focal point of inquiry.

Again, the social world is constructed by actors in complex interactions that occur in concrete situations. In turn, social interaction alters the interpretation of individual experiences and future behaviour. This emphasis on the construction of social action requires a concern for the situation. We cannot know why people do what they do unless we clearly understand what the situation means to them. The peculiarity of this theoretical approach claims that human beings interpret or define rather than merely react to each other's actions. These actions are based on their concomitant meanings. Thus, culture mediates human interaction. This mediation is equivalent to inserting a process of interpretation between stimulus and response in the case of human behaviour—that is, strategies of learning the meaning of one another's action. Mind, self and society are dynamic processes, continually created and re-created. Symbolic interactionism highlights the process-oriented and dynamic nature of definitions of self, others and situations. Humans act in a world that is interactively defined. Interaction, therefore, is the primary organizing unit of analysis.

TOWARDS "VISIONING" A CRITICALLY RESPONSIVE ALTERNATIVE

In teaching and learning, we can only begin to know ourselves and our locations by unmasking the privilege of conventional curriculum. Privilege is differentially distributed according to race, gender, class, sexuality and lifestyle-based differences. Traditionally, the discipline of education normalizes privilege, takes it for granted—especially the privilege of a white male (usually Anglocentric, certainly Eurocentric) heterosexist person. Overcoming this tendency calls for an ideological shift that is more inclusive of diversity. Teachers must come to terms with their respective privileges. They must come to terms with their privilege by "undoing" themselves, rendering their lives more knowable, more visible and more public. Because teachers' experiences of the world influence their approaches to teaching about that world, they must begin to redefine their "centres" as human beings and connect with other forms of consciousness. Understanding inequality requires making some tough choices. Positions of authority are sites of struggle, but successful struggles will result in greater pedagogical authenticity.

Authenticity means a commitment to resistance. As Trotman (1993) clarifies, authenticity moves beyond Western thinking to begin the work of constructing alternative social realities; authenticity encourages an awareness of the other, and envisions the self as a knowing being, a powerful person who possesses a clear understanding of his/her place in the world. In journeying towards pedagogical authenticity, we strive to dispute creatively, by means of a socially responsive teaching and learning process, normative conceptualizations of "difference." This work involves linking education and action to generate strategies for an equitable, sensitive and coherent set of immediate and long-term responses that enhance social justice (Visano 1994).

Our increasingly technological and skills-oriented culture often gives priority to employment skills over humanistic education. We believe that a critically responsive pedagogy (to be detailed in the next chapter) is a practical pedagogy, in that it provides specific concrete knowledge for living life dynamically and creatively. A more critical and emancipatory education provides us with roots—a historical consciousness. It allows for flexibility in thinking. At the societal level, a critically responsive pedagogy fosters an awareness of global issues and human suffering. This education provides analytical skills for understanding complex social conditions and human tragedies such as AIDS, famine, civil and political unrest, and war. On both the personal and interpersonal levels, critical education provides an understanding of the human condition, of the life cycle through which we all proceed, from birth to death. This education provides flexibility in making choices that help determine the shape of personal life, family life, social life and work life—that is, equipping us with the tools for self-analysis and other analyses. In sum, it provides a context in which we can come to a deeper understanding of the social world, of a world in which change can take place.

REFLECTING ON THE CONTROVERSIAL

As we embark on this pedagogical exploration, it seems appropriate to begin with some personal reflections. When we think about teaching controversy, endless ideas come to mind. In the first place, what issues are "controversial"? How should we approach controversial topics in the classroom? What kinds of risks do we take in dealing with themes and ideas that generate controversy? What kinds of resistance do we confront? How do we accommodate/negotiate the resistance that arises from different constituencies in the face of controversy, dispute and challenge? In trying to answer these questions we must remain cognizant of our responsibilities to those influenced by what we teach and how we teach it. Teaching about controversy demands accountability—both to our students in the classroom and to the related communities outside of the classroom.

When, as authors, we began to think about the most effective way of reflecting on our various experiences in relation to teaching controversy, we started out individually, highlighting experiences that each of us had in various contexts. It became increasingly clear to us that individual instances or reflections in no way captured the tensions, diversity or complexity of the experiences, or covered how we went about attempting to address controversy. As we sat and talked about the issues and experiences, we realized that "conversation"[1] was a necessary first step towards highlighting the complexities of controversy. The reproduction and analysis of our conversations became a necessary step en route to a more systematic articulation of the issues. In what follows we illustrate the main themes of our discussion using excerpts from our conversations (presented in italics).

UNRAVELLING THE COMPLEXITIES OF CONTROVERSY

1. The Context: Approaching Controversy; Negotiating Boundaries

One of the central issues we continue to face as teachers of controversy is how to invite participation in the classroom. We not only want students to be actively engaged in their learning but also want their participation to be "safe." To ensure this safety we have to create, negotiate, a familiar zone within which participation can occur. This "safe zone" can help to reduce the distance between instructor and student. In negotiating a "safe space," the first question we need to ask is who defines or sets the boundaries—the demeanour, the levels of formality and familiarity?

In negotiating the space for participation, we strive to find a balance between the formal and the more informal "friendly" interactions between teachers and students. Setting boundaries clearly has a role to play in this, because misinterpretation can be the result if the space is too "familiar." If things become too friendly, teachers can find themselves losing a certain necessary degree of respect, perhaps even being regarded as incompetent. The very concept of friendship needs clarification. Specifically, to speak of friendship is to speak about a level of trust; it is to speak about a relationship of mutual respect between teacher and student. A "friend" can be a person on the same side in a struggle. In the pedagogical context, the struggle for knowledge and growth, critical thinking skills and social justice can be the common ground on which both teacher and student are engaged. A degree of friendship, understood in this sense, is an important factor in fostering a healthy, mutually respecting, learning environment.

At the same time we cannot ignore how, even in the face of such friendship, a power imbalance remains between teacher and student— particularly in relation to the standard necessity of grading. We acknowledge this reality with students, but strive to reduce any associated anxiety and help students reach their full potential. For instance, students may be invited to submit drafts of their written work, and we will read and comment on these drafts in an effort to help the students improve the final paper. Similarly, to reduce anxiety and make studying more effective, we might give students their final exam questions in advance. We can reassure students that they will get the grade they deserve, even if that practice leads to a higher class average overall. Higher class averages, when the situation warrants it, are something we are prepared to defend.

In essence, the "friendship" we establish is anchored in instruction and serves to enhance trust, accountability and mutual respect. We work to facilitate, guide and encourage students and to help them excel within certain boundaries. When students come to us with issues that are more personal and unrelated to course content, the boundaries become particularly important. We can facilitate from the academic side, by listening with sensitivity, being understanding of the particular crisis and making the appropriate accommodation, where necessary. We will acknowledge our limitations and explain, when necessary, that we are not qualified to address certain concerns. We can and will direct students towards the appropriate professional office, if they make a request in that direction. In a healthy, mutually respecting teaching and learning environment, the need for explicit expectations and responsibilities—for both teacher and students—is vital.

The negotiation of pedagogical boundaries can, in and of itself, be controversial. In the completion of course requirements, for example, students may want to negotiate how certain projects will be undertaken. This is where one-on-one consultation becomes crucial. Students are urged to come and talk to us about the projects. If something does not seem to be a "good fit" for a student (for example, for cultural reasons), we will try to tailor it into something that works. Clearly, this attempt to be responsive to students' needs and concerns involves time. In striving to cultivate student talent and interest, we not only are always cognizant of the curriculum requirements, but also remember that instructors have a certain latitude in which they can fulfil those requirements.

Lisa Jakubowski (LJ): *I had a student who came up to me just before reading week, a First Nations student who had a paper due in the middle of March. This student, coming very much out of an oral tradition, said to me, "You've always been very open to me… to my approaches, to my ideas. I have a request for you that I don't know if you'll accept. May I do a video on the residential schooling experiences of First Nations people?" The student wanted to interview people who had lived the experience, who are much more comfortable telling their stories than writing them down.*

Livy Visano (LV): *But, why is she asking you? Why doesn't she just tell you—"I will be doing a video"?*

LJ: *Because in other courses, perhaps the student did not have the choice, and also, out of respect for me. She had a sense that I respect the students, and they, in turn, respect me. If I am completely uncomfortable with the idea, the student won't do it. As I think back, I remember my first thought was "video—no!" But then I thought to myself, "Wait a minute, if I truly practise what I preach, of course the video is an option." Because this person comes from a tradition that is primarily oral, as opposed to written, and the video is far more reflective of the person's reality, which is what I had asked them to put into those papers.*

Could it raise problems? Sure! I will have to deal with it if someone asks me "Why was this allowed?" But with critical pedagogy there is always a degree of risk. We try things that are less than conventional, and as a result, we may have to answer to someone for taking these approaches.

2. The Risks of Controversy

Throughout our conversations, the theme of risk surfaced repeatedly. As teachers we take many risks by utilizing controversial content and/or methods. We risk alienating students. We risk the difficulties associated with managing fear, resistance and dissent in the classroom. When dealing with material that can generate multiple viewpoints, teachers must be prepared for the possibility that differences of opinion can escalate into angry, frustrating encounters among students in the class or, alternatively, draw nothing more than silence as a response. In this instance, we risk being unable to build communicative bridges among those who disagree with one another.

LV: *Risk is important, then, it's a cornerstone for the evolution of change.*

LJ: *If you are not prepared to risk, it won't work. There's no question about that.*

LV: *You want the students to risk too.*

LJ: *Of course.*

LV: *But they are going to push your boundaries of risk-taking.*

LJ: *Sure they will… but that's okay.*

LV: *Because you can always default to your role as teacher to avoid trouble.*

LJ: *I would agree.… I don't think we should take risks mindlessly … that's inappropriate.*

LV: *Pushing the boundaries a bit beyond the traditional, and becoming more involved.*

LJ: *And going to the boss and saying, "This isn't the normal thing to do, but I want to do it anyway. I understand the risks involved, this is the reason I want to do it." A case in point is the time I took a group of students to the Canada/U.S. border as part of our participation in the Canada-Cuba*

Friendshipment Caravan. This was a social justice project designed to raise awareness about the economic and social implications of the U.S. embargo against Cuba. In addition to raising awareness, we gathered humanitarian aid in the form of school and medical supplies for Cuba, which was sent to Cuba with a caravan carrying goods from both the United States and Canada. These caravans are actually initiated by groups of American citizens who are critical of U.S. policy towards Cuba—they include Pastors for Peace and Pediatricians for Peace, to name just two. These groups travel through countries like Canada and Mexico, countries that have more neutral policies towards Cuba, en route to delivering their goods.

Rationalizing the trip as a concrete experience of social justice, I got approval from my boss and gave her my word that I would do nothing to jeopardize underage students, in terms of putting them at any kind of legal risk. As it turned out we were unjustly detained by the border patrol, and she was made aware of that. But at the same time, after their return my students, whether frightened or excited by the incident, all agreed that they learned more sociology through the experience than they had all year. They said, "No offence, Lisa. We've talked [in the classroom] about social control, but we were actually detained by these border guards, and weren't free to leave. Experiencing a lack of freedom and talking about it are two very different things." The message I received from them was that while they might forget the times I talked about social control, or things they had read about it, they would probably never forget the experience they had at the border.

LV: *But what happens if the students disagree with you? They don't see themselves as political or as politically active. They say, "No—we don't want this. Why do we have to go to the border?"*

LJ: *I wouldn't make them go. I, accompanied by another person—the college chaplain—took the handful of people who wanted to go. The rest of the class stayed behind and did in-class work. I would never impose such a trip or experience on the group. It has to be something that they want to participate in.*

The same thing applies to a trip I organized to the Oneida First Nations' community just outside of London. In fact, it was even done outside class time. A group of my honours students wanted to go. They were prepared to find a mutually workable time outside of class time to go. So, if I have ten people out of twenty-five who are excited about doing that, then I am going to make the time to accompany them.

Particularly because we were invited by a member of the community, it was a rare opportunity, not only to see the physical surroundings, but also to talk with people like the band council chief and the chief of natural teachings. At the same time, I told those who didn't express an interest, "This is not a mandatory trip, this is not to be imposed upon you as a course requirement. Those who are interested please come and see me." At this stage, I think this is the only reasonable way to proceed. You therefore don't risk a disgruntled student running to an administrator and saying, "I was forced to do this.... It was not listed on my course outline, and I'm not comfortable doing it." I think it's important not to have overblown expectations. These types of experiences engage some, but there is never a guarantee that you will engage all.

LV: *And those who are engaged—you clearly put the brakes on what they can engage in too. So, there are risks, but always boundaries imposed on risks. It's not free-flowing in challenging authorities. And if you try as "the teacher" to impose ... well you can't. But let's assume there are those who are more politically advanced. How do you tell them to behave? When they start attacking you, saying, "Come on Lisa! You aren't taking this seriously enough.... We want more revolutionary action ... an organized movement!"*

LJ: *You're right, and I had this very thing happen with a student when we were at the Canada/U.S. border watching the Americans violate their very own laws by crossing into Canada with goods clearly marked destined for Cuba. This student said to me, "Lisa, this isn't you. I want to go and protest in solidarity with the Americans. You won't let me, because suddenly you are worried about me being arrested." My reaction to this student was upfront and honest. I said, "X, you are underage, you are not a resident of Canada, and we are here as representatives of our college. We are not here, you and me, at a protest, free to do whatever we choose to do. We came here under certain conditions and this is the way it has to be. If you and I came here independently of the college, independently of the course, independently of me promising that there would be limitations on the type of action in which we would engage, then we could do what we want. Right at this moment, these are the reasons that can't happen." And that's the best you can do. She accepted my reasoning, not particularly willingly, but she understood. She understood it was a step forward being allowed to go to the border, knowing full well what would probably happen. That was a big step forward for her. The fact that there were some limitations ... well that wasn't acceptable, but it was understandable. It still was a learning experience.*

Overall I was comfortable taking the position that I did. I made it clear at the outset that we were not going to the border to get arrested. We are perhaps going to see others get arrested. But our primary agenda is to go and see, more concretely, what social justice is all about. We've partici-

pated, we've done our part as Canadians in the gathering of humanitarian aid to send to Cuba. By sending our particular aid with this particular caravan, we were in solidarity with those Americans who were breaking their laws by participating in this Friendshipment Caravan to Cuba.

LV: *The risk invites criticism and ongoing reflection.*

LJ: *Yes, and being prepared to defend the limitations you may be required to impose on any form of action.*

3. Negotiating Resistance to Controversy (The Question of "Voice")

Questions of "race" are notable for generating discomfort and resistance, but so too do many other subject areas. There are many instances in which emotions can arise, and at times students will feel not just uncomfortable, but also silenced or without voice. For example, in a class on social inequality, how does one deal with the position that employment equity is "nothing more than reverse discrimination and that women are no longer suffering from any form of discrimination"? When exploring First Nations' experiences of prejudice and discrimination (or, more strongly, cultural genocide), how does the facilitator manage the classroom when the lone First Nations student in the class asks of you: Why do they all remain silent when I speak? Why will they not answer my questions? React to my experiences? Say what they feel?

When we are studying media or, more specifically, how ads portray women, how do we deal with the young woman student who discloses that she has been suffering from anorexia nervosa for several years, and that this topic, as well as people's reaction to this topic, have triggered deep emotional feelings? On the question of sexual assault and violence against women, how do we simultaneously give everyone voice, regulate sexist, misogynist comments, and remain sensitive to women who have been victims of violence? How do we respond to the woman who gives voice to her violent experience, in the presence of her classmates, or in response to the comment of a classmate? How do we manage comments linked to morality and moral beliefs, in cases in which some students characterize abortion, euthanasia and homosexuality as sinful?

LJ: *The difficult part of the negotiation process becomes what do you do with the sexist or the racist or the severely homophobic student. This became a serious problem in one of my classes. There was some extreme homophobia among a few of the students I taught from abroad. These students were incredibly progressive in every other way, but when it came to "same-sex" anything, their tone, body language and behaviours changed. "Gays should be shot," one of them said. His friends seemed to be agreeing with him.*

A Teaching Experience: Silenced
by Lisa Jakubowski

For two years I used the book *Silenced* (Silvera 1989) in my introductory sociology course in a section addressing questions of social inequality. What we were doing was exploring, at a basic level, the interrelationship among "race," gender and class. In *Silenced* a number of Caribbean women who arrived in Canada between 1971 and 1980 provide oral histories of their experiences as workers in the homes of well-to-do Canadian families in the Toronto area.

The book is powerful, emotionally charged and hard-hitting. It provides evidence of exploitation at the level of class, "race" and gender. Indeed, the moving and couragous accounts reveal that elements of slavery are alive and well in Canada. The stories offer graphic accounts of sexual assault of the domestic workers by the men who employed them. They present accounts of how white women, as "managers" of the household, exploit and subordinate Black women and women of colour.

In the class, made up entirely of women (I teach at a university-level women's college), the discussions surrounding the book invariably proved to be extremely tense. The Black women and women of colour in the course generally appreciated the use of the text in the course. Many voiced their support for the work openly and passionately; others commented in written form, or in one-on-one conversations, on its value. But the reaction of the white women was more mixed. Some of them indicated that although they were quite shocked in reading about the domestic workers' experiences, they appreciated the new-found knowledge. Many, however, were extremely uncomfortable. They remained silent and "fidgety." Others were outwardly hostile in the discussions of the text and, in some cases, were also hostile towards me. That hostility was clearly linked to guilt. They became resentful towards me, they said, for "making us feel guilty" or, "for making us feel responsible for something that is not our fault."

The responses from students in my teaching of *Silenced* and similarly controversial themes include:

1) Lisa, why are you so anti-white?
2) Why are you making us feel so guilty? We didn't do anything wrong.
3) Why do you have to keep "shoving this down our throats"? We have never been exposed to all of this—it's too overwhelming—we can't handle it all at once.
4) Can't we talk about happier things once in a while? After all, things aren't as bad now as they used to be.

How do I deal with that?
LV: *Yes, how do you deal with that? Especially when their reactions are linked very openly to religious upbringing and personal biblical interpretation—in other words, matters of faith?*
LJ: *When one of these otherwise polite and personable young people, with whom I dealt every day, said this, screams erupted from the other side of the room.*

Students shouted, "How dare you? I have many gay friends." The reaction was, "Just kidding, I shouldn't have said that."

LV: *Then what?*

LJ: *So we had to take a few steps back. I made it very clear that there is an obvious and important line between expressing one's point of view and making assertions that are threatening to a particular group of people. The latter is not acceptable and will not be tolerated in my classroom. I pointed out to the students that in addition to this statement being extremely offensive and inappropriate, there is an inconsistency between their general perspectives on issues of inequality and their particular opinion of gays and lesbians. I then raise a series of questions to try to get a sense of where the anger and hostility are coming from, which will not make the situation better but may help those who are offended by the statement, including myself, better understand it. So what we end up getting into is a discussion of religion, and how the particular religions that these young people follow in their home country condemn homosexuality. There is no movement. They have been raised in really strict religious traditions and this is the first hurdle that must be greeted. Second, by their own admission, they come from an extremely "macho" culture where men are raised from birth to judge this kind of behaviour as absolutely wrong. So, minimally, what we are doing, through an exchange of perspectives, is getting to the root of the homophobia. And for those who are offended by the homophobia, there is now a dialogue going on—there are a series of questions and responses going back and forth.*

One who is critical of their homophobia asks, "What if you suddenly discover that your best friend, someone you have known your whole life, is gay?" The group starts asking these young men these kinds of questions, and they are forced to deal with them. The immediate response of one young man is, "How do I learn this? Does he 'come on to me'?" The reply—"No, he doesn't come on to you. He simply tells you, because you are his best friend. He has been there to help you out of many bad situations. Now he wants your understanding and acceptance. So what are you going to do?" Well, the homophobic male doesn't have an immediate reply.... He needs to think, but at least that is better than "Shoot them."

At least here there is some movement, however minimal. But crucial to movement is the dialogue among the students and myself. It's not to silence that person, for that is certainly not going to make the student any more tolerant or accepting of this form of difference.

LV: *What happens if this person gains converts?*

LJ: *Well, that's another risk you take. And isn't it better to risk here? At least if you put this stuff on the table, you know what you are dealing with. I spent several months prepping this particular group for the section on sexual orientation, and, no, I didn't convince those who are severely homophobic that their prejudicial attitudes are unfair. But I did get them to sit through the section without walking out of the classroom. And I did have some of those who had earlier expressed homophobic tendencies say to me, "We understand where you are going with this. We still can't necessarily accept your position, but hope in time we will be more tolerant." To me that's a baby step forward.*

When levels of emotion get high, the discussion has to be facilitated very carefully so things don't get out of hand. What I had to do especially was to make it very clear that statements like "shoot them" are inappropriate, offensive and threatening, and therefore not to be tolerated.

LV: *What if he responds, "It's because of my religion"?*

LJ: *There are ways of talking about a fear or intolerance of difference that don't involve that kind of violent, disrespectful reaction. I tried to highlight the inappropriateness of his homophobic comment by reminding him of a personal example he gave me in class. He had talked of how hurt he was when a group of white kids refused to get out of their car to use a bank machine, until he was about three blocks away. They seemed to be scared of him. He was angry, and justifiably so. How dare these people judge him on their irrational fear of a different skin colour? What he couldn't quite see was the parallel between his irrational reactions to gays and the youths' irrational reaction to him. He could see one as wrong, but not the other.*

No matter what subject matter gives rise to it, whether it is "race" or homophobia or something else, resistance to controversy poses a serious challenge to effective teaching and learning. Themes related to the power and politics of difference are difficult to address in class—and especially in large classes—but just because they are difficult does not mean that they can't provide a starting point for discussion: a place in which some form of dialogue can begin. Often most students, rather than bringing their frustrations out into the open, remain silent, possibly fearing repercussions if they speak out in a way that could be construed as "unfavourable" by either their classmates or the teacher.

Certainly, teachers may tend to avoid addressing controversial issues in class. Or, if a controversial topic arises, they may quickly move beyond it by cutting off the discussion between the individuals with differing viewpoints. But teachers committed to introducing and managing diverse viewpoints and uncomfortable topics in the classroom need to adopt an alternative approach. They may need to adjust their thought patterns— that is, "unlearn" their approach to teaching and learning. An alternative approach entails establishing a less conventional relationship with their students—a relationship based on a direct approach, on trust and friendship—in essence, building mutual respect. It involves recognizing that the same thing doesn't work in each and every situation. Context is vital to teaching, and what may work beautifully in one setting may well be completely inappropriate in another.

But teachers' responses to controversy may not be entirely related to their commitment to certain progressive ideals. Teachers labelled as being "radical," "critical" or "controversial" risk repercussions from academic administrations that are less open to alternative ways of teaching and learning.

4. Managing Controversy: Balancing Pedagogical Ideals with Institutional Constraints

Traditionally, in the context of teaching and learning what is presented as knowledge is limited and fractured. We are limited by our language and by our own ways of thinking. The language we use—the words we select—and our ways of thinking are culturally defined. Within our culture, there are certain things that don't get discussed and certain things that we know very little about. That which is omitted is often information that is uncomfortable, troubling or challenging, in essence the controversial. "Controversial" knowledge jars the sensibilities and sensitivities of the teacher and learner alike. For example, issues related to social justice, inequality and difference are controversial, and merit some consideration. Yet often, as teachers, when we introduce perspectives that usually "don't get discussed," we become identified as being too radical, too critical or too oppositional.

Recognizing the dominant influences of culture on how we think and on what we identify as controversial, we consider the question of why some claims receive primacy over others, and we offer an alternative. Our vision is one that includes a more meaningful, mutually respective and reciprocal relationship between teachers and students. For some people this pedagogical vision will, in and of itself, be controversial. Woven within the very fabric of this engagement is a process of teaching and learning that is political. It is a countercultural production that is critically responsive, responsible and action-oriented. It is a pedagogy that fosters an awareness of self that connects us to others.

Undoubtedly, the topic of "teaching controversy" is multilayered and complex. Teaching controversy is not only about course content, or the methods used to present the content. Ultimately much of what we do, and how we do it, must be understood in the context of a greater challenge: the balancing of pedagogical ideals with institutional constraints. The journal

Teaching Sociology (1998) once devoted the better part of an issue to this very topic (see, for example, Sweet 1998a, 1998b; Long 1998; Gimenez 1998; Gaianguest 1998), as critical sociologists debated how to accommodate "conflicting ideological commitments and institutional obligations" (Sweet 1998a: 106).

The teaching of controversy often involves a conflict between pedagogical vision and institutional commitments. Teaching controversy necessitates the adoption of a critical or radical perspective. In turn we also believe that one of the important aspects of teaching is to provide students with the critical tools and skills necessary for becoming engaged, active members of society throughout their lives. Sweet (1998a: 101) defines the "radical" ideal typically as "an outlook that questions the legitimacy of existing systems of hierarchy, as related to issues of race, gender, class, disability, sexual orientation or other socially constructed divisions between people." This perspective incorporates both curriculum and pedagogy. Radical curriculum provides "empirical and theoretical challenges to cultural practices and social structures that reaffirm dominance and privilege." In other words, it is "counterhegemonic." (For more on "hegemony" and "counterhegemony," see chapter 2.)

But radical pedagogy goes beyond exposure to counterhegemonic content: it demands a more equitable reconceptualization of the student-teacher relationship. In an ideal-typical Freirian sense, radical teachers can move towards equity by: 1) not testing or grading in the traditional fashion; 2) surrendering considerable power to students; 3) abandoning lecture in favour of dialogue; and 4) coupling learning with activism.

This seemingly simple overview summarizes Sweet's (1998a) ideal approach to the problem—in essence, "practise what you preach." But, in fairness, Sweet acknowledges that this ideal is far more complicated in practice. First, there are significant pedagogical variations among the many teachers who define themselves as "radical," "critical" or "humanist." For instance, some teachers offer a critical perspective and encourage critical thinking while using purportedly "traditional" methods (such as lectures and multiple-choice exams). This raises an interesting question: does a radical curriculum necessarily call for radical pedagogy?

Gimenez (1998: 117) suggests that a radical curriculum does not demand a radical pedagogy. Specifically:

> Radical teachers using conventional pedagogy might be more consistent than radical pedagogy advocates. To make sure students learn the basic intellectual skills necessary to be able to think critically and with self-assurance about their experiences, [conven-

tional] pedagogy is likely to be more radical—in the sense of challenging the status quo to a higher degree—than student-centered approaches that often cater to student prejudices and reaffirm them in the pragmatic, eclectic, and relativistic ethos dominant today. (117–18)

In dealing with radical or controversial content, which, then, is the more effective approach: radical methods, traditional methods, or diverse methods from both the radical and conventional traditions?

Many of these questions and themes emerged from our dialogue, albeit in a different form. For instance, we struggle with the issue of breaking down barriers between teacher and student by encouraging the evolution of a "pedagogical friendship" between the two. But what is the meaning of "friendship" in this context? Furthermore, how are we to set the boundaries for this friendship while simultaneously maintaining the trust of our students and some degree of legitimacy? Also, when we speak of teaching controversy, we have realized the need to clarify for ourselves what precisely is controversial about what we do—the content, the method, or some combination of both.

Beyond trying to better understand the particular combination of radical, critical and controversial content and method that produces the most intellectually developed and critically skilled student, we need also to grapple with how to address the institutional constraints associated with alternative pedagogical styles and curriculum. Institutions discourage radical or controversial pedagogies in many ways, including: 1) the criteria traditionally used in making promotion and tenure decisions; 2) the methods of evaluating teaching success; and 3) everyday, bureaucratic practices (Sweet 1998a: 105).

For example, if we advance a model that is action-oriented and more equitable and responsive to students, our class preparation time becomes far more time-consuming. We necessarily need to spend more time regularly modifying our readings, syllabi, lecture materials and means of evaluation in response to student concerns. We may need "a fresh approach" for each new group of students we teach. Furthermore, if our pedagogy is action-oriented, we will have more community-related obligations, above and beyond our classroom time. While teaching is one measure of "scholarly productivity," evidence suggests that "book and journal article publications played a stronger role in decisions regarding tenure, promotion and merit pay" (Marchant and Newman in Sweet 1998a: 105). Given these findings, Marchant and Newman (1994: 151) go so far as to suggest that the "career-minded" professor should minimize the time necessary to do quality teaching and devote as much time as possible to publishing.

Another institutional deterrent to radical pedagogy is the standard means of measuring teaching success. For teachers of controversy, success comes from using our knowledge to apply the very best lesson possible for our students and, in turn, learning what students can teach us. Ideally, success comes when both teachers and students achieve a heightened sense of awareness, which enables them to appraise social institutions critically, identify social injustice and, where circumstances warrant it, act in opposition to that injustice. From an institutional standpoint, the measure for successful teaching is the far more standardized teaching indicators that students use to evaluate the pedagogy of their teachers. If controversial or radical content cultivates resistance on the part of many students (see, for example, Bohmer and Briggs 1991) and teaching success is based "on indicators of how much students enjoy their classes" (Sweet 1998a: 105), teachers in probationary positions may well find themselves standing on shaky ground.

Some of the other everyday, bureaucratic practices of colleges and universities also undermine our abilities to implement radical pedagogical ideals. Books must be selected and ordered long before classes first meet, excluding student participation in decision-making around an important component of curriculum development. The very fact that teachers must evaluate students undermines efforts to reduce the power differentials between the two groups (Sweet 1998a: 106).

The struggle for balance between pedagogical ideals and institutional demands can create considerable stress for students too. In a practical sense, we appreciate the dilemma faced by the student of controversy. We live in a capitalist society, a society driven by market forces, and students are acutely aware of the dangers of not subscribing to those forces. As students forge their career paths, we hope through teaching controversy not to endanger their futures, but rather to equip them with the tools that will enable them not only to think critically about society but also to change themselves, their work, their lives, as need be.

NOTE

1. This conversation took place during Livy Visano's tenure as Dean of Atkinson Faculty of Liberal and Professional Studies, York University. Please note that in the conversation to follow no names of students or colleagues are reproduced. The interpretations of the events are ours alone, and we respect the right to privacy of those who participated in the events upon which we are reflecting.

2

Exploring the Process of Education
From Traditional "Schooling" to the Alternatives

Traditionally, educational institutions have been viewed as places used to transmit knowledge—including factual information and occupational skills, as well as cultural values and norms—to members of a society. People in these institutions are expected, specifically through the transmission of norms, to learn societal rules and expectations. More candidly, people, through "schooling," are expected to learn how to think, what to think, and how to behave. In this sense, "schooling" is intimately tied to the concept and reality of hegemony.

Hegemony is the term used by Gramsci (1971) to describe the process by which one group achieves domination over others using physical and/or ideological means. Here we are most concerned with the ideological dimension of hegemony. Conceptualized as "a set of ideas and ideals that provide an explanation for a particular community" (Fleras and Kunz 2001: 190), ideologies facilitate the maintenance of social order or the promotion of social change. In more explicitly political terms, ideologies can be defined as "a set of ideas and ideals that justify the prevailing distribution of power, resources and privilege in society" (190). In this sense, ideologies are an important persuasive tool for those in powerful positions. According to marino (1997: 105):

> Gramsci develops the notion of hegemony as the process whereby public consensus about social reality is created by the dominant class; whereby those in power persuade the majority to consent to decisions that are disempowering or not benefiting the majority.... In simple terms, hegemony can be defined as persuasion from above (by the dominant class) and consent from below (by the subordinate class).... Raymond Williams [1977] further extends the implications of this concept in cultural terms: "A lived hegemony is always a process. It is not, except analytically, a system or a structure.... It does not just passively exist as a form of dominance. It has continually to be renewed, recreated, defended, and modified. It is also continually resisted, limited, altered, challenged by pressures not at all its own."

As a means of "persuading from above," traditional schooling is very effective.

From early on in life, citizens are socialized to believe in the ideology of equality of educational opportunity and meritocracy. According to this line of thought, social differences stem not from lack of opportunity but from the lack of individual motivation or ability. A further implication is that social inequality is a problem rooted in the individual, not in the system. Following this logic, it becomes much easier to blame social inequality on the deficiencies of particular individuals rather than on systemic problems. However, countless studies (for example, Gramsci 1971; Bowles and Gintis 1976; Bourdieu and Passeron 1977) indicate that, traditionally, educational institutions have been guilty of both reproducing social inequality and reinforcing its "naturalness" (Jakubowski 1992: 71).

Freire (1970: 58) describes the learning process in traditional settings as analogous to "banking": "an act of depositing in which students are the depositories and the teacher is the depositor. Instead of communicating, the teacher issues communiques and makes deposits which the students receive and memorize." Like a form of indoctrination (Reimer 1972), traditional schooling is a sophisticated way through which the dominant value systems are transmitted intergenerationally (Giroux 1981: 1). Among other things, individuals learn about the value of competition, the "value of being taught, rather than learning for oneself—what is good and what is true" and the need to conform "in order to get along in the system" (Reimer 1972: 21–23). Schooling teaches individuals what behaviours are "right" and "good." Most importantly, children learn the importance of respecting and obeying those in authority (Henslin, Henslin and Keiser 1976: 308–309).

This method of instruction is often combined with educational practices such as IQ testing (see, for example, Murray and Herrnstein 1994; Rushton 1989; for a more critical look, see Rose, Lewontin and Kamin 1984; Jacoby and Glauberman 1995; and Ziegler et al. 1991: 77–84); tracking (Lazerson et al. 1985; Henslin, Henslin and Keiser 1976; Bowles and Gintis 1976), and "cooling out" (Goffman 1952). These hegemonic practices serve to psychologically reinforce, within the minds of the less advantaged, the naturalness and inevitability of their positions of subordination. Essentially, students are socialized to develop commonsensical perceptions about their differential qualifications based on, among other things, "race," class and gender. They become "objects of" rather than "subjects in" a learning process in which students' knowledge, stemming from both their past and present real-life experiences, is generally disregarded or relegated to the periphery (Jakubowski 2001: 63). Marcroft (1990: 64–65) acknowledges that these kinds of power differentials are quite "natural" in traditional classrooms. Specifically, "Teachers, those who naturally know more, distill skills and knowledge to students, who naturally know less." Here, students are portrayed as "emotionally and psychologically immature, underdeveloped young people, [who] cannot be forced too early into things that they are not ripe for."

While, in this context, the characterization of students as "underdeveloped" seems reasonable, we are more inclined to ask: is it correct to say that students are "underdeveloped young people" or is it more accurate to say that traditional pedagogical methods "underdevelop" students? Usually discussed in relation to dependency theory (see, for example, Gunder Frank 1967), the concept of "underdevelopment" represents a political and economic process through which "developed" countries work to "actively manipulate and therefore distort" (Mason 1997: 24) the growth of Third World economies. Here we are suggesting that traditional methods of instruction impinge on the intellectual and personal development of students and promote dependency. Students learn to become dependent on teachers to tell them how to think, what to think and how to act in order to function effectively within society. Because these methods perpetuate unilateral relations of dependence between student and teacher (as authority figure), there is little room to question or raise opposing arguments. Empowering students with the ability to critically analyze and challenge controversial or contentious course content is simply not part of this traditional pedagogical process (Jakubowski 2001: 64).

It is not difficult to see how ideologies perform the hegemonic function of social control through schooling. (For an interesting classroom exercise on clarifying how we reproduce hegemonic patterns, see marino 1997: 23–25, "Identifying Cracks in Consent.") But there is a more experientially based, subjective component to ideology. Specifically, ideologies represent individualized forms of adaptation by helping individuals to make sense of their social worlds. Miles and Phizacklea (1984: 9) suggest: "People can test ideas and interpretations they receive ... against their own experience of the world. Ideology is not only handed down. It is constantly being created and renewed by people in response to the world as they experience it." This responsive dimension of ideology invites social change and "counterhegemony" (Gramsci 1971). "Counterhegemony" as a process is oppositional and transformative. Clarke, Cavanagh and Cristall (1997: 14) elaborate: "If we see hegemony as a system that organizes consent, we have the choice of reorganizing or disorganizing that consent." For instance, if hegemony involves "framing"—"the process of imposing a preferred meaning ('framework') on an event" (Fleras and Kunz 2001: 190)—we can challenge that framework and work to "re:frame" our existing vision. A central theoretical concept in marino's (1997: 108–109) critical pedagogy, "re:framing"

> occurs when problems or experiences are represented in ways that both retain the realities of existing political relationships and transcend them by opening up new (for those involved) and real opportunities for acting on the inequities of those relationships.... [It] requires both teachers and students to co-construct new and useful frames on their experiences—ones that mobilize and empower them.

The process of "schooling" leaves little room for "re: framing," critical thought, empowerment or action. "Education," though, can be counterhegemonic. In the Freirian sense, education generally involves the articulation of experience, critical thinking and reflection, and action. It embodies a commitment to participatory, active learning. Such a pedagogy has been described as "humanizing" (Freire in Macedo 1997: 3), "engaged" (hooks 1994), "radical" (Sweet 1998a, 1998b), "transformative" and "critical" (Wink 2000: 123; Shor 1992: 189–90). Through a "constant unveiling of reality," education invites students to develop a critical awareness of their social worlds. It promotes both consciousness-raising and societal intervention. Students receive challenges in the form of problems relating to themselves "in the world and with the world," and they are urged to respond to those challenges. Education, thus, becomes a practice of freedom rather than domination (Freire 1970: 68–69).

Teachers who are committed to critical pedagogy in this sense recognize the importance of a continuing consultation with all those engaged in the learning process throughout all of its phases. This practice includes a recognition, on the part of educators, that the subjectivity of the student, articulated through experience, is an equally essential component of learning. To establish this education, the traditional role of the teacher must be altered. From the earliest stages of the learning process, the educators' role needs to become that of facilitator, someone striving towards empowering students with the ability to think critically and, if necessary, effectively intervene in immediate social realities. Within such a context, the teachers and students must collectively take responsibility for, and work towards creating, a liberating, pedagogical environment.

CRITICAL THINKING: THE ESSENTIAL COMPONENTS

Brookfield (1987: 7–9) suggests that critical thinking involves: 1) identifying and challenging assumptions; 2) recognizing the importance of context; 3) trying to imagine and explore alternatives; and 4) imagining and exploring alternatives in a way that promotes "reflective skepticism." He reminds us that critical thinking is not confined to the classroom (4). As it is now, from a practical standpoint the type of "critical thinking skills" generally taught in educational settings are not particularly useful in life beyond school. Sternberg (1985: 194) highlights the inconsistency between the requirements for critical thinking in adulthood and what is taught in school programs designed to develop critical thinking. As he puts it, "We are preparing students to deal with problems that are in many respects unlike those that they will face as adults."

Critical thinking is often understood as an intellectual skill that tends to be developed only by those involved in higher education (see, for example, Drake 1976; Young 1980; Meyers 1986; Stice 1987). Brookfield (1987: 11) outlines this rather elite conceptualization of critical thinking:

> It has been equated with the development of logical reasoning abilities (Hallet 1984; Ruggiero 1975), with the application of reflective judgment (Kitchener 1986), with assumption hunting (Scriven 1976) and with the creation, use and testing of meaning (Hullfish and Smith 1961). Ennis (1962) lists twelve aspects of critical thinking, which include analytical and argumentative capacities such as recognizing ambiguity in reasoning, identifying contradictions in arguments, and ascertaining the empirical soundness of generalized conclusions.... O'Neil (1985) proposes the ability to distinguish bias from reason and fact from opinion.

While Brookfield in no way dismisses the importance of learning to think critically in institutes of higher learning, he does argue that this is only one setting in which critical thinking occurs. It can also occur, he says, in the everyday interactions of adult lives—in relationships, in the workplace, in political involvements and in interpreting mass media (12). In this sense critical thinking is "a lived activity, not an academic pastime" (14)—and it is an activity is that is emancipatory, dialectical, and reflective (Jakubowski 2001: 64).

It is emancipatory in that participants become conscious of forces that have had an impact on their current realities and accordingly can take action to change some aspect of the situation. It is dialectical in the sense

that it focuses on how participants come to be situated in a world characterized by contradictory relationships and interactions, a world in which
life circumstances continue to change and evolve through the struggles of
real people (Brookfield 1987: 12-13). Critical thinking is reflective because it is "the process of internally examining and exploring an issue of
concern, triggered by an experience, which creates and clarifies meaning in
terms of self, and which results in a changed conceptual perspective" (Boyd
and Fales in Brookfield 1987: 14). Hutchings and Wutzdorff (1988: 15)
define reflection as "the ability to step back and ponder one's own experience, to abstract from it some meaning or knowledge relevant to some
other experiences." As they put it, "The capacity for reflection is what
transforms experience into learning." This form of learning has the potential for generating a new understanding about the surrounding social
world, an understanding that often requires "a corresponding change in
one's behaviour and relationships" (Schlossberg in Brookfield 1987: 14).

How then can we facilitate critical thinking in the classroom and make
it more applicable to life beyond the classroom? How do we begin to
improve classroom dynamics? How do we help students to critically
analyze, and ultimately overcome, their own discomfort in dealing with
controversial issues? In part, this pedagogical transition requires teachers to
become "critically responsive." According to Brookfield (1990: 23-24),
"critically responsive" teaching "is guided by a strongly felt rationale," but
the methods and forms of that rationale respond "creatively to the needs
and concerns expressed by students."

> Teachers help students to realize that dominant values,
> "commonsense," wisdom, generally accepted standards and pre-
> vailing social and political arrangements are cultural constructs.
> Because [these values] are cultural creations, teachers point out
> that they can be dismantled and reframed by human agency....
> The responsive component [represents] the willingness of teachers
> to adapt their methods, content and approaches, to the context in
> which they are working and to the ways in which students are
> experiencing learning.

In this spirit of responsibility, innovation and adaptability, we offer the
following philosophical and conceptual framework—keeping in mind
that because there can be no strict inventory of pedagogical methods, the
framework necessarily complements a multiplicity of techniques.

EDUCATION AS CRITICALLY RESPONSIVE

> I quite firmly believe that we cannot *not* learn. In the sense that teaching always involves learning from the point of view of the professor or faculty, even if it is unacknowledged learning, there is mutual learning going on even if this result is not discussed. I also don't think we can teach our students to be challenging and self-critical, socially critically, if we aren't struggling to get better at doing that ourselves.... Equally important is the notion that there is more to be learned than anyone currently knows. (marino 1997: 43–44)

Because of her emphasis on the challenging, ever-changing nature of teaching and learning, marino's words form an appropriate starting point for a discussion of critically responsive pedagogy.

By stressing creativity and sensitivity to context, critical responsiveness makes room for the creation of a pedagogical framework that accommodates a diversity of practices and techniques but refuses the "rigidity of models" (Macedo 1997: 8). For us, the framework in which pedagogical techniques or practices are grounded must include a number of concepts: collective responsibility, the Gramscian (1971) notion of the "intellectual," dialogue and intersubjectivity and the dialectic. At the root of this framework is the reconceptualization of the unequal, stratified relationship that traditionally exists between teacher and student.

This reconceptualization begins with the question of identities. For one thing, we need to abandon stereotypical images of the educator as "authority" and the student as "dependent." Instead, we need to reconstitute both actors, in a Gramscian (1971) sense, as "intellectuals." That is, "Regardless of one's social and economic function, all human beings perform as intellectuals by constantly interpreting and giving meaning to the world, and by participating in a particular conception of that world" (Giroux in Freire 1985: xxiii).

By treating all those who participate in the education process as "intellectuals," we take on the implicit understanding that they are social equals. Thus, teachers and students take **collective responsibility** for the advancement of teaching and learning. They will have equally significant, albeit different, roles to play as teaching and learning unfolds. Still, empowering the student in this way does not mean that the teacher is automatically disempowered. As Sweet (1998b: 128) observes, we should value the knowledge, expertise and credentials that teachers possess. But we must also openly acknowledge that students often have knowledge that teachers lack. We must encourage the sharing of this knowledge and welcome it as a significant component of teaching and learning.

This reconstituted relationship must be accompanied by philosophically compatible techniques. A teacher would, for instance, eliminate "guided" conversations in favour of **dialogue**. The notion of dialogue does not signify power and inequality. Instead, it facilitates "intersubjectivity"— that is, an authentic and open interchange of ideas among all educational participants, wherein each participant is respected as "an equally knowing subject" (Kirby and McKenna 1989: 129). Dialogue, in a Freirian sense, can also be viewed as a form of "social praxis so that the sharing of experiences is informed by reflection and political action" (Macedo 1997: 8). Effective critical skills will evolve within environments in which social equals engage in dialogue. When participants take a critical stance in dialogue, "They are committed to questioning and exploring even the most widely accepted ideas and beliefs. Conversing critically implies an openness to rethinking cherished assumptions and to subjecting those assumptions to a continuous round of questioning, argument and counterargument" (Brookfield and Preskill 1999: 7). Within such a context, the concept of the **dialectic** can be used to enhance the learning process.

Emerging from the works of Hegel and Marx, the dialectic is best understood as a method of inquiry that focuses on how people come to be situated in a social world characterized by contradictory relationships and interactions. For instance:

> The use of the dialectic assumes that every social phenomenon can be divided into (at least) two fundamental aspects or parts. Moreover the assumption is made that these parts or aspects are in dynamic interaction with each other (conflict) and that this relationship of conflict between the two parts is the driving force behind the social phenomenon of which they are a part. (Sociology On-Line 2000)

Given the conflicting nature of social relationships and interactions, the dialectic illuminates how life circumstances continue to change and evolve through the struggles of real people. Because people are continually engaged in a process of "movement and becoming, of development and change" (Norman and Sayers 1980: 4), the nature of the social world within which they exist continues to change.

When this dialectical method is applied to a classroom setting, it enables the teacher to more fully appreciate the importance of the student in all phases of the learning process. The dialectic acts as a stimulus for development and change. Towards this end, the real-life experiences of students play a crucial role in the identification, understanding and resolution of personal and societal contradictions. Thus, in examining any societal issue, a teacher has to consult and give equal credence to the views of all the participants.

Our framework, which incorporates the notions of collective responsibility, the Gramscian "intellectual," and intersubjectivity as well as dialogue and the dialectic, provides the philosophical foundation for an educational process that is action-oriented, critically responsive and flexible in its use of pedagogical practices and techniques. It is a framework designed to be "transformational":

> In this case the teachers and the students are not only doing critical pedagogy, they are living critical pedagogy. The fundamental belief that drives these classroom behaviors is that we must act; we must relate our teaching and learning to real life; we must connect our teaching and learning with our communities; we always try to learn and teach so that we grow and that our students' lives are improved, or for self- and social transformation. (Wink 2000: 129)

PHASES OF EDUCATION

There are many ways of fostering "action" among students. Reflective of a long-standing pedagogical tradition that supports education that is responsive to community needs (see, for example Dewey 1916, 1938; Freire 1970, 1985; Boyer 1990), the type of active learning we strive for begins in the classroom but then moves outward to the community (Wink 2000: 123). Sociologists commonly refer to the linking of classroom to community as "community-based learning." As Mooney and Edwards (2001: 182) put it, this applies to "any pedagogical tool in which the community becomes a partner in learning…. All community-based learning initiatives are experiential and in this way active learning." Like Winks (2000: 139) we believe that education, as critical pedagogy, is grounded in some variation of Freirian "problem-posing." Specifically, "Once learners have identified and captured (*named*) their concern, they take action, find solutions and extend the dialogue of the classroom to the real world" (Wink 2000: 141). Here we suggest that there are three very fluid phases in the process of education: experience and reflection, structured reflection and dialogue and action.

Experience and Reflection

In the first phase of education we invite students to share their experiential insights on a particular theme or issue. As Arnold et al. (1991: 52) suggest in their "spiral design model":

> Starting with what people know—with their experience—provides an important statement to the participants. It says that we value what they know, that their experience is important. It also helps people recognize their own personal resources: how much they can learn from each other; how much they already know about a theme.

Starting with what people know, we invite students to make a presentation that is somehow related to the theme under investigation. The presentation can take many forms, including poetry, dance, film clips and song lyrics (see, for example, Martinez 1994; Walczak and Reuter 1994). Following the presentation, we encourage all participants to give their reactions. In other words, *from the standpoint of their own experience*, participants think about the presentation and respond based on how they are affected by what they see, hear or read. There are no probing questions. Individuals simply rely on personal experience to guide their reflections.

Structured Reflection and Dialogue

After the initial meditation related to personal experience, the reflection becomes more "structured" (Mooney and Edwards 2001: 186). Structured reflection involves both individual and group processes. First, the students are required to make their earlier reflections concrete. The process of concretizing reflections—for example, in the form of a journal entry (see Roth 1985)—creates a **codification**, a concrete physical representation of a real-life situation (Freire 1985: 51). As Wallerstein (1987: 38) points out, codifications "can take many forms: a written dialogue, a story, a photograph, a skit, a collage or a song. No matter what the form, a code re-presents the students' reality back to the class and allows them to project their emotional and social responses in a focused fashion." The code is a "depersonalized representation" (38) of the issue designed to promote critical thinking and action.

"Structured reflection also has a collective or group aspect" (Mooney and Edwards 2001: 186). Specifically, the code becomes a starting point for dialogue among the participants. This codifying and sharing of experience alerts students to their creative and vital presence in education. Individuals begin to reflect anew on the codified experience(s) of their colleagues. After a period of reflection the students move into small groups and engage in a dialogue in which experiences begin to get "collectivized," which allows more voices to be heard and similarities and patterns to be identified (Arnold et al. 1991: 54). This collective reflection develops, within both students and teachers, a more critical awareness of the issue at hand. This reflection also marks the beginning of the **decodification** process.

Decodification invites the group as a whole to engage in an interchange of ideas, in order to highlight the significance, or simply the various elements, of the real-life experiences of students, as depicted in the codification. To some extent, the burden of responsibility shifts to the teacher/facilitator during the decodification phase: the teacher will work at drawing links between experience and pertinent theories (for a discussion of the value of a "concept-oriented" approach, see Downey and Torrecilha 1994). In continued consultation with students, the teacher draws from the discussion of the codification one or more **generic concepts** to facilitate a more general analysis of the issue at hand. In this sense, a generic concept is a panoptic tool that imposes order on diverse findings (Visano 1988: 231). In essence, generic concepts bring together themes or issues of the subject matter that the class as a whole has determined to be of fundamental significance.

How the teacher adds new information during the phase of structured reflection and dialogue can have wide-ranging effects on the process. As Arnold et al. (1991: 56) note, because we want to empower people, "Our process must affirm what people already know while suggesting new questions and frameworks for deepening understanding."

Action

Once experiences have been shared and analyzed, participants can begin to make links between classroom and community—in other words, to begin to act on what, thus far, has been learned. In this final phase, we feel it is important to point out that how students ultimately take action can vary considerably. We respect students' rights to have political visions different from our own (see, for example, Solorzano 1989). Furthermore, we acknowledge that previous experience with community-based learning can also have a sharp influence on a participant's degree of comfort when entering the community. Our main point, then, is that we welcome any form of action from our students—whether it involves interviewing others, writing a letter to the newspaper, boycotting a movie or marching in a demonstration—as we strive to keep them actively engaged in their learning.

CONCRETE APPLICATIONS: EDUCATING TOWARDS ACTION

The following examples are from courses that in some way address the theme of social inequality, and especially course sections exploring the theme of difference (where difference includes, among other things, "race," class, gender and sexual orientation) in relation to the social organization of institutions: specifically, how are unequal social relations reproduced, legitimized and/or challenged?

As the course begins, we invite students to sign up for seminar presentations. Depending on the size of the class, the presentation might be an individual or a group effort. One of the options for students is to do a seminar grounded in "problem-posing." As Wink (2000: 143) puts it, "Problem-posing takes place when people begin with a spirit of inquiry and questioning of situations that directly affect their own lives. Problem-posing ends with actions and transformations in their lives and their contexts." Although the guidelines provided vary depending on the course, a general overview might be as follows:

Problem-Posing Pedagogy Assignment:

This particular option definitely involves some degree of creativity. Grounded in a variation of the problem-posing pedagogy of Paulo Freire, this assignment challenges you to use "codes" as you critically analyze some dimension of difference in relation to a social institution. For instance, gender in relation to education, "race" or sexual orientation in relation to media and popular culture. A code, in some concrete way, represents your "take" on an issue. It is designed to encourage, among all participants, both structured, critical reflection and action strategies.

To begin the process, you are invited to provide for the class an example related to your particular theme. This can be anything from a newspaper article or image to film clips, poetry or music. Participants will then be invited to reflect on, and subsequently dialogue about, their experiences in relation to the issue, before they consider possible courses of action. If you find it useful, you might use Nina Wallerstein's (1987) problem-posing strategy to organize your seminar. Specifically:

1.   Describe what you see.
2.   Define/identify the problem(s) or issue.
3.   Share similar experiences.
4.   Question why there is a problem

5.   Strategize what can be done to address the problem.

For many students who choose this kind of an assignment, and who are interested in media, film clips are a popular way of presenting their examples. The clips become a means of critically analyzing how various forms of difference are constructed/represented in film. Around the theme of race, movies such as *White Man's Burden, American History X, Smoke Signals, Conspiracy of Silence, Hurricane* and *A Time to Kill* have been particularly effective. *Erin Brockovich* and *Dead Poet's Society* (see Giroux 1993: 35–56) are films that clearly address themes of class and gender. A film that looks at sexual identity in Cuba—a purportedly "macho" and socialist climate—is *Strawberry and Chocolate*. Students may also be interested in analyzing how television shows deal with the theme of difference. Examples range from "classic" TV like *All in the Family* or *Good Times* to more contemporary examples such as *The Cosby Show, Golden Girls, Will and Grace* and *Seinfeld*. Finally, these kinds of visual examples, in the form of documentaries, can also become a means of beginning to address how other social institutions manage difference. For example, the video *When Women Kill* analyses how the Canadian legal system treats abused women who kill their abusers. *Who Gets In?* documents how the Canadian government manages immigration. *A Class Divided* provides a wonderful illustration of how an American teacher, Jane Elliot, uses the education system to teach white children about privilege and discrimination.

Before students can do presentations and take on the responsibility of leading seminars, they must "learn the process" (Wallerstein 1987: 38). As an example of our attempts to educate towards action using a problem-posing model, we will outline an exercise centred on the controversial production of a popular musical in Toronto.

Show Boat

Based on the 1926 novel by Edna Ferber, *Show Boat* was a large, extravagant theatrical production that chronicled the lives of a white Southern family and the performers who work on a floating stage. As Henry et al. (2000: 277) point out: "In the world depicted in the novel, Blacks exist as a backdrop. Almost every reference to them in the novel employs demeaning and derogatory stereotypes." The original book has since been transformed into both stage productions and movies. While the various productions have been "revised and restaged numerous times … each version retained the negative and demeaning stereotypes of Blacks happily singing and dancing" (278).

When the play opened in Toronto in the 1990s, a large, diverse group of people from Toronto's Black community mounted an opposition to it, and a coalition was formed to stop the performance. Specifically:

> Concern centred on the ways in which the various productions of the play distorted the memory, history and experiences of Black People who lived through slavery and the Reconstruction period. Opposition to the play was based, in part, on the fact that it romanticized and trivialized one of the most oppressive periods of Western civilization and misrepresented the deep emotions, conditions and experiences of Blacks in those horrific times. (Henry et al. 2000: 278)

The opposition generated much controversy and emotion. Many of those who opposed the proposed ban argued against what they perceived to be censorship: "The Black community's call for greater sensitivity and responsibility in the selection of cultural productions in publicly funded institutions was seen as a violation of freedom of expression" (279). But, even with all the protest and debate, the "show went on."

In a course on social inequality, and in a section directed specifically towards representations of race in North American society, we decided to focus on the controversy and diverse points of view that emerged in response to the run of the show in Toronto. As part of this, we asked students to watch, listen and record their reactions to the 1951 movie version of *Show Boat*. In addition to offering their general perspectives on the film, the students were to provide specific commentary on two clips from the movie: 1) the arrival of the "Show Boat," with an emphasis on the image of Blacks presented in the scene; and 2) a scene touching on the issue of miscegenation, which includes the singing of "Ole Man River" by the character Joe.

In this case, more generally, the challenge becomes: how to effectively analyze the images that constantly bombard us? Specifically, in relation to *Show Boat* and the contemporary Toronto controversy, the question becomes, does the production simply reinforce negative racial stereotypes of Blacks? Can studying *Show Boat* in this way promote critical thinking and counterhegemonic movement?

In our class the students' written reflections on film clips and lyrics from *Show Boat* became the codifications. From these codifications, a number of generic concepts emerged: stereotyping, prejudice, discrimination; dehumanization; and resistance. The generic concepts were then linked to the more general themes of racism and injustice. After that, some of the students wanted to discuss more precisely how the analysis was connected to the Toronto controversy. Specifically, how does a revival of a story filled with discrimination, prejudice and stereotyping influence the current life situations of members of Toronto's Black community? What was the wider role of the media and popular culture in society—was the media of the 1990s failing to evolve in ways that would meet the needs of the community's growing ethnically, culturally and racially diverse population (Jakubowski 2001: 70)?

The dialogue on these issues raised—as it always does—the question of "discomfort." Only some of the students were eager to discuss the topic, and they tended to be those who were already active in the community protests towards the production, or at least sympathetic to the protests. Other students remained more or less silent. The challenge for us as facilitators was to explore why some people were uncomfortable talking about the *Show Boat* controversy.

To deal with this question, all of us had to return to a brief discussion of norms, and Lusk and Weinberg's (1994: 304) work on controversy was particularly helpful. We could begin by asking, "What norms underlie the discomfort?" But because this question is vague and general, we went a step further: "What were the major norms that you learned growing up that might affect your participation in class discussions of race and gender inequalities?" This discussion of norms could be linked to institutions. For instance, "What were the dominant institutions (for example, family, church) in your life before you came to university?" and "What norms did you learn from these institutions?" Following the discussion of norms, we revisited the original question: "How can we tie the dominant norms we have been taught by our families, schools, church/temple to the discomfort" surrounding *Show Boat*?

Often after this discussion, as Lusk and Weinberg (1994: 305) suggest, students begin to make

> connections between conformity, respect, notions of expertise and not wanting to make a spectacle of themselves, lose an argument, look foolish in front of friends (whom they will see later in the dorms) or say something that is not "right." They discuss how norms which they have taken for granted and which often facilitate interaction in some social situations actually interfere with discussion[s] of race and gender inequalities in this setting.

At this point, we generally reinforce the ground rules of mutual respect and dialogue as a way of breaking down barriers to dialogue and critical analysis (Jakubowski 2001: 70–71).

In discussions of *Show Boat* (or similar controversies), if classes can get past the discomfort and dialogue openly with one another as social equals, they can develop a critical awareness of their own social realities inside the classroom as well as a fuller appreciation of the dialectical relationship that exists between themselves and society. Students can become *empowered* and begin to develop action strategies. Again, though, we stress that action strategies must be specifically geared to the comfort level of the respective participants. Not all students associate education with social and political action. Among other things, cultural background, socialization and levels of self-confidence can have an impact on how active a person wants to become. Furthermore, as Wallerstein (1987: 42–43) acknowledges, action can take diverse forms, and we strive not to legitimate one form more than another.

On the various occasions when we have carried out this exercise, responses to the controversy have ranged from, on one side, a desire on the part of students to confront the racism perpetuated in *Show Boat* by organizing both an awareness campaign and boycott of the Toronto production to, on the other, an unwillingness to act at all. Specifically, some students were sceptical. They questioned the characterization of *Show Boat* as racist, because in their views prejudice and racism had significantly declined in society and the whole issue had been blown out of proportion. Taking this variability into account, yet wanting to maximize activity among students, we began by asking students to make "individual commitment statements" (Wink 2000: 155), which they would share with the rest of the class. For example, those more prone to political action might say something like: "I commit to boycotting the Toronto production of *Show Boat*." The commitment statements of students who do not support that kind of action might take a little more time to formulate. With some small-group discussion and facilitation on the part of the teacher, these students might eventually commit to exploring, outside the classroom, the question of whether racism and discrimination still do exist. In this case, a commitment statement might be, "I commit to more carefully investigating whether racism and discrimination are still serious problems in our society." For these students, we recommend a "Social Distance" assignment, as suggested by Morrissey (1992: 121–24).

To cultivate dialogue in the classroom, Morrissey uses an amended version of the classic Bogardus (1925a, 1925b) "Social Distance Scale." In essence, this Social Distance exercise is designed to measure the degree to which individuals are comfortable interacting with people from racial groups different from their own (Morrissey 1992: 121). For example, the scale includes items that require young adults to consider their degree of comfort in social situations ranging from conversing with someone of a different race to entering into a long-term relationship (121–24). The exercise requires each student to move outside of the university classroom and survey ten friends about their levels of comfort interacting with people from different racial and ethnic groups. In the context of a Canadian city, the designated groups might be European Canadians, Asian Canadians, African Canadians, or First Nations people, among others. The project guarantees anonymity and does not require demographic information except for gender. After completing the surveys, the students hand them in along with a two- to three-page discussion of "their findings in regard to ethnic and gender differences and desired social distance" (121–22). Students are also asked to address one additional question: is "social distance" the same phenomenon as prejudice? Finally, students discuss their findings and interpretations in the classroom. The whole process allows students who do not support political action to examine more actively and critically the phenomena of racism, prejudice and discrimination in contemporary society.

As teachers, we believe it is more appropriate to be receptive to diverse forms of action on the part of our students than to alienate students from teaching and learning. If we truly want to be critically responsive teachers, our experience suggests that students' choice of action will vary by context and we must readjust our expectations of our students accordingly.

The *Show Boat* example is only one way of working to make concrete our critically responsive philosophy. Any number of pedagogical techniques can be used to establish a politically literate and active population. Another variation of our conceptual framework that actively engages students in the struggles associated with teaching and learning about difference requires two things: a setting beyond the teacher's own university classroom, and willing student facilitators.

RISK AND THE ASSESSMENT OF STUDENTS' LEARNING EXPERIENCES

Many teachers have articulated the difficulties associated with teaching controversial material. Some of their comments—especially as they relate to inequality and difference—follow.

- "It has been our experience that students from privileged class and race backgrounds are frequently hostile, or at best neutral, to presentations on race, class and gender stratification; often they respond with guilt, anger or resistance" (Bohmer and Briggs 1991: 154).
- "I encountered tremendous resistance—overt hostility from some and

Taking Education to the Community:
When Students Become Teachers
by Lisa Jakubowski

The Context:

> *A big sweaty white man from the Southern United States that likes to drink beer, and drive big trucks and makes fun of people.* —Grade 10 student response to the question "What is a racist?"

During the winter of 1999 a teacher from a small-town, rural high school not far from London, Ontario, contacted me. She asked if I would be interested in facilitating anti-racist workshops for her two Grade 10 English classes. After explaining to me that the students were both "intolerant" and "unaware," and that they were dealing with a novel laden with racial themes, she said her hope was that some exposure to "race" and racial issues would help them to deal more constructively and critically with the material in their readings. I asked her about the racial composition of the classes, and she said that one class was all white, and the other had one student of colour.

I agreed to facilitate the workshops, but asked if I could bring three of my own students from Brescia University College as a way of facilitating small-group discussions during the workshops. The teacher enthusiastically agreed to my request. She told me there were some "behaviour problems" in the classes, but if the students in question were in any way disruptive they would be removed from the workshops.

When the time arrived, I went along with my three students, two from the Caribbean (one black and one white, both with accents) and one a Muslim. When we greeted the first class, the high-school students were quiet, seemingly nervous. The second class was much more boisterous and far more challenging to manage. In both cases, I very quickly realized that their attention spans were short, and the exercises had to be altered accordingly. We made every effort to involve the students in the workshops as much as possible, and, indeed, they were expected to participate in different ways throughout the various phases. When I told the classes that we were very much interested in what they had to say, and that hearing their points of view was important to the effectiveness of the overall workshop, some of them seemed quite surprised.

In the first class, one of the students asked, "Are you really interested in what I have to say?" He was, we were told, normally considered to be the "class trouble-maker." Before we began he took a seat at the very back of the room, perhaps hoping he would have more opportunity to "goof off" with his buddies. Much to his surprise, I had an opposite strategy. I called upon him first of all to answer questions and to participate in various phases of the workshop. Soon, when he realized that what he had to say did truly matter to us, he became attentive and animated, one of the most actively involved.

In the second class we made similar efforts to engage the most "troublesome" students, although there were significantly more of them there. For the most part the second group provided a far more lively discussion, expressing their points of view (often racist) quite openly. At the end of class one student went so far as to ask one of my facilitators to listen to his portable CD player and some music by a purported "hate-rock" band. He told us that the band was wrongly labelled and not into "hate-rock" at all. What was interesting about the exchange between my student facilitator and this young man was that at least the young man showed a willingness to listen to alternative perspectives on racial issues. It seemed likely that he had previously had no exposure to other points of view.

For our part, the most striking observations of the day centred on the lack of both awareness and exposure to difference. Some students indicated that they were uncomfortable with people of colour and "difference," because they had little exposure to difference in their town. Some talked openly about racism in the town, and some had no problems with it. Others were at least somewhat aware of the problems of stereotyping, intolerance, prejudice and discrimination, yet were uncomfortable when it came to looking at ways of addressing the problem, even in the microcontext of the classroom. This discomfort generally led to much giggling, laughing, joke-making (as reflected in the remark about the "big sweaty white man" from the U.S. South) or silence. Most of the students in both classes, usually by their own admission, fell into the "uncomfortable" category. A few spoke out against racism and racist practices. Interestingly, the one person of colour said not a word throughout the class, expressing discomfort by laughing and giggling along with others when "controversial" questions were asked. Regardless of the level of the discomfort, the highest degree of participation and exchange of perspectives occurred in the small-group discussions facilitated by my undergraduate students—what we consider to be the "educating" part of the process and particularly significant when it comes to formulating the critically responsible alternative.

A Tentative Workshop Outline

Note that the following workshop outline is necessarily tentative—again we emphasize that there can be no strict inventory of pedagogical rules and techniques. We make adjustments according to the level and reaction of each workshop group. In the end, what actually happens in practice is very much subject to context.

Overview:
- Introductory comments
- What is "race"? racism?
- Student responses: oral and written
- Student reactions to video clips
- Types of racism*
  red-necked, polite, institutionalized

* While there are various and more complex ways of pursuing this topic, we made revisions "in the moment" after assessing the academic level of the class and the students' previous exposure to the topic.

• Case studies:

I am going to divide you into three groups—each one will be given a case study with a question or group of questions to consider in relation to the incident. With the assistance of one of my three students, what I want you to do is to discuss the question in your group—try to come up with some consensus in relation to your particular case—then present your case and your group's position to the class for wider discussion.

Possible Case Studies:

1) Faced with the choice of two equally competent applicants for a part-time sales position, the manager of a sporting goods store decides to hire a white student rather than an Asian student, arguing that the white student "would be better for business."

  • Is this discriminatory action or a sound business decision? Why?
  • If you think it is discriminatory, what type of racism would you say best describes this scenario?
  • Would you respond to these questions in the same way if the hiring decision had been the opposite—i.e., the Asian youth got the job and you, as the white student, did not? Justify your answer.

2) An all-Black basketball team from Toronto arrives at your school for a day-long tournament. During warm-up one of the team members is wearing a T-shirt with the words "White Men Can't Jump" written on it. Your team (predominately white) complains to the officials that this shirt promotes racism and the student shouldn't be allowed to wear it. The Black student argues that he isn't intending to be racist; rather, he is simply wearing a shirt bearing the title of a favourite movie.

  • Is the shirt racially prejudicial? Why? Why Not?
  • A related question: is racism a two-way street? In other words, can members of a minority group (generally in a position of powerlessness) display racism against those in "the majority"?

3) A group of white youth arrive at a high school to distribute literature that describes: 1) the immorality of interracial marriages; and 2) the need to protect the "superior" white race from extinction. Both students and school officials ask them to leave the premises and take their racist material with them. The youth refuse to leave, arguing that they live in a democracy and have the right to express their points of view.

  • What kind of racism does this scenario describe?
  • Can the dissemination of this kind of information be justified by appeals to the ideal of democracy, and the accompanying right to "freedom of expression" or "free speech."

4) With the help of a few dedicated teachers, a large contingent of Native students at a local high school lobby for a history course that is more representative of their experiences—for instance, a course entitled "First Nations Perspectives on Canadian History." After much struggle, the course is approved and placed "on the books." A white man, who admittedly knows nothing about the subject matter, is hired to teach the course. His only knowledge will come from a crash course he will be required to take on "First Nations Issues" the summer before he begins to teach. The school board was provided with a list of Native teachers, whose knowledge and experience made them far more qualified to teach the new course. However, the board chose to ignore the list and go with their own candidate. The students, frustrated by the decision, accuse the board of racism.

- Were the actions of the school board racist? Why? Why Not?
- If yes, what type of racism seems to best describe the act?

From the standpoint of facilitation, the workshops were very much a team effort. In inviting my students to participate in them with me, my motivation was not to make my job easier but to create a valuable pedagogical experience for several motivated and committed young scholars. The workshops, for them, were extra, non-credit experiences that would allow them to develop an appreciation of the challenges that teachers face when approaching controversial subjects such as racism.

The use of workshops helps to remove the stratified, unequal relationship that traditionally exists between teachers and students. In this case, my three students and I reconstituted our relationship to reflect the more equitable, Gramscian (1971) notion of "intellectual." Each of us brought to the experience different credentials and expertise that were equally weighted throughout the activity.

The first step was an open dialogue around the format for the workshops. Because these students had never acted as facilitators or even been involved in an anti-racist workshop, they had minimal comments to make on structure. But because of various experiences with racism in their own lives, and their exposure to the process of teaching and learning about racism in the classroom, they could offer strategic comments on content. They were able to help clarify what content was appropriate for the particular level of the class, and what types of pedagogical experiences would be most stimulating and helpful in addressing the content. This dialogue created a more enriched framework within which we could operate.

The involvement of the students in this workshop was a way of bringing to life the theoretical notion of "dialectic." The students came to understand how the combined effects of their real-life experiences and facilitation can have an impact on the process of social transformation. Even in the microsetting of the classroom, the process of development and change is initiated by awakening the consciousness of one young man or woman. Just in having one person thank you for presenting a different point of view, for saying "I never thought about it that way," for acknowledging the need to challenge prejudice and discrimination, teachers and students alike can experience a positive step forward.

The small-group discussions facilitated by my students were the most enriching part of the workshops for them. They had a chance to exchange ideas with seven to ten Grade 10 people around the first three of the four case studies in our outline. They faced the challenge of directing a discussion filled with diverse perspectives—from youth who had a strong anti-racist stance to those who were extremely racist in their actions and/or words, but seemingly unaware of their racism. Specifically, how do you allow all voices to be heard, while ensuring mutual respect in the process? (Jakubowski 2001: 73–74).

Following the workshops, the four of us had a debriefing session, with each of us sharing our views on what was positive about the morning and what required improvement. All of us thought that everything had seemed rushed. There was little time to go into any depth in any one phase of the workshops. This was particularly true of the case studies: there was not enough time to adequately hear all the positions on the questions. But we also acknowledged that given the attention span of the audience, "in-depth" was not necessarily a realistic option.

We also decided that the third case study, dealing with the dissemination of hate literature, was too remote from the students' experience. In each workshop, the group assigned this case had minimal discussion because, by their own admission, they really couldn't appreciate the issues. All three of my students recommended constructing a case study dealing with the problematic nature of jokes based on supposed race-based characteristics or backgrounds.

a wall of silence from others—in response to materials that make vivid the experiences of racial discrimination, hatred and violence" (Cohen 1995: 87).

- "Teaching social stratification is a challenge because students may have little awareness of stratification and may have many stereotypes about the disadvantaged" (McCammon 1999: 44).

Becoming "critically reflective" is an incremental process. It does not happen overnight; and it is not without challenges and pain. Once we make a commitment to subject our pedagogical practice to regular evaluation by students, we must be committed, in practice, to adapting to the changing needs of students. We must also take care not to personalize students' suggestions for change and negative reactions to particular methods. A teacher must avoid what Brookfield (1995: 138) calls "the trap of conversional obsession"—that is, "the process of becoming obsessed with converting all of your students, even the most hostile, to becoming enthusiastic advocates of whatever educational process you are trying to encourage."

Being adaptable, though, does not mean giving up every method or exercise that students don't like. It means hearing student concerns, discussing them in an open forum, and then together negotiating the options. Regular solicitation of critical feedback from students should not have, as its ultimate goal, the achievement of total student satisfaction in every class. Rather, the point of the exercise should be "to situate your teaching in an understanding of the emotional, cognitive and political ebbs and flows of group learning" (Brookfield 1995: 139). The journey towards critical reflection is thus accompanied by "the gradual realization that the dilemmas of teaching have no ultimate solution ... that becoming a skillful teacher will always be an unformed, unfinished project—a true example of lifelong learning" (239). An acceptance of critically responsive teaching as unpredictable and experimental provides the necessary foundation for an assessment of our pedagogy through the eyes of students.

How, then, do we begin to see ourselves through the eyes of our students? How can we begin to adapt our teaching to reflect their concerns? How can we begin to build a pedagogical friendship between teacher and student? Some argue that annual teaching evaluations provide access to student opinion. But that technique can be criticized on two grounds. First, it often provides only a way of measuring the popularity of the teacher, rather than a way of indicating how students are experiencing learning. If students like the teacher, the teacher scores well. If students feel threatened or intimidated by a teacher who is challenging them to think more critically, or in ways that make them uncomfortable, the teacher can score poorly on the evaluation.

The second ground for criticism is the timing of the evaluation. It is usually administered at the end of a course so that it doesn't give teachers the opportunity to respond or adapt. Teachers need to have a mechanism for receiving regular feedback from students during a course. Here, relying heavily on the expertise of Brookfield, we will suggest two methods: 1) the Critical Incident Questionnaire (CIQ) (Brookfield 1995: 114–39); and 2) student learning journals (97–101).

Brookfield (1995: 114) identifies the CIQ as his most effective method for seeing his practice "through students' eyes." Tripp (1993) describes critical incidents as events that people, for different reasons, remember as significant. Brookfield (1995: 114) argues that in every class students will experience critical incidents, and to respond effectively to those incidents teachers must be aware that they are happening. Thus, at the end of each week, a teacher can give students five questions to answer on a sheet of paper.

The Classroom Critical Incident Questionnaire

Please take about 5 minutes to respond to each of the questions below about this week's class(es). Don't put your name on the form—your responses are anonymous. When you have finished writing, put one copy of the form on the table by the door and keep the other copy for yourself. At the start of next week's class, I will be sharing the responses with the group. Thanks for taking the time to do this. What you write will help me make the class more responsive to your concerns.

1. At what moment in the class this week did you feel most engaged with what was happening?
2. At what moment in the class this week did you feel most distanced from what was happening?
3. What action that anyone (teacher or student) took in class this week did you find most affirming and helpful?
4. What action that anyone (teacher or student) took in class this week did you find most puzzling or confusing?
5. What about the class this week surprised you the most? (This could be something about your own reactions to what went on, or something that someone did, or anything else that occurs to you.)

—based on Brookfield 1995: 115

Teachers will have to justify the need for the CIQ to students. In doing this they can emphasize how serious responses to this exercise can improve the overall quality of learning in the class; how the exercise will allow students to get the most out of their educational experience in the class; how it is a way for the teacher to address student concerns regarding the class as these concerns are unfolding, rather than after the course is over. If teachers feel the need to change something about their pedagogical methods in response to comments on the CIQ, they can explain this adaptation to the class. They can clarify matters of content or process that are fuzzy. They can make sure that controversial or contentious issues are discussed so that everyone who wants "voice" receives it (Brookfield 1995: 117).

Although use of the questionnaire adds a great deal more work to the tasks of teaching and learning, the CIQ (or some variation of it) has its advantages: 1) it can alert teachers to potentially serious problems in a course; 2) it encourages students to be reflective learners; 3) it strengthens the argument for diversification in teaching methods; 4) it can build trust between teacher and student; and 5) it suggests possibilities for teacher development (Brookfield 1995: 118-23). All in all, some form of the CIQ can be an effective means of building an open, sensitive and critical learning environment. We encourage teachers to explore Brookfield's writings and to consider experimenting with the variation of the CIQ most suitable to their respective pedagogical styles.

Encouraging students to commit to this reflective learning process is a challenge. One way of highlighting its importance, and "winning over" the sceptical student, is to build into the course grade a participation component of 10–20 percent that will be assigned to a "student learning journal" (Brookfield 1995: 99–100). Essentially, this component requires students to write, in their own words, weekly summaries of their learning experiences (again, the CIQ, if utilized, can be helpful in this exercise as well). Students will summarize the main themes of these descriptions twice throughout the course in report form, submitting the summaries to the teacher for evaluation. Students, as Brookfield (1995: 100) suggests, should be graded on the amount of detail provided and the seriousness of their approach to the assignment, not on the nature of the content.

For the assignment to be successfully completed, teachers must: 1) provide specific guidelines; 2) convince the students of the personal value associated with keeping an educational journal; and 3) acknowledge and reward the effort involved (Brookfield 1995: 97). Brookfield offers guidelines for a learning journal in his work (97–98). Below we offer a variation of those guidelines, a model used by students doing community-based learning in a public school setting. As part of a sociology of education course, students were offered a placement called the "Homework Club," which involved tutoring children in grades 4 to 6. One of the associated responsibilities of doing the placement was keeping a journal.

Instructions on Keeping a Placement Journal

The purpose of this journal is to trace, in a self-reflective way, your experiences as a Homework Club tutor. The idea is to write an entry each week, describing or reacting to, some aspect of the program. For instance, was the program what you expected it to be? If not, what is different? What is positive about the program? What do you feel could be improved? From a more personal standpoint, what has this experience taught you about the process of teaching and learning?

I must stress that you should include in your entries *whatever seems important to you* as you reflect on your experiences as a tutor. If you would like some structure to help with the entries for the first few weeks, try writing a few lines in response to the following questions. What have I learned this week about myself as a tutor? What were the highest emotional moments in my interactions with the children this week? What responsibilities gave me the greatest difficulties this week? What was the most significant thing that happened to me as a tutor this week? Of everything I did this week in my tutoring role, what would I do differently if I had to do it again?

Sharing your journal entries with me will help me to see, through your eyes, the strengths and weaknesses of the Homework Club as an action-learning educational experience. It will also help me to see how future sessions of the program may need to be modified. Ultimately, it will help me to enhance what I perceive to be vital connections between the university classroom and wider community. —modified from Brookfield 1995: 97–98

Brookfield's work reinforces, for us, the tremendous value of regularly soliciting student input. By whatever means a teacher chooses, the gathering of this input, regular debriefings on student concerns, and negotiating solutions that reflect adaptation to these concerns will build a community of trust in the classroom.

There is no doubt that moving towards critically responsive teaching is a risk for teachers. We run the political risk of being marginalized by our colleagues and/or administrations in an environment that is becoming less tolerant of critical diversity in pedagogy. We run the risk of feeling or being labelled incompetent if our pedagogical experimentation is not as "successful" as we might have hoped it would be. And we risk being unable to devote ample time to the other side of our professional identities— research and publishing. But what does it say about our teaching if we choose not to be critically reflective? As Brookfield (1995: 263) states:

Not to live and teach this way is to see yourself as a victim of fate, to be open to exploitation, to live with no sense of promise or forward movement, to be unable to say what you are doing is important, and to think what you do when you show up to teach makes little difference to anyone or anything.

3

Exploring the Controversial
Oppression and First Nations Peoples
with Ursula Elijah, John Elijah and Julie George

Today the Aboriginal people and other Canadians stand on opposite shores of a wide river of mistrust and misunderstanding. Each
continue to search through the mist for a clear reflection in the
waters along the opposite shore. If we are truly to resolve the issues
that separate us, that tear at the heart of this great country ... then
we must each retrace our steps through our history, to the source
of our misperception and misconception of each other's truth.
The challenge is to define, clearly, new visions and pragmatic
mechanisms that will allow our cultural realities to survive and co-
exist. We must seek out those narrow spots near the river's source,
where our hands may be joined as equal and honourable partners
in a new beginning. —Nishga Rod Robinson in Barnaby 1992:
228

One of our First Nations students used this powerful quotation as an
opening to a sociology of law paper, "'You Can Always See the Stars
Brighter When It Is Dark': An Exploration of Justice from a First Nations
Perspective." The ultimate message of her paper was a call for understanding along with an acknowledgement of, and respect for cultural differences
(Shawana 1998). Drawing on the ideas of Rupert Ross (1992, 1996), she
suggests that we will never be able to truly see, hear or appreciate things
that are different—that is, outside our normal frame of reference—until
we recognize that our culture dictates how we translate everything we see
and hear (Shawana 1998: 12).

With this advice in mind, we turn to the question of how, pedagogically,
we can most effectively shape the process of teaching and learning around
the concept of "oppression" as it relates to peoples of the First Nations.
Paraphrasing Gloria Steinem (see the quotation opening chapter 1 here), we
would say that the first task for all of us is to "unlearn" how and what we have
been "schooled" to think about First Nations issues. This unlearning
necessarily involves critical reflection, or the uncovering of hegemonic

assumptions. It involves becoming aware of how the dynamics of power "permeate" educational processes (Brookfield 1995: 1) to shape our understanding of Native culture in relation to non-Native culture. Taking up this approach will mean directly confronting the practices of oppressors by asking uncomfortable questions and most likely finding few gentle answers. This critical reflection also demands a consideration of our "schooling" in Canadian history. That schooling, merely by including some perspectives and excluding others, reinforces Eurocentric biases that marginalize First Nations peoples (for an elaboration, see Jakubowski 1992).

In addition to exploring the inadequacies and inaccuracies of a Eurocentric/Westernized interpretation of history, we must also provide students with an alternative perspective—in particular the perspective of those on the receiving end of colonization. The challenge is to reduce the distance between the Native and non-Native cultures by welcoming into our learning the ideas of those who "think and see with de-colonized minds and hearts" (Monture-Angus 1995: 229).

One way of generating a more inclusive understanding of First Nations' oppression is to explore, via a critically responsive, "problem-posing" (Wallerstein 1987) pedagogy, the related elements of colonization, popular culture and justice. Here, "the controversial" includes both the methods utilized and the content taken up by non-Native instructors teaching this form of oppression to a predominantly non-Native audience.

SETTING THE CONTEXT: CONCEPTUALIZING OPPRESSION AND PRIVILEGE IN RELATIONAL TERMS

In our work, consistent with the approaches of progressive educational scholars such as Bohmer and Briggs (1991), Lucal (1996), Moulder (1997) and Pence and Fields (1999), we have found it effective to conceptualize the study of oppression in "relational terms." We begin by discussing an "absence/presence" approach and considering why, for us, this approach is a less effective way of exploring the different dimensions of oppression (such as race, class and gender). Adopting Lucal's (1996: 245–46) logic, we argue that the "absence/presence" model oversimplifies matters by inadequately addressing how the oppression of one group leads to the privileging of another group or groups. Lucal (245) refers to the "current widespread conceptualization of race as an 'absence/presence' approach," because "race" comes to be treated as "something possessed by people of colour that affects their lives. It depicts whites (usually implicitly) as having no race and as people whose lives are not affected by race." Lucal (246) continues:

> In this model, white is normal and natural…. As a result, because they are not people of colour, many white people do not think racism affects them; they do not consider whiteness as a racial identity…. As a signifier of dominance, whiteness remains invisible (Brah 1992; Lorber 1994)…. [Because] racial inequality is explained in ways that do not implicate white society, white responsibility for the persistence of racism is obscured (hooks 1994; Sleeter 1993). As a result whites can look at racial discrimination with detachment (Feagin and Sikes 1994).

Because whites are generally not taught to see privilege as the flip side of oppression, the power dimension of racism remains obscured (Lucal 1996: 246).

A relational definition of oppression is more inclusive. Viewing oppression and privilege in relational terms urges us to move beyond theoretical abstractions towards an examination of how oppression and privilege are experienced in our everyday lives. According to Lucal (1996: 246), "If race is regarded as something that gives some (white) people privileges, even while it oppresses other people, then it is difficult to believe that race only affects people of colour." Furthermore, to deal with "whiteness" in an analysis of racial oppression is to "assign *everyone* a place in the relations of racism" (Frankenberg 1993: 6).

McIntosh's (1995) article on white privilege and male privilege is a particularly useful starting point for illustrating this relational approach. A relational model of oppression and privilege clearly locates everyone connected to the subject, and the discussion, in societal relations, and makes power relations more transparent. We can begin to speak about "systems of oppression/privilege" as "those attitudes, behaviours and pervasive and systemic social arrangements by which members of one group are exploited and subordinated while members of another group are granted privileges" (Bohmer and Briggs 1991: 155).

From a pedagogical standpoint, the use of a relational model of oppression and privilege helps to reduce students' resistance and discomfort in dealing with controversial material. In our practice, we highlight the idea that both oppression and privilege have an effect, in some way, on the lives of *every* member of society, and that therefore these conditions provide a necessary site for investigation. We try to reduce guilt and discomfort by stressing that, in most cases, people "cannot choose whether they belong to an oppressed or privileged group, because this status is typically ascribed" (Bohmer and Briggs 1991: 156). A white man, for example, can be anti-racist and anti-sexist in his beliefs and actions but still derive benefits from his group memberships. Analyses of oppression and privilege must always be located, then, in their appropriate social contexts.

PROBLEM-POSING AS A CRITICALLY RESPONSIVE ALTERNATIVE

In *Pedagogy of Freedom*, Paulo Freire (1998: 31) reminds us that there can be no teaching without learning. He stresses that while the teacher and student are obviously different, they each have "subject" roles to play in the process: "The person in charge of education is being formed or re-formed as he/she teaches, and the person who is being taught forms him/herself in this process…. Whoever teaches learns in the act of teaching, and whoever learns teaches in the act of learning." Freire's comments reinforce education's role as an ongoing process of knowledge construction for which teachers and students are mutually responsible. Essentially, teaching and learning emerge from the knowledge and life experiences of the various educational participants.

Theorist and teacher Nina Wallerstein (1987) offers a critically responsive, "problem-posing" alternative appropriate to exploring First Nations' oppression. Wallerstein (34) describes problem-posing as "a group process that draws on personal experiences to create social connectedness and mutual responsibility." This method involves three phases: listening, dialogue and action (35). The "listening" includes determining which issues are of central importance to an analysis of oppression. Given our relational conceptualization of oppression and privilege, this assessment of issues cannot be completed before the class begins, nor can it be done exclusively by the teacher. Rather, "as content is drawn from learners' daily lives, listening becomes an ongoing process involving both teachers and students as co-learners and co-explorers." This first step can occur both in and outside of the classroom and can include observation, interviews or analysis of documents. The students individually record what they hear, see or observe in a "code" that is, according to Wallerstein (38), "a concrete physical representation of a particularly critical issue that has come up during the listening phase." These codes become the "objects" around which "dialogue" occurs.

The codes become an important tool in the mediation of dialogue. They help participants deal with issues that may be "too threatening to approach directly or too overwhelming or embarrassing to confront individually" (Wallerstein 1987: 38). A codification exemplifying a dimension of First Nations' oppression, for example, allows individuals to think critically and to express their concerns on the problem—in a depersonalized, less threatening way. Within the dialogue phase, Wallerstein (1987:

38–39) uses a five-step questioning strategy to promote movement from critical thinking to action. In relation to the code, students are invited to:

- describe what they see, hear or read;
- define the problem(s);
- share similar experiences;
- question why there is a problem;
- strategize what they, individually or collectively, can do about the problem.

The fifth step of strategizing facilitates movement into the action phase: what kind of small action steps can students take in their daily lives to ameliorate oppressive conditions?

Action begins when students envision themselves as social and political beings. The development of this level of social and political awareness depends on many factors, including internal classroom dynamics, external societal factors, and the level of self-confidence and cultural experiences of the individual actors (Wallerstein 1987: 42). Action can also take diverse forms, both in and outside the classroom (42–43). Expectations of "action" will vary by context. For example, strategies for change might be more modest among a class of students who have traditionally been more passive and apolitical in the classroom than they would be for a group of students who have already either participated in social movements or have expressed interest in doing so. Because we would rather have students choose activity over passivity, we remain flexible in our definitions of "action."

Adopting the philosophy embedded in Clyde W. Ford's (1994) book *We Can All Get Along*—that is, "All positive change starts with one person who cares"—we strive to move a controversial component of the course towards a "hopeful" course of action. While its content focuses on steps towards ending racism, Ford's book is extremely helpful in suggesting many different opportunities (fifty of them) for action—towards ending racism specifically and oppression more generally. Frances Moulder (1997: 124) describes her experiences in relation to promoting diverse forms of action:

> It is important that instructors provide many choices, so that students do not feel forced into a personally uncomfortable situation. My students write a brief, one page report on each of their "action steps," and also discuss their experiences in small groups during the class.... I find that almost anything a student chooses

to do will give them some insight into the possibilities of change. The small group discussion also begins to create a mini-community in the classroom, which reinforces the notion that change is possible.

COLONIAL EFFECTS: A FIRST NATIONS PERSPECTIVE

Given the preceding pedagogical context for our analysis of oppression, our task now is to apply this method in relation to colonization, the role of popular cultural and justice.

Over the centuries, the dominant society has created and perpetuated the Native as "other," through means of numerous overlapping discourses that have served to regulate the discussion: from the spiritual (programs of religious conversions) and the physical (strategies of territorial confinement) to the moral (popular culture) and the legal (prisoning of the mind, body and spirit). Here, striving to break with mainstream discourses that see people of the First Nations as the "other," we proceed with a more constructive pedagogical exploration, returning to Native tradition and natural teachings. Integral to this approach is a deep respect for, and utilization of, the knowledge of several of our First Nations colleagues, who have generously provided textual "codes" to facilitate our exploration of, and dialogue about, the subject of oppression. Focusing on the use of "first voice," "the circle" and "story-telling" as teaching tools (Graveline 1998), we begin outside of our "normal" frame of reference with the voices of those traditionally silenced in the cultural mainstream.

The Residential School Syndrome
by Ursula Elijah

As a reader, open your mind, acknowledge my voice, and understand the words I speak, and accept my reality. I speak these words with a clear mind, an honest heart, and a perished soul. Envision there are two worlds that separate our paths. Your path and my path. These paths will forever clash, causing external conflict and turmoil between our people. The path I choose to speak of is my truth. My truth tells me that our truths are not the same. Your eyes tell you one thing; and my eyes tell me another. The truth I speak of reveals the vivid recollection of horrible past events that are real to me. Because I live with these recollections, and they will never be forgotten. These horrific events have demoralized, humiliated and belittled my very soul. Even today, I wear these scars. These are the scars I pass on to my children, and my children's children. This is my history. Hear me!

At one time or another FIRST Nations people have been made to endure the ill effects of the residential schools. Many live with the invasions upon their lives.

It goes deeper than people actually realize. These past experiences have left emotional scars on the personal and social being. The negative implications of these schools have affected many, from our infants to our elderly population. In order to understand the residential schooling syndrome, acknowledgement has to be made of the injustices that First Nations People have had to endure, especially within the confines of the educational institutions; as a result, CULTURAL GENOCIDE PREVAILS. There are three crucial areas in need of investigation: European Contact, the assimilation process, and the effects of these processes upon the First Nations populations.

European Contact

Picture the year 1492. The historical era known as the INVASION OF THE AMERICAS, by none other than CHRISTOPHER COLUMBUS. Needless to say, it was a voyage that changed the lives of many people: First Nations people and Europeans. This increment of time was the start of the colonization period. The colonization process, itself, was first introduced to the original inhabitants that occupied the vast, prosperous, and nurturing lands of North America, the First Nations populations. As the colonization period progressed, the process took a special form of domination. Where the European country sent immigrants to North America to settle it (according to European standards) and take political, social and economic control. However, this process only served the self-interests of those who travelled the seas: to rape, brutalize, and forcefully possess what they could physically claim as their own. These people had dispossessed natures. In a sense, their focus was on the material possessions in life: money, land, natural resources—oil, gold, silver, copper, etc. Their belief consisted of the more you have and are in possession of the wealthier you are, as an individual, and the greater your status and stigma in society. This ideology as a belief transpired in a cultural clash which evolved between First Nations peoples and the European newcomers. While the focus of First Nations peoples was forever on the land. Their life cycles were in accordance with the RESPECT of the land, namely Mother Earth, and the bountiful gifts she gave in return. First Nations peoples' identities came from the land and were further incorporated into networks of the individual's responsibilities, the family's unity and the community's surroundings as distinct nations.

The Assimilation Process

Speaking of conformity, the key to understanding First Nations peoples and the injustices inflicted upon them is to grasp the techniques used. Let's begin with exploring some new concepts. We'll begin with assimilation: it has been defined as "to make or become like...." In reference to First Nations communities, the vast array of people suffered from the verbal attacks to their beliefs, morals and life-long practices. They endured negative backlash and numerous attempts to stigmatize their lifestyles.

The Europeans played on the defence mechanisms that the First Nations exemplified, to make their position of power legitimate. They believed that these people were in need of resocialization. As they stood, these people were less than adequately equipped to meet the needs of the greater society. It then became a quest to properly equip these savages with the necessary skills of reading, writing, and mathematics. These were the skills defined as the tools to interact on a daily basis with the European settlers. Therefore, the European concept implied the ability of those in power to transform these nations in accordance with European ideology. The task was to make the First Nation residents like themselves.

The assimilation process was confirmed by First Nations people and their alcohol abuse, broken homes, and single mothers raising numerous children. Out of this type of thinking grew the construction of residential schools. These schools were the most appropriate means—to resocialize, teach academics, fulfil religious quotas and eliminate or erase the cultural sanctities in each and every child. They provided the perfect opportunity to house these children and legitimize their system of assimilation, not to mention alienation. These schools would never be under the scrutiny of others, nor would anyone question the religious orders, which followed their beliefs in order to help these disadvantaged children who live in sin. The children who occupied these schools were forced from their homes, taken from their families and ripped away from their communities. They were thrown into foreign environments that were cold, harsh, and restricting to their nature. Most times, these environments cared little about each child's identity; except to change it.

Many of the methods used were volatile acts of conformity. Conformity was to a new way of life. A child's emotions were never nurtured and the soul was in constant turmoil. The worst part of these schools was that the children had limited access to their own siblings. Children received physical punishment if they spoke their language. Their way of life was constantly attacked. These children suffered from broken spirits, especially in the midst of all the commotion, including all the transitional elements. The loss of identity results from the mind and body being separated (these components are no longer whole and no longer in unity with one another). The spirit can no longer feel the emotions that make the First Nations person feel human. These educational institutions teach the tiny victims to shut down their systems of emotions, not to feel. The task of these authoritarian figures is to erase the "Indianness" out of the Indian. The only reserves that First Nations children had to fall back on were their links to family ties and the craving for family unity. Maltreatment within these institutions has never been denied. The facts remain and the voices tell all. A case study of actual events follows: **A note of caution to the reader: very sensitive issues and emotions are expressed in the following passage.

I am a child of dark skin, long brown hair, and raven eyes. I am eight years old. I have seven brothers and four sisters, excluding myself. I live in a small community outside the city. My mom and dad are no longer together. I don't know why! The drinking hasn't stopped, but the beatings my dad laid on my mom have stopped. She walks around our tiny home sad and lonely. She spends less and less time at home. White strangers came knocking at our door today. My mom said they want to take all us children away. I know I don't want to go, neither do my brothers or my sisters. They said they would return for us tomorrow. I'm so scared, I just want to cry; or even run away. My mom talks to us our last night home. She says she loves us and we have to be strong. Her final words are I'll visit you, and never forget I love you.

All I remember next is riding in a car. Ahead of us is another car carrying my brothers. We've been driving for a long time. We finally arrive at the boarding school. It looks cold, dark and scary. I don't like this, I want to go home. Take me home. We're led down this long hallway. My brothers, sisters and I are divided. And that's the last time we are together as a family. These women here are mean and very forceful. They don't treat us very nicely. They make me change my clothes. They took all our clothes, put them in a pile and burnt them. I don't know why they did this. They then rush us into another room, and they chopped my hair off. I just wanted to cry as I saw my hair fall to the ground. I never said they could cut my hair. But I don't think they would have listened anyway.

The food is rotten, not fit for my dogs to eat. There sure is a lot of dishes to wash and dry. It takes us a long time to do all those dishes. It seems like nobody cares. I hardly see my brothers and sisters anymore. When I do, they look like me, lifeless. I just can't wait until I get out of here. I saw a little boy today. He can't speak very good English. He sure got one hell of a beating for speaking his language though. I see the expression on his face; they can't hurt him. The night time is the worst. I don't even remember the night time being so long, dark, cold and scary. All us girls hate going to bed, especially when the lights go off, the hallway is quiet. You can hear a pin drop. We all wonder who it's going to be tonight. If I lay still enough, I can hear the other girls weep on their pillows. These beds offer no comfort at all. The door opens ... the Priest comes in, gently shuts the door behind him. My heart is beating fast, I dare not breathe. He walks past my bed. I sure am relieved, my heart slows to a normal pace. He walks to Nancy's tiny little bed. I hear her weeping. She whispers, "No, don't, it hurts, oh ... it hurts." He doesn't hear her.

She cries softly, and I can't help her. I close my eyes and wish I was someplace else. You know if I close my eyes hard enough I can remember running in the fields, playing tag with all the kids and having fun until dark. I long to return to that time not so long ago and have that same freedom again. The days go on and on and on. I've only seen my mother twice in the last three years. I know I have another little sister. She's a year and a half old. "Boy, I sure hope she never ends up here." I have never heard from my dad or even seen him. I guess he's busy and can't come see us.

I'm tired of this lifestyle. The names they call me don't hurt anymore;

I'll never let them know it. I tell myself, I'm not a dirty little Indian, and I'm not a savage either. "You know what, I am good for something." It seems like the only thing that keeps me going these days is knowing they can't keep me forever. One of these days I'll get out of here, one of these days. And I'll show them. I've learned to forgive, but I'll never forget.

This scenario is a combination of true events that actually took place inside the walls of these residential schools. A lot of heart-breaking violations were directed towards the children. In most cases innocent children experienced physical, mental, emotional and sexual abuse. As adults we live our lives protecting all children from these acts of violence. "Who was protecting our children?" The most serious violations came from those persons in positions of authority. The authority these people possessed became a weapon they used uncontrollably against the children they were in the midst of assimilating. As far back as history retracts, not once did the First Nations populations ask to be assimilated. Throughout history, the First Nations' political power, as a group, has been one of resistance. The resistance the Nations used was their form of protection (of the natural ways, including the natural surroundings: in all actuality, their distinct identities). Europeans took these ways as negative acts of resilience that needed to be addressed and virtually put to an end.

The European settlers could not for the life of them see or acknowledge the cultural differences. They were the ones who wore blinders and tunnelled their own vision to reality. The only reason that comes to mind is that the power of the dollars has a greater significance than human lives, and is treated so. The transitional process they set in place became CULTURAL RAPE. They actively induced physical force, brutal means and violent acts to strip these cultures of their heritage and the burial of their ancestral ways. A majority of First Nations were dealt a horrible fate, while the outsiders looked on and wallowed in the glory of the aftermath.

Remember, the First Nations never asked to be converted; but were made to endure the hardships that followed and to relinquish their ties to themselves, and the rights to Mother Earth. The history books of the past presented only one side of the story. And the Indians were the only ones made to pay the price. The stereotypical attitudes that evolved denigrated Indians. Everything an Indian was or did was wrong. It was bad, they are all dirty, and they are all savage, like in nature. Still these depictions are the reality of many people who are ignorant of past historical events. A judgement cannot be made, unless an understanding of the past prevails and the truths are revealed.

In the context of today's society, our Mother Earth has been made to endure untold abuse (her resources are not as plentiful as they used to be). She has been exploited, physically assaulted and raped of her assets. Damage to the ozone layer is a constant threat to the existence of us all. The air and waters are polluted, and the fear of implacable diseases is overhead. It is time for change because the environment is telling us so. Where is the focus geared to ... the NATURAL WAYS? Who are the people who possessed this knowledge? FIRST NATIONS

PEOPLE. It seems as though the greater society is retracting its steps, but is it too late? With the shift in time, the question is: were First Nations populations in need of assimilation to change their naturalness in accordance with the world?

As a closing remark: the implementation of European values proved to be detrimental to the nature of First Nations peoples. Many of these communities are in turmoil today, and attempts are being made to restore their cultural balance. But currently the struggle is in overcoming the negative self-esteems that many people are victims of. These poor self-esteems are directly linked to the ill treatment that many experienced within the residential schools. As a consequence the residential schooling syndrome has hurt the children of children in these schools, as well as the children to come. The greatest sacrifice has been the loss of LANGUAGE.

A TEACHING SUGGESTION

From our standpoint, the ideal way to discuss an essay like the one you have just read is with its author present or with someone who has shared a similar cultural experience. In our teaching both Ursula Elijah and her partner, John Elijah (Past Chief of Natural Teachings, Oneida Community, Lambeth), have regularly and generously shared their wisdom with us. They have never turned down our invitations to give guest presentations on First Nations issues. As Moulder (1997: 125) notes:

> Not surprisingly, many students have never interacted face to face with people who could be role models for participating in social change.... [Yet], some teachers may feel there is not enough time in a semester to spend valuable class time on the view of people who are not sociologists. However, if an important aim is for the students to understand change, and not come away cynical and despairing, then I believe the time "lost" is more than made up for by lessening students' alienation from the topic.

In our case, Ursula and John, coming from an oral tradition, introduce these issues to non-Natives with a non-threatening, direct eloquence. They welcome any and all questions and comments from the audience. Oral narration is central to Native cultural preservation. With "first voice," "the circle" and "story-telling" as teaching tools (Graveline 1998), a relationship can slowly build between the teller and the listener.

"First voice" as a critical pedagogical tool is closely associated with anti-racist, feminist, experiential and First Nations discourse. More specifically, "the voice of experience" is used to guide our knowledge base. From the standpoint of First Nations' ancestral traditions, "First Voice poses a necessary alternative to the truth claims articulated in the voice of the White 'expert,' who 'knows' what we 'need'" (Graveline 1998: 118). First voice is an essential component of "story-telling," which is combined with the circle to create the "talking circle" as a form of pedagogy.

In Talking Circle ... in "circle time"
We open our Hearts
Speak what we know to be True
Share what we Care deeply about
As Honestly as we can ... as Respectfully as we are able.
We are able to enter into another's experiences through their Words.
A doorway to self-examination ... a social context for
a "personal experience." (136–37)

Through the talking circle, dialogue unfolds in a way that builds the community values of respect, honesty, caring and sharing (137–38).

Mi'kmaq Elder Isabelle Knockwood (1992: 7–8) makes the talking circle eloquently concrete when she describes the "talking stick" process:

> Our Mi'kmaw ancestors used the Talking Stick to guarantee that everyone who wanted to speak would have a chance to be heard and that they would be allowed to take as long as they needed to say what was on their minds without fear of being interrupted with questions, criticisms, lectures, or scoldings, or even being presented with solutions to their problems. An ordinary stick of any kind or size is used. Those seated in the Circle commit themselves to staying to the end, not getting up to leave or walk about because this behaviour is considered an interruption. Anyone who leaves the Circle can return and sit with the latecomers whose only role is to observe and listen. This is because they have missed some information and therefore cannot offer advice or make an informed decision. The person who has a problem or issue to discuss holds the Talking Stick and relates everything pertaining to it especially everything they have done to solve it. After they are through, they pass the stick to the person on the left, following the sun's direction. The next person, Negem, states everything they know about the problem without repeating anything that was already said. They tell what they and others have done in similar situations. They neither agree nor disagree with what others have said.
>
> The Talking Stick goes around until it returns to the person with the problem or issue, who then acknowledges everyone

present and what they have said. Sometimes the solution or answer comes as soon as everyone has spoken. Maybe the person has already thought it out, or it may come as an inspiration on the long trek back home. Or else, it could appear in the form of a vision or dream. Dreams were a very important part of problem-solving with the First People of the land. Maybe a Spirit Guide will come, or some new information will be brought to light or a series of events will fall into place.

A note of caution with respect to use of the circle as a pedagogical tool: Graveline (1998: 240–41) reminds us that in using the circle for sharing information, we must be careful to highlight that in a school setting it represents an "adaptation" of the spiritual process used by shamans and elders. Beyond this acknowledgement, we must be careful not to appropriate and misuse something so sacred to First Nations peoples. While Graveline (242) believes that First Nations traditions need to be taught to non-Natives to "assist in healing the earth," the adaptation and application of the circle must be carried out with the utmost respect.

For this reason, we strongly encourage teachers, before utilizing this pedagogical tool, to consult extensively with an elder or traditionalist who has used the circle in different contexts (244). Ideally, have a traditionalist or elder come to your classroom to teach via the circle. Such a person is in the best position to contextualize the method, "articulate the Ancestral wisdom that guides the process" (241) and distinguish for non-Native participants how their experience of the talking circle will differ from the healing process used by elders and shamans in First Nations communities.

While we are fortunate to have some strong connections to traditionalists in different First Nations communities, this is not the case for all teachers. It may be necessary to do some networking and seeking out of traditionalists before it is possible to invite them to the classroom to facilitate. For example, one of us participated in a First Nations pedagogical "circle" that was based on principles similar to the talking circle. This experience was part of a cross-cultural, anti-racism education conference held for youth in the Southwestern Ontario region. The circle was taught by a group of First Nations young men and women from across Ontario who are part of an organization called WI CHI HI TOOK ("Helping Each Other").

This information-sharing circle generated knowledge about First Nations' heritage through open and interactive dialogue. In addition to technical research, the perspectives offered were based on the personal and community experiences of these young men and women. This particular adaptation involved the use of two circles. The larger outside circle was for the audience members; the smaller inside circle contained a seat for each First Nations person, with an open chair for audience participants. Participants from the audience were invited into the inner circle one at a time. Once there, participants could pose questions to their Native hosts, who would then share their knowledge on the topic.

Throughout this procedure, it was clear that every question is valid and every voice is equal. Questions ranged from issues associated with justice and self-government to stereotypes, language, life on reserves and the purpose of ceremonies like the "pow wow." As the experience unfolded, the group's working philosophy of "Friendship, Peace and Respect" became clear in practice. The audience, including children, youth and adults, was actively engaged in this process designed to further the understanding between cultures and generations.

This adaptation of a "traditional" Native practice embodied the goals of contemporary critical pedagogy that so many of us regularly strive to achieve. There were no power differentials, no reference to titles or positions. From the start, we were all on a first-name basis with each other. There was respect for all voices in the room; no one spoke while another was speaking, and no voice was silenced. The mutual respect that developed within this setting was facilitated by the group's use of a two-circle model. The outer circle remained focused and attentive to the discussions of the inner circle. No question was repeated, and in responding to the questions each individual spoke in turn, adding only new information to the discussion. If nothing new could be added to the discussion on a given topic, the next Native facilitator would simply refrain from commenting. People could re-enter the inner circle more than once, as long as their movement did not preclude a person in the audience from first-time participation.

Following the formal process, there was time for informal, one-on-one dialogue with the facilitators to further discuss substantive issues. In addition, the facilitators were anxious for feedback, in written or verbal form, from the audience on the strengths or weaknesses of the circle. What was good about it? What could be improved? This phase clearly highlighted a commitment to context and a willingness to maximize the effectiveness of the approach by taking into account the experiences of the participants, just as the participants had grown (to varying degrees) through knowledge shared in dialogue with the facilitators. In essence, the sharing of experience in an environment respectful of all participants is a defining feature of this "community-building" pedagogy (Graveline 1998: 171).

Ursula Elijah's account provides one example of the kind of content that might be used to begin a conversation. Following are other examples of ways of taking historically silenced voices into account.

EXERCISE NO. 1: COMPARING THE COLONIZED TO THE COLONIZER

Codifying the "Eurocentric" Colonizer's Voice

Consider here how French explorers Jacques Cartier and Samuel de Champlain described their first encounters with Canada's First Nations people. The Eurocentric "savage" imagery initially appeared in 1534 when French explorer Jacques Cartier encountered Canadian Native people for the first time. When commenting on the costumes and clothing of the first inhabitants he saw, Cartier noted:

> There are people on this coast whose bodies are fairly well-formed but they are a wild and savage folk. They wear their hair tied upon the top of their heads like a handful of twisted hay, with a nail or something of the sort passed through the middle and into it they weave a few birds' feathers. They clothe themselves with furs of animals, both men as well as women. (Cartier 1924: 22–23)

Considering another community of Native people he encountered on this first voyage, Cartier noted:

> This people may well be called savage; for they are the sorriest folk there can be in this world.... They go quite naked except for a small skin with which they cover their privy parts and for a few old furs which they throw over their shoulders.... They have their heads shaved all around in circles except for a small tuft on the top of the head, which they leave long like a horse's tail. This they do up upon their heads and tie in a knot with leather thongs. (60–61)

When commenting on some of the customs, beliefs and habits of the Huron people, Cartier creates even more negative imagery:

> This tribe has no belief in God that amounts to anything; for they believe in a God they call *Cudouagny*.... After they had explained things to us, we showed them their error and informed them that their *Cudouagny* was a wicked spirit who deceived them and there is but one God, who is in Heaven, who gives us everything we need and is the Creator of all things and that in him alone we

should believe. Also, that one must receive baptism or perish in hell. (179–80)

Similarly, while discussing religious beliefs with a First Nations chief, Samuel de Champlain (1971: 72–76) expressed even harsher sentiments: "I then asked him how they prayed to their gods and he said they didn't have any ceremonies, that each man prayed in his own way. This is why they have no principles and know nothing of God and behave like animals.... They are a brutish people."

How then, do these reactions compare with the North American Native peoples' reactions to colonization and the colonizer?

Codifying the "Authentic" Colonized Voice

In 1775 a member of the Stockbridge tribe told the Massachusetts Congress:

> Brothers! You remember, when you first came over the great waters, I was great and you were little—very small. I then took you in for a friend, and kept you under my arms, so that no one might injure you.... But now our conditions have changed. You are great and tall. You reach to the clouds. You are seen round the world. I am becoming very small—very little. (Safire 1992: 90)

Likewise, another Native leader, Chief Red Jacket of the Seneca nation, was equally indignant with the efforts of the Christian churches to convert Aboriginal peoples. Chief Red Jacket, born in 1758, was given the Indian name of Otetiani when he became chief, and he enjoyed the title of Sagoyewatha. Known by the red coat given to him by the British, he became prominent through his lifelong struggle to maintain Native culture against the introduction of white customs. He opposed attempts to bring European values to his community and became a spokesperson for all indigenous cultures. In 1805 he spoke publicly to Christian missionaries trying to baptize his followers:

> We have listened with attention to what you have said.... All have heard your voice, and all will speak to you now as one man.... Brother listen to what we say. There was a time when our forefathers owned this great island. Their seats extended from the rising to the setting sun. The Great Spirit had made it for the use of Indians. He had created the buffalo, the deer, and other animals for food. He had made the bear and beaver. Their skins served us

for clothing.... All this he had done for his red children.... But an evil came upon us. Your forefathers crossed the great water and landed on this island. Their numbers were small. They found friends and not enemies. They told us they had fled from their own country for fear of wicked men and had come here to enjoy their religion. They asked for a small seat. We took pity on them, granted their request, and they sat down among us. We gave them corn and meat; they gave us poison in return.... You have now become a great people, and we have scarcely a place left to spread our blankets. You have got our country, but are not satisfied; you want to force your religion upon us.... Brother, we do not wish to destroy your religion or take from you. We only want to enjoy our own. (Safire 1992: 532–33)

Another great orator, Chief Seattle, who led the Duwamish and Suquamish nations of the Pacific Northwest, delivered a speech on the Chinook language on January 12, 1854. His call for justice has an ominous tone:

Today it is fair; tomorrow it may be overcast with clouds.... The great, and I presume also good, white chief sends us word that he wants to buy our lands but is willing to allow us to reserve enough to live on comfortably. This indeed appears generous, for the red man no longer has rights.... There was a time when our people covered the whole land as the waves of a wind-ruffled sea cover its shell floor. But that time has long since passed away with the greatness of tribes almost forgotten. I will not mourn over the untimely decay nor reproach my paleface brothers with hastening it for we too may have been somewhat to blame.... Your God loves your people and hates mine.... The Indian's night promises to be dark. No bright star hovers about the horizon.... The white man will never be alone. Let him be just and deal kindly with my people, for the dead are not altogether powerless. (Safire 1992: 574–76)

When Chief Joseph of the Nez Perce, known to his people as Thunder Travelling to the Loftier Mountain Heights, surrendered to the U.S. army in 1877, he addressed the depths of defeat:

Tell General Howard I know his heart.... I am tired of fighting. Our chiefs are killed; Looking-Glass is dead, Ta-Hool-Shute is dead. The old men are all dead.... He who led on the young men is dead. It is cold and we have no blankets; the little children are freezing to death. My people ... have no blankets, no food. No one knows where they are—perhaps freezing to death. I want to have time to look for my children, and see how many of them I can find. Maybe I shall find them among the dead. (Safire 1992: 108)

Critically Reflecting on the Codes

To maximize participation, we encourage participation in a pedagogical "circle," if the setting permits and if an appropriate facilitator for the circle is available. Alternatively, we would invite two modes of reflection: oral participation in a small-group discussion and/or writing journal-like entries (Roth 1985). The value of small-group discussions prior to a facilitated plenary group discussion is that those who traditionally won't speak in the larger group may share their ideas and become more involved. However, even in small groups some participants will feel that they have gained much from the presentation and reflective exercise, yet will not be confident enough to share their ideas orally. In this instance, the written reflection can become another form of participation. The facilitator can take a look at the piece of writing and then share it anonymously with the class. Writing can become a mode of learning: asking questions, and attempting to answer one's own questions, in this journal-like form, becomes a way for each individual participant/writer to begin the process of making connections between theoretical and experiential forms of knowledge—in other words, making links between the classroom and the outside world.

At this point we make every effort to link critical reflection to some form of action. For example, following Ford's (1994) guide, we may invite students to:

- inventory their life experience with this form of racist oppression (Ford 1994: 28–31);
- examine their personal views about racism (32–35); or
- release the stereotypes they have of others (39–42).

Oppression, Regulation and the Role of Popular Culture

Popular culture, as expressed in film, television, literature and entertainment, consistently misrepresents Aboriginal peoples. From the "wild west" movies to contemporary television and literature, Hollywood has subordinated Native peoples by providing grossly inaccurate portrayals of a savage and pagan culture and a lazy, drunk and irresponsible people. Any pre-European history is virtually non-existent on the screen. According to La Roque (1975: 33–34) contemporary literature advances competing stereotypes of Natives. On the one hand, they are condemned as hostile savages attacking white settlers, as "Dirty Indians"—irresponsible, lazy, superstitious, drunk and perpetually on welfare. On the other hand, they are romanticized—the "noble red man" in harmony with nature, the hero of freedom, simplicity and dignity.

In the shape of the so-called "Hollywood Indian," the motion picture industry sells stereotypes to entertain the white culture (Price 1973: 154), with fictitious language, inappropriate costumes and an overwhelming theme of conflict. Friar and Friar (1972: 47) described the predominant image of the Indian as "a grunting, mentally retarded, monosyllabic idiot," an image that ignores the rich cultural diversity of well over 560 languages in North America (Price 1973). Until recent times, western movies almost always used non-Natives to play prominent Indian roles—as in *Stay Away Joe* (Elvis Presley), *Apache* (Burt Lancaster), *The Outsider* (Tony Curtis) and countless others. Although the image—similar to that of Tonto in the Lone Ranger—is slowly changing, the re-romanticized stereotype of the "Noble Savage" armed with a magnificent landscape, obedient horses and weapons, as evident in *Dances with Wolves*, *The Last of the Mohicans*, and *Geronimo*, maintains the central role of the white man as he dictates to the Native people, who exist in supporting roles only. These reformulated sidekicks are also subordinate to the horses, guns and scenic landscapes. Alternatively, as in *The Quest* and *Poltergeist II*, Natives are portrayed as medicine men, the shamen.

In North America, racism is so much a part of the landscape that we most often no longer recognize its painful consequences. For example, during the widely televised baseball playoff and World Series games of the 1990s—and into the new decade—tens of thousands of Atlanta Braves baseball fans were swinging or "chopping" with their stadium-supplied tomahawks—the then owner of the Atlanta team, Ted Turner, and his wife, former activist Jane Fonda, among them. Throughout their regular season the Cleveland Indian fans sported traditional headdress, painted their faces, and shouted what they considered to be Indian war chants. In other professional sports, the National Football League's Kansas City Chiefs and their Arrowhead Stadium, the NFL's Washington Redskins, the Canadian Football League's Edmonton Eskimos, the National Hockey League's Chicago Black Hawks, and the Florida State Seminoles in the college football league, among others, contribute to the perpetuation of deep-seated bigotry that rejects the rich contributions of Natives in favour of dangerous images of violence, war and savagery. During the Persian Gulf Crisis, the U.S. military was equipped with "Tomahawk" missiles and Apache helicopters.

Common pejorative expressions have proliferated. "Indian giver," for instance, is defined by the *Webster's New World Dictionary* as "a person who gives something and then asks for it back; from the belief that American Indians expected an equivalent in return when giving something" (*Webster's New World Dictionary* 1974: 715). According to the *Random House Thesaurus of Slang* (Lewin and Lewin 1988: 200), a number of common idioms and colloquialisms are considered synonymous with the word "Indian": "injun, redskin, buck, brave, red man, apple, Uncle Tomahawk (white establishment oriented)." None of these general terms received the routine "derogatory" designation that accompanies the descriptions for other cultures and races in the thesaurus. The racist exploitation of distorted aspects of Native traditions as celebrated commodities at sporting events, in battle and in language is the outcome of historically rooted structured inequalities.

EXERCISE NO. 2: A PROBLEM–POSING APPROACH TO POPULAR CULTURE

Teaching and learning can take many diverse and creative forms, most of which are linked to dialogue around popular cultural "codes." For example, defining movies as popular cultural codifications, we have invited students to compare *Dances with Wolves*, the high-budget Hollywood extravaganza, with *Smoke Signals*, a more recent, less publicized movie about Native peoples.

Smoke Signals was billed as the first film to be written, directed and acted by Indians (Howell 1998a: C6). As Howell (1998b: C1) notes: "*Smoke Signals* presents Indians in a way not often seen on screen: as people with human strengths and weaknesses, capable of both laughing and crying. People who would rather raise their children, than raise their fists." Irene Bedard, an actress of Cree and Inuit heritage who stars in the film, states:

> I think what is great about this film is that finally it has our eyes going out into the world.… Before *Dances with Wolves*, every film had John Wayne battle scenes with lots of death and we were the cause of it all. And then *Dances with Wolves* happened and we went through our roots era, where we were telling stories of famous native people. But it was still constantly through Eurocentric eyes. This one has our eyes. (quoted in Howell 1998b: C1)

Students might do a comparison of the content of each movie. For instance, how are First Nations' characters portrayed in each film? What are the implications of these portrayals? Furthermore, students might do some informal interviewing of friends (for the purposes of class discussion) asking various questions, such as 1) Have you seen both movies? 2) If you have not seen *Smoke Signals*, what do you know about it? 3) Why would you find *Dances with Wolves* more appealing? Setting up a series of questions will allow students to develop a better appreciation of the reasons why people attend movies, and whether there is a "social distancing" from certain types of movies, and why?

Alternatively, some may choose to be a participant observer at a sporting event where a team is in some way identified with First Nations' culture. The observer might note the reaction of the crowds towards the particular team, the types of uniforms worn by the team, and how the various symbols or behaviours portray the culture/cultural symbol they have appropriated: in other words, an analysis of the imagery associated with the league's regular season competition or playoffs. Or one might do a content analysis of advertisements for vehicles in some way identified with First Nations' culture, and consider how these ads perpetuate oppression.

In each of these instances, critically reflecting on movies, sporting events or advertisements can potentially lead to positive forms of community action, such as doing an evaluation of different aspects of popular culture in terms of their impact on eliminating or perpetuating First Nations oppression (Ford 1994: 112–14, 141–42); or generating a strategy for eliminating racism in popular culture (138–40). This kind of action can be a short-term initiative or something more elaborate, in the form of "service learning." According to Parker-Gwin and Mabry (1998: 276):

> Service learning enables students to apply classroom material to community service.... Through partnerships between a college or university and community groups and agencies, students receive course credit for volunteer work and for reflecting in journals, class discussions, papers or class presentations on how their service relates to course material, their academic discipline and larger social issues.
>
> As a form of experiential learning, service learning allows students to apply what they are learning to "real life" issues and to cultivate a commitment to community service and understanding of social processes.

The value of service learning comes in breaking down discriminatory barriers, student development, moral development, an increase in civic responsibility, and an improved ability to analyze and explain the causes and consequences of social problems (see Myers-Lipton 1998; Marullo 1998; Lowe and Reisch 1998; Everett 1998; Parilla and Hesser 1998; and Rundblad 1998.

CRIME, JUSTICE AND THE LAW

Despite its attractive rhetoric, Canadian law tends to be an exclusive domain of privilege and, for those who are marginalized, an inaccessible resource. To participate in law creation requires a mastery of procedures that are all too well concealed from, or foreign to, Aboriginal peoples. "Western" and "traditional" (First Nations) approaches to law and justice differ radically in philosophy and application. Rupert Ross's (1996: 269–72) work eloquently summarizes these differences.

Applying Western Approaches to Law and Justice

Western Law	Traditional wisdom and law
* Advocates for "absolutes"—i.e., there is one truth, one way of speaking, one way of seeing, one way of knowing, that is, the "Western" way (269).	* Is relative—"each person, family, community and nation should be as free as possible to put their own wisdoms into practice within their own spheres of activity" (269).
1. "Offenders can be effectively dealt with on their own, whether within deterrent or rehabilitative contexts" (270).	1. "Traditional wisdom suggests that we are all substantially the products of our relationships. Traditional law thus commands that justice processes involve all people within the webs of relationships that surround every offender and every victim" (270).
2. "Western law seems to assume that we are captains of our own ships and that each of us is equally capable of moving out of anti-social behaviour on our own, just by deciding to do so" (270).	2. "Traditional wisdom suggests that each of us rides a multitude of waves, some stretching back centuries, which we cannot fundamentally change and which will still confront us tomorrow. Further, it suggests that each of us is confronted by very different wave

combinations, some more powerful and destructive than others. Traditional law thus commands that a justice system focus on healing and teaching offenders so that they become more, not less, capable of dealing with their unique and continuing realities" (270).

3. "Western law focuses very narrowly on particular acts, for it is acts that are alleged, subject to proof, and if proven, substantially controlling of the court's disposition" (270).

3. "Traditional understandings suggest that such acts are no more than clues signalling relational disharmonies between individuals, between individuals and other aspects of Creation, and between the physical, mental, emotional and spiritual dimensions of each individual. Traditional law thus commands that these be the areas of investigation and intervention, and that acts no longer occupy centre stage" (270).

4. "Western law puts the parties through the adversarial process that inevitably adds to the level of antagonism between them" (271).

4. "Traditional wisdom suggests that antagonism within relationships is in fact the cause of those adversarial acts, and traditional law thus commands that justice processes be structured in ways to reduce that antagonism and bring health and understanding back to those relationships" (271).

5. "Western law labels and stigmatizes offenders, to others and to themselves" (271).

5. "Traditional wisdom suggests that we are all in constant processes of reformation within ever-changing relationships. Traditional law thus commands that justice processes be structured to help people begin to believe they are more than their anti-social acts, that they too have worth and dignity, and that they too are capable of learning how to cope with the forces that surround them" (271).

6. "According to Western law, 'taking responsibility for your act' means little more than acknowledging the particulars of the illegal act, then paying a proportionate price in punishment" (271).

6. "Traditional wisdom suggests that acts are important only for their consequences on the mental, emotional, spiritual and physical health of all those affected, including all those within the *offender's* relationships. Traditional law thus commands that justice processes be structured so as to incorporate the 'felt' responses of all those people in respectful, dignified and 'non-blaming' ways and to help the offender truly 'take responsibility' for his act by coming to feel some portion of the pain he has caused all those other people" (271).

7. "According to Western law, 'solutions' are best provided through reliance on professional, third-party strangers like judges, psychiatrists, probation officers and the like" (271).

7. "Traditional wisdom suggests that the only people who understand the complexities of their relationships thoroughly enough are the people actually involved. The proper role of third-party professionals is to act as regulators of respectful processes, teachers of values upon which respectful relationships can be developed, and real life demonstrations of what those relationships look like in action. Traditional law thus commands that the responsibility for problem solving be restored to the parties and that the experts step down from their thrones" (271–72).

Despite the differences between approaches, we continue to treat, judge and punish Natives using Western standards. Consider, for example, the case of *R. v. Warren George*. Shirley Honyust, president of WIICH KE YIG (Friends Who Walk with Us), the London Chapter of the Canadian Alliance in Solidarity with the Native Peoples (CASNP),[1] summarizes the situation of George:

> Warren George is a Stoney Pointer who was defending his native land, and his fellow residents in particular, at the time Dudley

George was shot and killed by the OPP. Because of this he was charged and convicted of criminal negligence causing bodily harm and assault with a weapon (his car). He is being labelled a criminal and scapegoated by the courts because of the actions he took to defend his people.

The following codification by a young First Nations Woman speaks, in compelling ways, to the case of Warren George specifically and First Nations justice issues more generally. (For a full transcript of the decision in *R. v. Warren George*, see Appendix.[2])

Injustice in the Criminal Justice System: A Historical and Contemporary Analysis of First Nations' Involvement with a Westernized System of Justice
by Julie George

The overrepresentation of First Nations people in the criminal justice process and in various correctional facilities across Canada is the result of prejudice and discrimination on behalf of the system and the people working within it. This is prejudice and discrimination that stems primarily from a lack of appreciable understanding of First Nations cultures and the issues that most concern First Nations people.

In a commentary on the differences between the First Nations cultures and the dominant Canadian culture in *Dancing with a Ghost: Exploring Indian Reality*, Rupert Ross talks about how Canadians have a responsibility to react differently to First Nations people than they have in the past. They must learn not to so readily come to negative conclusions about the actions of First Nations people. It became clear to Ross in the midst of his studies that, first of all, the reactions of First Nations people to the judicial process are based on experiences that do not mesh well with Canada's procedures for dealing with misconduct. It also became clear that while we disproportionately have to pay fines and are present in jails and prisons, unlawfulness on our behalf is not exclusively to blame for this phenomenon. This becomes evident as Canada's policies and methods of invoking justice are more closely investigated.

One of the areas I will examine to develop the argument that First Nations people are unfairly assessed in the criminal justice system is the decision of Judge Gregory A. Pokele in the case of *R. v. Warren George*. George stood charged with and was convicted of three offences under the Criminal Code: criminal negligence causing bodily harm, assault with a weapon, and operation of a motor vehicle in a manner dangerous to the public, causing bodily harm. Beyond this case, injustice and overrepresentation are also linked to methods used by early settlers to undermine the integrity of First Nations people, the reactions of police officers to First Nations people, and the failure of society to respect the fundamental rights of First Nations people.

The white majority in Canada has developed conventions of justice that are composed of its own values. The white majority has in so doing deemed the values and subsequent concerns of First Nations people irrelevant and therefore separate from the execution of justice. The popular approach to criminality—which presents transgression from the law in the context of individual and cultural inferiority—fails to implicate unequal social relations and organizational racism in the creation of social problems that inevitably lead to criminal behaviour. The history of the residential school, for example, makes it clear that the vision that premised the institution was racist and in many ways resulted in the misfortune of an entire people. The ultimate objective that First Nations children establish themselves in the white community was a failure because of racial prejudice and because whites did not, and do not, provide First Nations people with employment. The consequence has been anomie. Despite the assumption that students go to school to learn and use what they learn to think for themselves, the First Nations children who attended residential schools were never permitted to use their intellectual capabilities. When released from the imprisonment of the schools the children-turned-adults were left with no sense of what was appropriate and were incapable of using their creative processes to favourable ends. And in acting upon ingrained beliefs that they were inferior, many residential school survivors became victims of disorientation—that is, in having trouble adjusting to life as independent adults, many turned to alcohol and drugs as temporary relief of the detached and insecure feelings that they had acquired.

In almost every aspect of the criminal justice process there is a general failure to see crime for what it really is. Crime in many ways seems to be the result of alcohol and substance abuse. Racism, discrimination, and barren socio-economic circumstances seem in turn to contribute to the abuse. In 1970, 90 percent of the crimes committed by First Nations people in Manitoba involved alcohol, and in 1984 the involvement of alcohol decreased only slightly, to 75 percent (Wotherspoon and Satzewich 1993: 195). Crime among First Nations people therefore seems to be less about the individual, and more a manifestation of years of discrimination that has led to the various social problems. Consider that the Canadian government has now acknowledged that a multitude of First Nations children who attended residential schools experienced not only the pain of being separated from their families, but also the type of pain that would result from physical and sexual abuse. We have all heard stories about teachers inflicting extreme forms of punishment on children in the form of food deprivation, confinement and beatings with sticks and chains when they were caught speaking their own languages. Our children were in fact so afraid of being beaten that they often ran away from the schools in spite of the cold and the risk of death. The Canadian government did little to nothing to protect the children and until very recently turned a blind eye to treatment that would not be tolerated in any other institution. First Nations victims were left with little recourse, and many First Nations people, being left without any real means of obtaining retribution, remain victims of the residential school experience. The distress experienced by the young First Nations children who attended residential schools inevitably followed them back to their homes, and to this day it continues to reverberate and be passed on from parents to children. In emphasizing the damaging effect of the residential school experience, Phil Fontaine, a prominent Aboriginal leader, made note of the difficulties that arise when "the same people who tell you to be pure are violating you. You don't know what's right or wrong. The abused become the abusers. Then we blame ourselves and those around us" (Wotherspoon and Satzewich 1993: 125).

There are multitudes of social problems experienced by First Nations people that did not exist before European contact. First Nations people typically live six to seven years less than the average Canadian, have a suicide rate among youth that is eight times higher for females and five times higher for males, and are more likely to suffer from chronic and acute respiratory diseases. Many of these problems stem from intense poverty, overcrowding and poor housing (Frideres 1998: 115–80). But, perhaps most disturbing, some 22 percent of First Nations youth are self-proclaimed abusers of solvents, 62 percent believe alcohol to be a major issue in their communities, and 48 percent believe that drug abuse is a major issue in their communities (Stevens 1997: 30). Some First Nations people, particularly those from the remote reserves of the North, commit crimes with the intent of being caught and with the hope of being sent to correctional facilities. Many look at jails, prisons and detention centres as havens that provide a place to sleep, warmth, access to television, activities to keep them occupied, and three meals a day, things that most people take for granted.

It is not surprising that First Nations youth are overly and increasingly involved in drug and alcohol abuse. Such things as hunting and fishing have fallen into decline as industrial development works to deplete resources. And as economic development destroys traditional ways, it does not typically accommodate for this loss by providing the First Nations people with work. Where there are no jobs, there is subsequently little to no incentive to go to school (York 1989: 142). The poverty in itself contributes to the overrepresentation of First Nations people in jails and prisons. Poverty forces people to steal food and clothes, for example, and it leaves people unable to pay fines when they are given the choice to either do so or go to jail (York 1989: 144). So while the First Nations people in such circumstances are committing the acts, capitalist enterprise—characterized in the cutting of trees and the building of factories on resource-laden and fertile land— is as much to blame for the crime. It has left many First Nations people impoverished and without hope. The structure of social ranking in Canadian society works to place First Nations people outside the mainstream and without the mechanisms necessary to gain access to the corridors of power (George 1999: 7).

Whites have always and in many different ways worked to impose their ways on First Nations people. From the outset of their contact with the original inhabitants of this land, whites have undermined their integrity with claims of barbarism. As Dickason (1992: 92) reports, the early English settlers "appear to have shared with Europeans in general the belief that all New World peoples were cannibals," and the descriptions of Native people became more sensational with time. Speaking of the Indians, one Canadian-born interpreter of the early eighteenth century remarked, "When they kill or capture any of their enemies, they eat them raw and drink their blood." These are indeed the nature of the attitudes that have stood the test of time, that are manifest in the eyes of the white majority today, and that have allowed for action deemed for the benefit of First Nations people to be taken without our consent. The result has been the development and subsistence of procedures of disciplinary authority over the lives of First Nations people, widespread feelings about our abilities, and therefore ways of thinking that facilitate the continuity of extreme social control from generation to generation of Canadian citizens and leaders. Consider what Chief Justice Allan McEachern said in his chronicled judgement concerning the desires of the Gitksan and Wet'suwet'en people to reside as their ancestors did, on land with sufficient economic resources:

> It would not be accurate to assume that even pre-contact existence in the territory was in the least bit idyllic. The plaintiffs' ancestors had no written language, no horses or wheeled vehicles, slavery and starvation was not uncommon, wars with neighboring peoples were common, and there is no doubt, to quote Hobbes, that Aboriginal life in the territory was, at best, 'nasty, brutish and short.' (Menzies 1999: 236)

Policing First Nations

Because most police officers are predominantly ignorant to the reality of First Nations people, their responses to perceived acts of misconduct are often based on racial bias. First Nations people fall prey to stereotypes that see them as being lazy, uneducated, unemployed and unconstrained abusers of alcohol. These stereotypes are evident in the comments that officers make. During the Oka crisis in 1990 there were numerous complaints about discrimination and harassment, and about displays of racial intolerance linked to security checks made at police barriers. One officer was said to have told a young Mohawk man that he would not let cans of beer past the barricade because he did not want to have to clean the streets when the conflict was over. Another officer who was looking through a woman's grocery bag told her that her food would not help to make anyone past the barricades smarter (Rochon and Lepage 1991: 25). Comments like these incite First Nations people into being uncooperative and violent, and the provoked outrage perpetuates the image of First Nations people as criminal in nature. Police officers emerge from such situations feeling justified in assuming that First Nations people are threats to social order.

Although First Nations people are certainly guilty of perpetrating offences, we are often arrested for behaviour that would not be considered criminal when perpetrated by white people. For instance, First Nations police working for First Nations police forces make far fewer arrests than members of outside forces, even though they are in much greater contact with community members. Research shows that they spend most of their time providing services—services that often end with the officers referring people to other agencies such as social or health services or psychiatric specialists (Goff 1997: 143). They most typically do not lay any charges, and when arrests are made, the offences cited are the least serious. This practice is in stark contrast to the work of officers who are not of First Nations ancestry; in that case First Nations people are overwhelmingly more likely to be arrested for, and convicted of, both minor and major offences. In the Prairie provinces almost 32 percent of the federal jail population is made up of First Nations people; across Canada as a whole, First Nations people make up 10 percent of the population in federal correctional institutions (Stevens 1997: 28). These staggering numbers are particularly astonishing when we consider that First Nations people represent only a tiny portion of the entire Canadian population.

Crime has long been a problem in First Nations communities and is symptomatic not solely of the discriminatory practices of the justice system, but also of the various social problems that we are confronted with as a result of the discrimination. First Nations people face a complex set of social problems, such as alcoholism and suicide, that cannot be solved in the short term. Any approach to the delivery of policing services must be proactive and, with the help of community members, must attempt to negate social problems. Ontario Provincial Police officials have made recent efforts to, among other things, provide officers with training that can better equip them to deal with First Nations people. They have also established a First Nations Operational Liaison Unit dedicated solely to First Nations-related issues, and have been host to numerous cultural awareness seminars both within and outside of the organization. Beyond these initiatives, the government has made little attempt to meet our needs. So we are more and more deciding to live our own lives, according to our own norms and values, which has not been without costs. The clash of cultures has resulted in many violent acts and confrontations. Because First Nations people are steadily pulling away from them, it is important that policing organizations across Canada make efforts to understand where First Nations people are coming from, and why they are committing crimes. The question that remains, however, is whether the relationship between First Nations people and constabulary forces is sufficiently intact for such efforts to be productive. Time will tell.

First Nations constables are far more sensitive to the issues of internal politics and fractions in the First Nations community than are white constables. An awareness of the local ways of doing things is a useful tool in the investigation of a serious crime and in determining who is responsible. The First Nations community is respectful of its elders and assigns them much authority. Before going into a community and risking an unnecessary confrontation, an officer from an outside agency might want to visit an elder and ask him or her for information regarding the misconduct. The legitimacy of outside policing organizations is extremely weak and will remain so as long as those organizations persist with their dominating and controlling practices. There is no evidence to suggest that these current attitudes and methods are about to change. Therefore a white officer would typically be unwelcome in the home of a First Nations elder, or not be regarded well enough to be entrusted with incriminating information. The dominant Canadian culture tends to give little respect to its elders, but rather hides them away, which in its own right prevents white officers from taking such action.

The Sentencing of First Nations People: *R. v. Warren George*

While evidence suggests that the police, their attitudes, their behaviours and discretionary powers contribute to the overflow of First Nations people in the system, the role that judges play in determining guilt is equally consequential in perpetuating stereotypes of criminality. Judges' discrimination against First Nations people is difficult to prove, due both to the complexity of the criminal justice process and to the aura of righteousness and impartiality attached to the position of judge. This difficulty is unfortunate, because a fair share of judges are blatant racists who, to the chagrin of First Nations people throughout Canada, have been given the authority to decide guilt despite their attitudes concerning minorities.

In the matter of *R. v. Warren George,* Judge Gregory A. Pokele showed his bias. Of utmost concern is his pronouncement that the evidence of the trial was considered within the context of a tightly framed snapshot (Pokele 1998: 3). The court in this instance and in other instances involving First Nations people failed to take into consideration the unique realities and standpoints of First Nations people. Rupert Ross (1996: 23), in *Returning to the Teachings,* talks in depth about how the most glaring problem with the criminal justice system is that "everything is shoved into it as if all crimes are identical and raise the same issues and concerns." A narrow approach to defining criminality fails to acknowledge the vast difference in the experiences of Warren George and the experiences of most white people. A narrow approach also fails to acknowledge the difference in the circumstances that caused Warren George to drive recklessly on September 6, 1995, compared to the circumstances of most other people. Judge Pokele's decision makes no note of the historical struggle for land and does not acknowledge that the land known as Ipperwash was supposed to be returned to members of the Stoney Point Reserve or that the struggle was testament to the dereliction of Canada to recognize land-claim issues. There is no mention of the frustration that many of the occupiers must have felt in knowing that the government no longer recognized the existence of Stoney Point as a separate band. There is no mention of what it must be like to be First Nations and to truly believe that the ground in which your grandparents and great-grandparents are buried was for years and years used as a place where complete strangers could swim, play games, pitch tents and have bonfires.

Judge Pokele talks in his judgment about Warren George's attempt to portray the police generally as assaultive, violent and unreasonable. He goes on to say that the accused appeared to be projecting his beliefs upon the police: that police would not listen to the occupiers, that police were trying to intimidate the occupiers, that police would try to murder the occupiers. His judgment on this particular matter was that the evidence given as such by George was exaggerated, unsubstantiated and unsupported (Pokele 1998: 13). Are these beliefs null and void? Past incidences of police brutality and unreasonable use of force against First Nations people suggest that police officers are capable of actions that extend beyond the boundaries of their job descriptions. They are capable of intimidation tactics and of killing innocent First Nations people. Interaction between First Nations people and paramilitary and military forces has historically and increasingly been violent in nature. The roles played by the Ontario Provincial Police in Ipperwash, the Quebec Provincial Police in Oka, and a multitude of other policing agencies across Canada indicate why police have come to symbolize the victimization of First Nations people by dominant society. In 1979 a Mohawk man from Kahnawaké was shot three times and fatally wounded by Constable Robert Lessard of the Quebec Provincial Police. Although Lessard testified that he felt his life was in danger when the Mohawk man opened the front door of his cruiser and lunged at him with a baseball bat, testimony from numerous witnesses showed that no such incident took place. Testimony also showed that he fired his weapon without any warning (York and Pindera 1991: 124). In 1988 a well-known Indian leader by the name of John Joseph Harper was shot and killed by a Winnipeg police officer while walking alone in the early hours of the morning. The officer, who was at the time looking for a twenty-two-year-old car thief, was aware that a suspect fitting the description of the thief was in custody, yet still chose to confront the thirty-six-year-old Harper, who he testified fit the description of the man he was looking for (York 1989: 150). In Ipperwash, in 1995, Anthony Dudley George was shot and killed by Sergeant Kenneth Deane, who was at the time, and still is, a member of the Ontario Provincial Police. The Ojibway man, who had never before displayed violent tendencies, was not in possession of a weapon at the time of his death and presented no physical threat to the officer. More recently there have been allegations that officers from a Saskatoon detachment were involved in the deaths of at least two First Nations men found frozen in a field near a power plant. This is a story that broke not upon the discovery of the bodies but upon later complaints from a third man, who recalled two officers driving him to the outskirts of the city, stripping him of his jacket, and making him walk home in below-freezing temperatures. Adding to the pressure of all of this is the promise of new information involving the unsolved death of a seventeen-year-old First Nations youth whose body, in 1991, was found frozen in an open field in an industrial park. These examples are not exhaustive. A myriad of First Nations people have fallen victim to the effects of being Indian in a racist society. The list of instances of police brutality is extensive, and the existence of such a list is understandably enough to incite First Nations people to react to police officers (especially police officers sporting helmets, protective shields, bullet-proof vests, batons and guns) with caution, irreverence, and quite often a fighting instinct.

The judge in the Warren George case exemplifies an action that supports the continuation of the assimilation of First Nations people into mainstream society. This is an action that opposes the granting of special rights and considerations to First Nations people. Support for such movements is evident across the country in the form of riots and demonstrations such as the ones that occurred during the Oka crisis in 1990. The violent protests there were characterized by the chanting of racist remarks and by visible effigies of tortured First Nations people. Mobs of protestors, in response to the blockading of the Mercier Bridge by First Nations people, swarmed and threw large rocks at a caravan of women and children who were attempting to leave the area. But while support for the continued assimilation of First Nations people into the mainstream and lack of support for assertions of sovereignty are quite often discernible, so too are they indiscernible. These are the types of movements that emanate intelligence, dignity, and prestige and in so doing have an even greater impact on the denial of distinctiveness and on the abolition of the concept of inherent rights. The decision of the judge in the matter of *R.* v. *Warren George* denies that First Nations people are unique.

The judgment denies that First Nations people have customs that are different from those of the white majority, and it denies that we want a system of criminal justice that is different from the one that we are now involved in. The judge also in effect denies that First Nations people once comprised self-governing nations. This denial comes despite the historical existence of successful systems of justice within most traditional societies. Governance was a collective right delegated to leaders, whether they were elders or hunters, or men or women, and all members of a community were, as a result, respectful of the leaders. Constructed as such, social and political organization was extremely effectual. For example, the Iroquois Confederacy, made up of the Mohawk, Oneida, Onondaga, Cayuga and Seneca peoples, was composed of a council of fifty elected chiefs. Although they arbitrated on problems, and on issues such as when to partake in warfare, it was not their responsibility to control people (York and Pindera 1991: 108–10). Law existed within the jurisdiction of the people. Crime against persons or property was therefore infrequent, not only because people of close relation dealt with it, but also because property belonged to everyone. The reality that we had our own institutions and that we have inherent rights to self-government is what separates First Nations people from other groups of people in Canada—from whites, from other ethnic groups, and from immigrants. We are unique in that we never agreed to become part of this nation we call Canada or to conform to legal processes that we did not have a hand in creating. The rigidity of Judge Pokele on the matter and his refusal to move beyond the borders of his comfortable outlook are not based on his assertion that it is not the function of the court in adjudicating criminal charges to admit to precipitating factors. Rather, his words demonstrate that he holds long-standing and negative beliefs about First Nations people and that he has a predilection to observe all cultures from his own vantage point. His prejudice therefore encumbers First Nations people in fighting for what is rightfully their own.

Prejudice ensures that when an accused person is First Nations, he or she is never cloaked throughout a trial with the presumption of innocence. This is why Judge Pokele describes all of the actions taken by the police officers as being both necessary and honourable and all of the actions taken by the occupiers as being unnecessary and dishonourable. "The Ontario Provincial Police cordoned off the park and set up checkpoints outside Ipperwash to warn and protect innocent passersby" (Pokele 1998: 5). Their actions are at the same time justified. "As the Crowd Management Unit advanced, occupiers outside of the park boundary lit up the Crowd Management Unit with portable halogen-type lights and with headlights from vehicles parked inside the park. This backlit the occupiers and negatively affected the vision of the Crowd Management Unit members as their visors and shields generated glare" (8). The judge offered other statements of vindication. "Members of the Emergency Response Team and Crowd Management Unit were not designed, trained, or intended to respond effectively to the type of attack unleashed upon them" (6). The statements were in complete contrast to the language used to describe the behaviour of Warren George and the other occupiers. "The activities of the occupiers were not peaceful, respectful, and dignified. There was vandalism to vehicles and other personal property, weapons were brandished, threats were made to police officers, and citizens made complaints to police" (7). But perhaps most damaging and certainly most unwarranted was the judge's assertion that the occupiers and Warren George in particular were responsible for the death of Anthony Dudley George, the First Nations man shot and killed by police officer Deane during the altercation. "The occupiers commenced a course of conduct which was extremely dangerous, violent, and assaultive. The activities constituted the proximate cause of all violence and injuries which occurred that night, and the death of a man" (8). Although what he was touching on was not of relevance to the proceedings, Judge Pokele appears to have wanted to indict the occupiers and in so doing declare that Deane was simply at the wrong place at the wrong time: an innocent man unfairly accused of wrongdoing.

This is strangely reminiscent of other cases in which First Nations people were blamed for crimes they did not commit. In this regard the case of Donald Marshall Junior is classic. Marshall was convicted in 1971 for a murder he did not commit; he was cleared only in 1983, after spending eleven years in jail. The case made clear that persistent problems of racial bias operated throughout the criminal justice system, including in the courtroom, and are committed not just by police but also by lawyers and judges. Geoffrey York, in *The Dispossessed*, gives an account of the type of comments that prosecutors and senior officials made about First Nations people during the Marshall proceedings. Junior prosecutor Lewis Matheson recommended that "a fence be built around one of the Micmac reserves 'so that the Indians couldn't get out to come to Sydney to cause problems.'" A senior provincial official and director of criminal prosecutions, Robert Anderson, reportedly told the lawyer for Marshall, "Don't get your balls caught in a vice over an Indian." Both Matheson and Anderson later became judges (York 1989: 165). In 1982, after key witnesses admitted to giving false testimony, the case was referred to the Court of Appeal, yet problems associated with prejudicial judges endured. The five judges appointed to the matter accepted the argument made by prosecutors that the public would suspect something wrong with the system if a man could be wrongfully convicted of a murder that he did not commit. They

therefore ruled that Marshall was most likely convicted because of evasive statements that he made during his trial. They also ruled that Marshall triggered the
death of the victim by trying to rob the actual killers and thereby instigating a
deadly chain of events that ended in murder (162). Together the pronouncements
in the Marshall and Warren George cases demonstrate severe flaws in the system
hinging on racism. The judges used their positions as upper-class Caucasian men
to attempt to exonerate white men of murder and incriminate First Nations men
of foul play regardless of the facts.

Judge Pokele deemed the testimony of Warren George to be unbelievable
because the evidence of the police officers contradicted it, and the result was a
skewed depiction of what really happened on the night of September 6, 1995.
The popular, government version is that in July of 1995 First Nations protestors
demanded a return of land that they claimed as a traditional area. When their
demands did not bear immediate fruit, First Nations protestors walked onto an
army base without permission and began to live there. The cadets who were
staying on the base were forced to leave. Soon after the cadets left, the protestors
established blockades and began to claim that the area accommodated a burial
ground that they also wanted to have returned to them. The illegal occupation of
the land meant that the Ontario Provincial Police had to confront the protestors
in an effort to solve the problem. On September 6, demonstrators began to throw
large rocks at a group of police officers standing outside of the blockaded area and
to drive cars and buses at them. Warren George attempted to injure the officers
with his vehicle. The police began to shoot their guns in efforts to protect
themselves from imminent injury. Anthony Dudley George was inadvertently hit
by a bullet in the exchange and died soon after. In spite of not intending to kill a
man, police officer Kenneth Deane was found guilty of criminal negligence
causing death.

An understanding of the events from the standpoint of a First Nations person
leads to a much different depiction. The unpopular but equally viable version is
that a small group of protestors were in occupation of the Ipperwash Canadian
Forces Base and Ipperwash Provincial Park because the government was effectively in illegal possession of it. On September 6, without warning, the government deployed a large group of armed officers to confront the occupiers. More
than two hundred officers, including a number hiding in bushes and trees and
others stationed in nearby homes, were deployed, many armed with sophisticated
weapons. As the officers approached a sandy lot outside of the blockaded area, a
councilor from nearby Kettle Point Reserve confronted the officers in an attempt
to convince the officers to retreat. His intention was not to fight the officers,
because they were heavily armed, he was without a weapon, and they were greater
in number. Cecil George was attacked by a group of the officers as he approached
them and was struck in the head and beat unconscious. As fellow occupiers came
to his assistance they were threatened and attacked. Fearing that the occupiers
would be seriously injured, Warren George made the decision to drive his vehicle
towards the officers in an attempt to disperse them from that area and to hinder
them from further beating on the protestors. It can be assumed that he was aware

of the implications of injuring an officer. Police began firing at the vehicle and at the protestors, one of whom was Anthony Dudley George.

The "popular" depiction of events is the one that Judge Gregory A. Pokele declares to be reality. He justifies his taking of sides by arguing incessantly that the evidence of the occupiers shows a lack of logic. He poses a question throughout: why would Warren George think that he or any of the other protestors would be shot at if they were not endangering anyone? As well, he goes on at length to maintain that all of the police officers were subjected to forceful and unwavering cross-examination concerning every detail related to the incident. Police witnesses were called upon to recount an incident that took place over a few minutes, in a situation of stress, in which they were under lethal attack, accompanied by concerns that the occupiers might have access to firearms. Judge Pokele places much importance on the officers' statements to the effect that they believed their deaths were imminent—this despite paying very little respect to the same admitted fear of death on Warren George's part. "Over and above this there was a great consistency with respect to the important elements of the prosecution's case" (Pokele 1998: 28–29).

But the consistency in the testimony of the police officers—plus the finding that their testimony was more consistent than that of the occupiers—is by no means surprising. The police clearly knew (and the occupiers did not) that they were about to be deployed and that a confrontation was about to take place. In performing their assigned duties, the police would therefore be most likely to follow and remember in detail the sequence of events. This is not to say that their portrayal of events was any more accurate than that of the occupiers, because points of view and bias will always influence perception. The point is that the police were at an advantage in being able to prepare mentally for what they were about to experience and for what they might have to say later in a courtroom.

Westernized vs. Traditional Definitions of Criminality

Over and above the prejudices exhibited by professionals working within the system there are differences in perceptions regarding what constitutes crime. Specifically, First Nations people seem to have tolerance for a broader range of behaviour. Such descriptive terms as assault, battery and false imprisonment are meaningless to many traditional First Nations people, but are grounds for severe punishment in Canadian courts (Denis 1997: 92).

One particular case that shows the collision of Canadian and First Nations law involved a group of First Nations men from Vancouver Island. In 1992, acting on the request of a female community member, the men took her husband to a secluded place where they performed a traditional ceremony on him known as "syewen" or spirit dancing, which involved confinement, fasting, and a resulting elated state that led the husband to singing and dancing. The ceremony was meant to connect him with, and to teach him to live harmoniously with, his guardian spirit. The men used some physical force on him during the process, and against his will made him perform certain acts, such as jumping naked into a cold lake.

The purpose—a purpose difficult for a white person to comprehend—was not to injure or punish the man for having a hostile marriage, but to heal someone who was a well-known alcoholic with a violent temper and to promote better relations between him and his wife. Remember that many First Nations people continue to think in terms of what is best for the community, not necessarily one individual, and consequently do not function in a context that would see this activity as deviant. In this instance, the First Nations men situated the needs of a community member in the spiritual realm, and they carried out their actions not in the privacy of their individual lives, but as members of the greater group (Denis 1997: 14). The husband eventually took the matter out of the hands of his own people and launched a lawsuit. The judge in the matter found in favour of the husband on the grounds that people cannot provide their help to another if that person does not consent to the help.

Very serious consequences arise from situations in which First Nations people carry out acts that they consider to be legal but that the dominant society treats as illegal. Most serious is the gradual dissolution of tradition. Individuals within the community are allowed to avoid healing by taking matters out of the hands of their people; and when the situation is placed in the hands of the Canadian justice system, it is treated the same as cases that have dissimilar meanings attached to them. In the eyes of the court, the case of the Coast Salish First Nations men who performed the traditional ceremony of spirit dancing on a reluctant initiate becomes simply the same as a multitude of other very dissimilar cases—treated in the same way, for instance, as a case in which a group of college students jump a man outside of a bar, take him to an abandoned building, and beat him until he is unconscious. The First Nations men committed their act out of concern for their community. The college students attacked the lone man because he made a pass at one of their girlfriends earlier in the evening, or perhaps because he was simply in the wrong place at the wrong time. The result of the ignorance of tradition is the stripping of the spiritual context that underlies the conduct of the First Nations men. When First Nations people are punished for maintaining their traditional customs, it becomes less likely that the ceremony will be performed again.

But in the court procedures themselves—and in particular with those running the show—even the supposed equal treatment of whites and First Nations people can lead to inequality. Numerous problems arise as white people try to determine whether or not First Nations people are telling the truth in the courtroom. Stemming from the principle of non-interference, a First Nations person is reluctant to suggest that his or her version of fact is superior to that of another. The ethic of non-interference is a principle central to the conduct of First Nations people, more so in traditional times but still evident today. It means that First Nations people will rarely interfere in any way with the rights, privileges and more importantly the activities of others (Ross 1992: 12). Giving evidence, even when it is in favour of the position of another, is forbidden, and doing so while in the presence of that person only adds insult to injury. According to the point of view of a First Nations person, interfering in the business of another is not only a criticism of another's judgement, but also an insinuation of one's own superiority. The ethic of non-interference was and continues to be evident in innumerable aspects of traditional life. In decision-making each and every individual takes part and the people involved do not ignore any opinion. The main objective is to accomplish some sort of overall consensus. Therein lies the notion that the ethic of non-interference is more than anything else about making sure that everyone within a group is in equal standing.

The ethic of non-interference is exceedingly pertinent to the issue of justice in that judges and members of juries will usually translate an unwillingness to intervene as uncertainty. In a judicial courtroom, a sense of uncertainty will often lead to the assumption that the witness is not believable, in which case the testimony will be disregarded in the determination of guilt or innocence. Court officials may also assume that someone following the principle of non-interference is trying to conceal culpability. The ethic of non-interference has, consequently, resulted throughout history in the wrongful convictions and subsequent sentencing of many First Nations people. In the 1870s, for instance, a First Nations gentleman was sentenced to fifteen long years in prison for the murder of a woman, a crime he did not commit. Due to the looseness of the procedures that existed at the time, the man was imprisoned—not because he was found guilty of killing the woman, but because he did not disclose the name of the real assassin (Wotherspoon and Satzewich 1993: 204).

The notion of respect is encompassing and fosters not only the ethic of non-interference, but also the ethic that anger not be shown. This ethic leads to the general lack of emotion exhibited by First Nations people when they talk about uncomfortable events, indeed if they choose to talk at all (Ross 1992: 28). A testimonial given in court may be unconvincing because of the dull tone in which it is offered. A dull tone does not mean that a person on the receiving end of a crime, as defined by the Canadian courts, is not angry; rather, it may mean that the witness would rather bury past hurts and allow all parties to move on with their lives. The reluctance to show anger is therefore closely related to the general unwillingness to relive past events. History has proven to be a destructive and perpetual force that works against the efforts of the First Nations people.

It may also be that anger is not felt as strongly as it is by whites in similar circumstances. First Nations people see themselves as being connected. Not only are we born into large families, but historically we have also had to depend on each other to provide food and shelter; and more recently we have had to depend on each other as social and psychological supports in a very unequal world. Perhaps it is this feeling of connectedness with the family and the community that allows us to be more at ease in uneasy situations. Countless other problems and misunderstandings—too numerous to be cited—arise as white people misinterpret the response and behaviour of First Nations people after a crime has been committed.

First Nations people also suffer terribly from discrimination in sentencing. The extent to which discrimination exists in sentencing is most evident in the case of Donald Marshall, who was sentenced to life in prison for a crime he did not commit, while the real criminal, a white man, several years after the crime was committed, spent a mere year in prison. The case of Kenneth Deane, the Ontario Provincial Police Tactics and Rescue Unit officer who killed Anthony Dudley

George at Ipperwash Provincial Park, is also a testament to this discrimination. He was ultimately convicted of criminal negligence causing death despite his insincere and cowardly pleas of not being guilty. He was sentenced to community service in the form of two years less a day, to be served in his own community. This result contrasts with the case of a man from Six Nations who unintentionally killed a middle-aged white man while driving impaired. He pleaded guilty, took responsibility for his actions and was convicted of criminal negligence causing death. His sentence was a severe punishment of three and a half years, to be served in the federal penitentiary in Kingston. Neither of the men had previous criminal records. The First Nations man was regarded as an exemplary figure in his community and in work. The apparent message is that the life of a white man is more valuable than the life of a First Nations man (Miller 1997: 5). This is the type of discrimination that has been apparent for many long years, although more recently in more subtle and roundabout ways.

First Nations-Style Justice

Justice among First Nations people means restoring peace and equilibrium in society, and bringing the offender to correct or proper standing with his or her own family, with the victim, with the victim's family and with members of the community as a whole. Sentencing must therefore consider the penalty's impact on all parties (Goff 1997: 85). This concept of total healing in small communities, in which peace is a must, cannot be fulfilled if an offender is banished and sent to a correctional facility. Also because all aspects of the community must be taken into consideration, strangers in the form of judges and jury members cannot adequately bring action against an offender. Canada's adversarial system of justice has proven to be ineffective in dealing positively with First Nations offenders. The involvement of elders in determining sentences increases the likelihood of rehabilitation. Elders are respected and thought to have much wisdom, and their wisdom holds First Nations communities together. The need to submit to the reflection of the elders can drive an offender to try to regain their respect.

The Navajo of the United States control their own police, as do many First Nations in Ontario, where the Anishinabek Police and the Six Nations Police are examples. The difference is that the Navajo also control their own courts and rehabilitation programs. The consensus among First Nations leaders in Canada seems to be that all First Nations peoples need to have separate justice systems. The dilemma lies in determining the exact form of such systems.

Some First Nations people believe that the practices of the Canadian system simply need to be modified to accommodate the needs of First Nations people. This modification would supposedly ensure the integration of First Nations peoples' values into the current system of justice. Indigenization of the criminal justice system would generate changes in relations with First Nations people, so that the system becomes more sensitive to our needs. It would ensure representation by First Nations at all levels of the planning and delivery of criminal justice. The work could involve more First Nations police officers, more translators in the courtroom, efforts to secure more First Nations judges and the involvement of elders in judgments of criminal offences (Frideres 1998: 186).

The problem with accommodative strategies is that First Nations people have very different ideas than the dominant society concerning the functions of criminal justice: for instance, that all parties must be involved in finding a solution to a dispute, and that to prevent future crime within the community, it is most important that offenders be rehabilitated (Frideres 1998: 185). These perspectives do not mesh well with Canada's procedures for dealing with misbehaviour, which predominantly involve punishment in correctional facilities. So no matter how many First Nations police officers are employed by the Ontario Provincial Police for instance, or how many First Nations people are working in the courtroom, it still remains that they are working within a foreign system. This is not only a system that responds to perceived acts of misconduct based on conventionalized stereotypes, but also a system that has different ideas about such things as what type of behaviour is considered criminal, and how one should act when testifying in court. Due to historical dominant-group/minority-group relations, it would seem that the Canadian practice is not sufficiently compassionate to make these accommodations.

Others believe that First Nations people should have their own courts, in their own communities—courts that would, for the most part, be free of Canadian criminal law influence and therefore be based exclusively on traditional rules and methods. The establishment of First Nations courts on the basis of sovereignty, where sovereignty is not fully recognized in Canada due to the effects of treaties, would be a difficult endeavour, but an endeavour no more arduous than having to live through the past five hundred years of extreme exploitation. A true "tribal court," as described by Bradford Morse (1990: 15), provides the most likely model for the First Nations people of Canada. Tribal courts obtain their structure and methods from the tribal government alone, and the judges within it administer law as it stems from traditional customs (2). There are of course foreseeable problems with tribal courts, especially when the courts would only be able to enforce tribal law on First Nations people, on the reserves. The inherent limitation of this is that it allows offenders to escape any action that may be taken by the courts. The simple fact, however unjust it may seem, is that First Nations people live in a larger society that has very different ideas of what constitutes misbehaviour, and how misbehaviour should be dealt with. This will never change. Tribal courts are nevertheless progressive insofar as those under their jurisdiction are willing to adhere to them. Having jurisdiction over matters arising on reserves, between First Nations people, is at least a step in the right direction, and talk of other issues concerning the territorial command of the courts would have to follow.

More in-depth discussions of what mechanisms can be put into place for the creation of tribal courts, to whom the authority of the courts should apply and, most importantly, whether such courts are even feasible in Canada, certainly need to take place. The issues are broad and complicated. What is clear is that First Nations people need to be increasingly involved in the delivery of their own services, justice included. A tribal court can help to promote increased involvement. As well, separate justice systems are not as out of reach as people may think:

"What seemed unlikely—if not impossible—several years ago, is now being regarded as a serious alternative and, in some areas, is being accepted as part of the future of Canada" (Morse 1990: 30). First Nations people should therefore begin to seriously consider (at least where this has not already been done) the steps that should be taken to begin such a rewarding undertaking.

Looking Ahead

The measures that we will take to make it clear to Canada that we are more than a group of insignificant savages living on reserves is evident in the beliefs and actions of the Mohawk of Kahnawaké. They are constantly fighting for their independence, are constantly in conflict with the government and with the police as a result, and are becoming more and more militant in their stance of sovereignty. Increasing numbers of young children are attending the Kahnawaké Survival School, where they study from textbooks written from a Mohawk point of view and re-enact and voice their disdain for historical interplay between their ancestors and whites, and where it is compulsory to learn and speak the language of their forefathers. Although the warrior movement is not an official subject for classroom discussion, the school has become a breeding ground for warriors (York and Pindera 1991: 116). Increasing nationalism among First Nations was predictable, especially in light of a statement made years ago by Georges Erasmus, National Chief of the Assembly of First Nations:

> Canada, we have something to say to you. We have a warning for you. We want to let you know that you're playing with fire. We may be the last generation of leaders prepared to sit down and peacefully negotiate our concerns with you.... Canada, if you do not deal with this generation of leaders, then we cannot promise that you are going to like the kind of violent political action that we can just about guarantee the next generation is going to bring to you. (Anderson 1992: 479)

The Erasmus statement seems eerily foreboding. The potential for violent outbreak seems to have only increased, and a new generation of young people and future leaders does appear to be less willing to cooperate peacefully with Canadian officials. First Nations people are more and more resorting to protest and extreme actions to make it clear that they are frustrated with the current nature of justice in Canada. If the consciousness of the young people in Kahnawaké is any indication of the consciousness typical of all First Nations youth, a confrontation would seem to be inevitable.

Conclusion

Issues of injustice extend far beyond the institution of justice. Canada's democratic system of government requires that voting citizens elect governmental officials who will presumably act on their behalf. The democratic system prides itself on the idea that people control their own destiny with the vote, and that all supposedly have a voice through the vote. Unfortunately, the political arena has become a playing field for a myriad of actors and reactors, each of whom has very different and definite opinions and goals. Zones of conflict exist between First Nations and Eurocentric approaches to justice. While citizens are assuredly given the opportunity to vote, a privilege that was only recently in history granted to Aboriginal peoples, the opportunity to run for political positions of influence exists only for those with high social standing. It is fair to say that most of Canada's Native people do not belong to this group. Political parties especially are largely made up of society's white elites, which have the education and the resources needed to make connections and pursue agendas. First Nations people cannot fully pursue their own interests in our democratic system of government.

First Nations people have more recently come to form into credible groups with the common objective of no longer being subject to foreign practices. Ideologies that centre around notions of individualism can actually work in positive ways to incorporate First Nations people into the dominant framework of social life. Ideological systems assuredly work to alter the thoughts of the op-pressed, and they have also, in the case of First Nations people, worked to alter their actions (Ritzer 1992: 178). Increasingly common individual endeavours, such as attending university, have helped First Nations people in their efforts to more fluently and eloquently express their opinions concerning inherent rights based on history. First Nations people have as a result developed new capabilities, new ideas and new communication techniques that have put them on the same intellectual level as those within the system (Ritzer 1992: 160). The leaders of Canada are no longer justified in ignoring the concerns of First Nations people.

Traditional justice systems, as well as a multitude of other systems dealing with such matters as education and economics, have been the targets of assimila-tion policies. Social control based on foreign ideology has had a very negative impact on First Nations people, and on the relationships between First Nations people and whites. New ideologies are constantly being created that work to justify the control of the powerful over the powerless. The underlying ideology that exists in all of Canada's social institutions is one of compliance. The younger of the First Nations people have relentlessly been exposed to mainstream society, through education, for example, and have consequently been exposed to the rules by which all are supposed to abide (Frideres 1998: 328).

Yet First Nations elders remain active in maintaining cultural traditions, and adamantly encourage their juniors to do the same. This is where the reluctance to accept foreign ideology originates, and where the struggle for recognition of the ways of First Nations people takes root. Despite all that has been done since European contact to negate First Nations families, unique viewpoints, customs and ways of life remain. This very act of survival has given First Nations people across Canada the incentive to carry on traditions and pave the way for children to come. We realize that the problem of justice lies not with the First Nations people and our inability to adjust to the structure and methods of justice, but rather with the system itself. We have no doubt that it is time that the system was taught more about the values and characteristics of First Nations people.

EXERCISE NO. 3: CASE RECONSTRUCTION USING NATIVE WISDOM AND LAW

As Julie George suggests, "Western law" fails peoples of the First Nations. Adopting our critically responsive pedagogical philosophy, how then can we work collectively to find more equitable methods for dealing with individuals who come in contact with the law? Having worked through the process with Julie in a reading course, we would invite her to facilitate a similar discussion on her codification in a larger group. Adopting the pedagogical tools of "first voice" and the "circle," and utilizing as a reference point Ross's comparison of legal approaches, the class would discuss the components of Western law that were used in arriving at the decision in *R. v. Warren George*. Then, using the principles of traditional wisdom and law as outlined by Ross and clarified by the guest speaker, we would ask students to work first individually and then in small groups to reconstruct the case in a way that illustrates how an alternative, more "traditional" judicial process might be taken up. The summary by Ross and the reflection by George would serve as the codes for critical reflection.

Moving beyond critical reflection, class participants would strategize about action that could be taken to ameliorate racism in the criminal justice system. Action might begin, for instance, with the gathering of information on the justice system's treatment of First Nations people in a student's local community. Ford (1994: 135–36) offers a number of questions and suggestions that can be used to help begin the investigation.

- Do criminal justice workers (police, court officials, lawyers, judges) reflect the ethnic composition of your community?
- Have there been cases in which law enforcement officials have been charged with excessive use of force towards First Nations people?
- Compare the arrest records of Aboriginal peoples with whites and other minorities. Are Aboriginal people overrepresented in the criminal justice system in your community? Why?
- Question members of First Nations organizations about information they have on the fairness of law enforcement in the community.

Becoming more informed and sharing information are the first steps towards challenging racism in the justice system.

Towards Healing and Justice—The Struggle for Identity: In Retrospect
by Ursula Elijah and John Elijah

We live in a diverse society, where things are not as they seem. Our lives are structured around social context: the people, places, things and circumstances we greet in life. All of these elements of social context are significant when it comes to identifying the self. It seems that the struggle for identity gets lost amid all the diversity and transitions around us. Because of all of the diversity that we are regularly exposed to, First Nations people often tend to behave in "unnatural" ways. We justify these "unnatural" behaviours as responses to the social variation around us. The result is that we unnaturally eliminate or abandon our natural upbringing and adopt convenient methods for achieving our more immediate needs and wants.

We, as First Nations People, generally neglect the things that are important to us—our morals and values as a people. We downplay trust, friendship, respect and honesty and toss them aside. We neglect these morals and values because our social context invites and rewards conformity to the larger society, instead of respect for our natural teachings. The methods used in the larger society are considered the norm, the standard by which behaviour should be judged.

Because of the influences of the dominant society, First Nations people begin to doubt their own identities. The questions that often arise are: "Do I conform? Or, do I resist the Westernized mode of thinking?" As we all know, it is easier to conform, go with the flow and make life easier all around us. But to adhere to this mentality is to make a great sacrifice: the loss of identity. For a First Nations person, the identity is the key to the soul and spirit.

As historians have increasingly documented, First Nations people have endured numerous acts of domination at the hands of colonizers, from cultural genocide to imposed conformity to an imposed "Western" lifestyle. First Nations people "learned" the ways of the larger society through residential schooling, training schools, the Children's Aid Society, and incarceration to curb inappropriate behaviours. Currently First Nations communities are beginning to see the effects of these institutional experiences among members of their populations, through the dysfunctional lives they are leading.

The purpose of this reflection is to begin to correct these wrongs, by helping readers to understand what, from a review of First Nations teachings and philosophies, is "natural" behaviour, and what is "not natural" behaviour.

Natural Behaviours

Natural behaviours involve the teachings from the Creator that give meaning and purpose to our lives as First Nations people. These teachings also take into consideration how we treat ourselves, others and those outside forces around us. Natural behaviours intend for us to be conscious of four very important elements. Specifically, in order to understand us as a people, it is necessary to understand:

- the creation story;
- the ceremonies;
- the great law and the government; and
- the faith and religion.

What natural teachings do is answer the questions of how we came to be, in the hopes of teaching us how to understand, and better participate in, human relationships. Natural behaviours are based upon using the knowledge and life skills that we have acquired to make decisions clearly and rationally, taking into account both personal and collective concerns.

In the past, for example, if a person made a decision, it was necessary to consider the impact of the decision on the self, one's family, and ultimately the family's clan. If the person did not consider the impact of the decision on the wider community, she or he could disgrace both the family and the family's clan (determined by matrilineal descent). And no one ever wanted to disgrace him/herself or the family. Thus people made decisions in a way that benefitted the individual specifically, and the wider community more generally. There was never any time to think selfishly; thinking had to be done holistically.

The best way to understand natural teachings is to chart in sequential order the elements or behaviours associated with the four principles or messages from the Creator:

- thinking = creation story;
- actions = ceremonies;
- attitudes = great law and government;
- feelings = faith.

Thinking = Creation Story

Thinking is a mental activity that all people are capable of performing. The thinking process relates to the natural teachings that the Creator gave to the people. The first message the Creator gave to the people was the "creation story," which speaks of how we came to be. The creation story reflects the identity we are given. When we think of identity, we also think of the creation story.

Actions = Ceremonies

Following the thinking process in relation to the creation story are our actions. These actions make our thoughts concrete and reinforce our identities, which have been shaped by the Creator. Our actions tend to follow the second message that the Creator gave, which corresponds to the ceremonies that First Nations people perform in acknowledgement of, and for, the Creator.

Attitudes = Great Law and Government

Next, we acknowledge attitudes, which are tied to identity. Actions and attitudes together, for us, represent a sense of consciousness that we have for ourselves, as well as for others. Our attitudes are tied to the third message from the Creator, the great law and the government.

The significance of this part is that the great law, in conjunction with government, applies equally to all people. It represents the responsibilities that men, women and children have to one another, the clan, the community and the nation. This natural lifestyle is strongly based upon living honourably and conducting the self appropriately, because there are consequences for unacceptable behaviours.

It should be easiest to cultivate strong Attitudes, because the Creator has laid out everything for the people to live by, as a foundation upon which to build. However, this is not the case, especially today.

Feelings = Faith

The last central component of the identity of First Nations people is feelings. Our feelings are so important because they visually express our attitudes, actions and thoughts. Our self naturally includes the interconnection among the four elements—that is, thinking (mental), actions (physical), attitudes (emotional) and feelings (spiritual).

These elements should be a natural, functioning part of our identities. The feelings we are all capable of expressing are reflective of the fourth and final message from the Creator, which is intended to highlight our faith in: life, who we are and what we are, and our purpose in life. These four elements provide us with all the answers that we are looking for.

Unnatural Behaviours

The discussion of unnatural behaviours cannot be related to a precise code of conduct. Rather, unnatural behaviours are sporadic, inconsistent and illogical. When First Nations people engage in unnatural behaviours, it shows how they are caught up in a lost state of being. Their purpose in life has become diluted. In relation to the teachings of the Creator, there is a lack of thinking, a lack of actions, a lack of attitude and a lack of feelings. When this pattern emerges, we have a neglect of the natural being. Unfortunately, this pattern is present in society today.

In today's reality, natural teachings are only used for symbolic purposes and for show. The people place neither meaning nor pride in the ways of our ancestors. We choose instead to eliminate the natural philosophies and adopt unnatural methods that neglect the issues of values, morals and loyalties for one another and among one another.

This unnatural process is three-tiered. First, it begins when a person learns to become self-centred. Second, the person becomes uncaring for his/her family, friends and community. There is an uncaring attitude towards people, animals and the environment in general. The person is consumed by materialism and personal possessions. He/she views individual gain as more important to his/her concept of self than are family, clan, community or nation.

Rather than being taught healthy attitudes through examples that highlight respect, our children, at an early age, are taught the wrong attitudes by fraudulent authority figures. This means that children are only taught part of the four messages from the Creator. The natural teachings are not meant to be used in bits and parts when it is convenient to do so. Natural behaviours require respect for the whole process; they require being able to apply all four components of the process to our daily lives. When this natural process begins to diminish and deteriorate into bits and pieces, it does not hold the same meaning in an incomplete state.

Today we teach our children how to carry the burden of the adults. We break the bonds with our children when we cannot show them trust, friendship, respect or honesty. As parents, we need to know who we are and what we are as human beings, with a strong and nurturing concept of the self.

One way of illustrating natural versus unnatural tendencies is to compare two sets of children of the same age and with similar backgrounds but different upbringings. What will automatically become clear is that whether children grow up to be "healthy" or "unhealthy" depends upon the parental directive in life.

NURTURING

Healthy	Unhealthy
The parents have a clear understanding of their children and the four parts of being: the mental, the physical, the emotional and the spiritual. The primary caregivers do not give their dislikes to the children, nor do they transfer their unresolved issues to the children.	The primary caregivers are not at all concerned with the four parts of being. The children are conditioned and taught to behave in a certain way. Their lives are based upon the plentiful burdens of the primary caregivers, who in turn have never dealt with their own internally threatening issues.
The children receive unconditional love; they are able to feel for themselves based upon the body language given by others.	The children learn to adopt adult attitudes and learn to mistrust siblings and extended family members, adults and children alike.
At this point, the children can form their own internal foundations if intuition develops into trust.	At this point, there is no clear and concise foundation upon which to build an individual identity.

Self-Perception	**Shame and Doubt**
Naturally, the children over time are consistently more open and secure with themselves and with others.	Since adult issues are given to them, the children are continuously scolded and condemned and they see for themselves that they are influenced by behaviours

associated with their primary caregivers' unresolved issues. The older the children get, the more unnatural their behaviour becomes, starting with self-shame, guilt and anxieties that they exhibit towards others. The children work with their anger from the inside out.

Initiative

The children begin to explore and expand their boundaries as a means of testing the waters. They are able to form concrete boundaries for themselves based upon their premature interactions with others, from peers to adults around them.

Productivity

These children begin to form and internalize morals and values along with deserving acts of loyalty, while understanding why things are the way they are.

Visually, these children grow mentally, physically, spiritually and emotionally. For example, children learn to distinguish a good decision from a bad decision in the case of a stove. If they touch the burner when it is hot, they will get burned. This is the result of a poor decision. But, at the same time, the children know the stove is useful in preparing meals.

The lesson children learn is how far they can go before consequences determine otherwise. Children have to balance their decisions with the understandings gained from the primary caregivers, of the consequences of inappropriate judgements.

Responsibility

These children can carry themselves in a more responsible manner, practising morals, feelings and values. They can

Guilt

The children are afraid to make mistakes verbally, emotionally and intellectually. They are underdeveloped because of the primary caregivers' negative influences. The children find themselves in a no-win situation.

Inferiority

These children have accepted the adult burden as their own. They have accepted the notion that this is the way things are going to be and carry out that behaviour without questioning.

These children face defeat and they are not able to experience their own self-growth, never having the opportunity to ask "why." They are always told why.

For example, the children are taught who to associate with, while their loyalty is tested to side with the primary caregivers. The children are fooled by the disguise of morals and values. As it turns out, these are not really morals or values. Rather, the children become the carriers for their primary caregivers' burdens.

As a result, the children are unable to experience any type of emotional, spiritual, physical or mental growth.

Irresponsibility

They begin to practise their learned customs. They look for others with similar traits and ways of understanding. What change judgements into personal choices and accept the consequences of their actions, whether they are proper or improper acts.

Also, the children create an internal balance within the self, which includes some incorporation of the viewpoints of their primary caregivers and peers. At this point, everything is based upon the decisions they make.

Intimacy

The young adults have physically, mentally, emotionally and spiritually matured and they are not afraid to show the self or reveal their identities to another.

Stimulation

These adults experience upward mobility. They are aware of the seven generations and know the differences between love and nurturing with the knowledge of what bonds are all about. These adults use events of the past and present collectively to shape the future.

These adults are able to show compassion for themselves, the family, a partner's children, and others around them.

They understand what it means to have and show trust, friendship, respect and honesty towards others, and vice versa. As people get older, the intensity of relationships change, as others come and go. They allow room for those changes.

constitutes caring for these people is defined in relation to conditioning received from primary caregivers.

They look for external remedies such as drugs, alcohol or promiscuous behaviour as a way of disconnecting from the primary caregivers. At the same time, the children break any acts of loyalty to those other persons, because they have established new loyalties with their peers.

Isolation

These young adults are physically, mentally, emotionally and spiritually immature because of lack of nurturing. They tend to push others away and to clear the self because they don't have true identities of their own. They adopt bits and pieces of others' desirable traits as their own personalities. They live in a world of fantasy that neglects reality.

Deprivation

These adults live a rich fantasy life. There is a constant struggle between fantasy and reality. They tend to reflect back on the past to justify the present.

These adults lack a clear future because they are caught up in personal grief, which is used as a cover-up.

External stimulation or remedies are used to release the emotional anxieties.

At a certain point, depression sets in. The only way to relieve the tension in the self is to deal with the childhood grief that is affecting daily life.

Childhood trauma varies according to the person. Life is subconsciously structured around childhood traumas so that people are unable to get past them, if they don't deal with the issues. If the issue is not dealt with before they have children, the remaining issues do affect their children as well as their parenting styles.

Living	Surviving
These people are at peace with themselves and have accepted life and life's challenges and frustrations. They see both gains and losses as signs of personal growth and maturity.	These people blame others for their current situation and circumstances. They have learned at an early age that it is easier to blame others than to accept responsibility for personal actions.

Final Thoughts

At one time, we knew what internal peace was. We also knew what was expected of us at all times. The boundaries were clearly marked, and we understood the internal as well as the external relationships around us. Spiritually, we have connections with the Earth, the Creator, the people and the children. Today we have forgotten these connections because we are too caught up in ourselves to see any differently.

Even as we speak, our roles and responsibilities are still clearly defined and outlined by the natural teachings of the Creator, as was intended. The natural ways are the most sacred and important tools on earth. There is so much to be learned and to be practised. However, our people are not taking the time to reacquaint themselves with the natural knowledge that has the potential to enhance and enrich our identities, and that can give us the strength and encouragement to carry on with pride and dignity.

Understanding the natural ways requires a person to accept all the ways equally and unconditionally. The natural ways mean nothing if we can't accept the whole package. By only accepting half a package, we disrespect the teachings and ourselves. The natural ways are not meant to be used when it is convenient or suits the purpose we have in mind. It requires inner strength, and a commitment to fulfil and live up to.

Society places a lot of pressure and stress on us to conform to the larger picture. As a result, First Nations people get caught up in this lifestyle and forget who they are, and what their roles and responsibilities are to one another, to the Earth, as well as to the Creator. What emerges is the loss of identity.

Our people need to understand what "natural" versus "unnatural" methods are, and decide towards which one we shall strive. Are we willing to strive towards "natural methods," recapture our true identities, and preserve our distinct First Nations culture? The way in which we recollect the past, and act in the present, will shape the future of our people.

NOTES

1. According to Honyust, "CASNP is an independent organization with chapters all across Canada. We support specific Native issues such as Stoney Point, the fight against water pollution at Walpole Island, and Native fishing rights for Chippewas of Saugeen and Nawash, by hosting speaking engagements on these crises. Also, we lobby and rally against political injustices and racial issues such as the relocation and resettlement of the Stoney Point Nation on their native land base."

2. References to *R.v. Warren George* in Julie George's essay correspond to the page numbers found in the original court transcript.

4

Methods of Learning to Learn
The Controversy of Youth

Character and moral development are necessary to give the critical
intellect humane purposes. —Martin Luther King, Jr., 1947

In the teaching of and learning about controversy, context and content are
key. Context and content shape the teacher's identity and social interactions. Moreover, context—structural and experiential—conditions the content of teaching and learning. Both social contexts (affiliations, resources
and skills) and personal contexts (ideology, motivations and self-concept)
mediate the message—the subject matter of learning. The coterminous
forces of context and content are, then, not only integral to teaching
controversy but also, as concepts, integral to recent theoretical develop-
ments in critical pedagogy. Accordingly, teaching controversy leans on
contemporary debates in education theory and practice oriented towards
issues of identity and difference.

Critical pedagogy challenges normative patterns of teaching and learning and urges "a social praxis"—an approach that, as Freire (1985: 125)
puts it, helps "to free human beings from the oppression that strangles
them in their objective reality." Towards this end, the concept of "difference" plays an important role in revealing the different forms and elements
of power in various "zones of culture"—the circumscribed areas of the
dominant culture (Giroux and Simon 1988). For Peter McLaren and
Tomaz Tadeu da Silva (1993: 40), the task of teaching:

> is to provide the conditions for individuals to acquire a language
> that will enable them to reflect upon and shape their own experi-
> ences and in certain instances transform such experiences in the
> interests of a larger project of social responsibility. This language is
> not the language of the metropolitan intellectual or the high-
> priests of the post-avant-garde, although it may borrow from their
> insights. It is a language that operates critically by promoting a
> deep affinity for the suffering of the oppressed and their struggle
> for liberation, by brushing common-sense experience against the
> grain.

Critical pedagogy enjoys a rich intellectual history (Young 1971; Bowles and Gintis 1976; Willis 1977; Anyon 1980; Freire 1985, 1993, 1995; Apple 1986; Giroux and Simon 1988; Kozol 1991; Kanpol 1994; Giroux and McLaren 1994; McLaren 1994; Giroux 1995, 1996, 1997; Yeo 1997). These progressive perspectives are replete with diverse theoretic tools that can enhance our understanding of education; and the literature both highlights and challenges how most learning reflects the values of the dominant social order.

Unlike the traditional view which reduces teaching to simple instrumentalist transmission models of "skill and drill," critical pedagogy connects the cultural politics of difference within a perspective that connects identity to a politics of ethics and justice (Saltman 1998; Kanpol and Brady 1998; Petruzzi 1998). Critical pedagogy challenges all forms of alienation, oppression and subordination. Critical pedagogy, as a set of practices, challenges the historically constructed dominant and oppressive ideologies. It forms and informs teaching in relation to conflicting (controversial) social narratives of the self and subjectivity. How should controversy be articulated? How can it be empowering to teach about marginality in a context of privilege? By developing an awareness of difference, teaching controversy is not disempowering but enabling. In turn, the concepts of content and contexts and the exploration of codes mediate the relationship between teaching and learning. Critical pedagogy can be conceptualized as a process of "reaching in," "reaching out" and building trust, which leads us to focus here on the controversies of youth, risk and resistance as substantive sites of investigation.

CRITICAL PEDAGOGY: FOCUS AND LOCUS OF CONTROVERSY

In the processes of "reaching in" and "reaching out," the personal and social converge rather than diverge as opposing interests. In addressing the question of agency or, alternatively, the role of the teacher and student in constituting social relations and forms of consciousness, teaching controversy is evolutionary and built from the bottom up, rather than imposed by teachers alone, from the top. The emphasis is on a commitment to "being" and "becoming" aware, thereby moving well beyond the mindless "doing" of routines.

1. "Reaching in" (Intrapsychic): Knowledge and Identity

Pedagogy cannot be separated from the teacher's own set of ontological assumptions, intellectual traditions and knowledge. As Giroux (1995: 133) puts it, "The act of knowing is integrally related to the power of self-definition." But as Nietzsche (1973) observed, of all the knowledge that we seek, self-knowledge is the most difficult to achieve. After all, the self is not ordinarily self-conscious. Since most of our understanding of the world is filtered through our understanding of self, introspection or inner conversation enables the self to think through its many activities. Reflexivity is a condition in which groups or individuals reflect back upon themselves, upon the relations, actions, symbols, meanings, codes, roles, statuses, social structures, ethical and legal rules, and other socio-cultural components of life (Brunner 1999). Self-consciousness, the active process of creating or constituting inner personal meanings, serves to connect the past through the present to the distant future (Barresi and Juckes 1997; Bruner 1990; Carr 1986; Dennett 1992; Hermans, Kempen and van Loon 1992; McAdams 1990; MacIntyre 1981).

Success in teaching controversy depends heavily upon a teacher's self-awareness and sense of freedom—the ability to move into an altogether new space. As Hooks (1990: 157) states, for instance, "One of the deepest expressions of our internalization of the colonizer's mentality has been self-censorship." Certainly, a basic fear of movement often dominates the actions of the privileged (teacher and student alike) and arrests the development of empathy and growth. Self-censorship is a matter of self-protection, with an attachment to the deeply engrained benefits of privilege placing strict limits on educational gains and experience. The self-reflective and contemplative teacher should be able to identify and recognize the role of privilege in her or his work and life and thereby be able to work at breaking down barriers. As part of this teachers must come to terms with their own positions, recognizing their privileges, their power, and the resulting limitations in understanding the experiences of the marginalized, let alone the experiences of most students. Writing in reference to racism—though it is equally applicable to privilege—activists Stokely Carmichael and Charles Hamilton argue:

> One of the most disturbing things about almost all white supporters has been that they are reluctant to go into their own communities—which is where racism exists—and work to get rid of it.... Only whites can mobilize and organize those communities along the lines necessary and possible for effective alliances with black communities.... [The] political modernization process must involve the white community as well as the black. (Quoted in Lines 1992: 27)

In other words, only by entering another world—that of the student or the participants in the controversy under investigation—can teachers become aware of their own condition of privilege and manage to work effectively from within it.

Noddings and Witherell (1991: 3) note that "to educate is to take seriously both the quest for life's meaning and the meaning of individual lives." Reflexivity or internal dialogue, like psychoanalysis, can dredge up the repressed unconscious, the fixed meanings embedded in the indirectness and disconnectedness of identity and knowledge (Saltman 1998).

2. Reaching Out (Intersubjective): How to Interact Pedagogically

A commitment to teaching controversy recognizes the importance of intrapsychic and intersubjective relations. Learning to teach is transbehavioural in the sense of making ongoing connections between inner and outer perspectives. The inner perspective emphasizes the ability of teachers to know themselves, while the outer urges teachers to understand others through sympathetic introspection. Given that teaching is a set of negotiated interpretations, the interactional contexts of student–teacher relations shape the respective identities, roles and rules. The solution, therefore, is inclusion rather than exclusion, readmittance rather than isolation, reinterpretation rather than adjudication—a system guided more by the altruistic than the adversarial (Kirkpatrick 1986). A methodology of "appreciation" (Matza 1969: 25) invites us to suspend predefined categories in favour of learning the language of our students. An appreciative stance demands a certain sensitivity and willingness to explore matters that are significant or important to the students. Listening to what students know and feel about a particular situation makes the crucial difference in "demarginalizing" (Barak 1998) teachers and students alike.

Intersubjectivity is the capacity for exchange based on mutual recognition, and its potential exists in all forms of social and cultural interactions. Intersubjectivity recognizes the complexity of multiple involvements with students, along with the value of incorporating diverse voices and experiences into education. Intersubjectivity brings students closer to the learning process because it implies various forms of collaboration with other students and teachers. As a process of identification through mutual recognition, intersubjectivity informs the discourses and practices of teaching. This process not only includes the intrapsychic positions of teachers and students but also focuses on the interactions between "self and others" (Rose 1996: 56–74). The inherent tensions of likeness and distinction—that is, the processes of asserting the self and recognizing the other—allow for various possibilities in understanding the relationship between self and other. Intersubjectivity is a form of mutual recognition of both the similarities and likeness of the other. This mutual recognition is a mechanism by which people perceive each other's pain and pleasure as well as the possibilities for appreciating a connection between the self and the other.

In teaching about privilege, for example, teachers can encourage students to contemplate and examine their respective attitudes and beliefs and then help them connect themselves to others in a cooperative learning arrangement. Working in small groups, for instance, students can look at both at their own actions in terms of group dynamics and at their commitments to each other as the key to an equitable and just life together. At the core of any controversial issue is a reconciliation of the values of social justice (the collective, social or community) and dignity (personal, private individual). A second step is to consider the context of the prevailing value systems, including the philosophical, sociological, and anthropological examination of the elements that foster privilege. As a general methodology, critical pedagogy displays an "omnibus quality" by incorporating an array of well-reasoned exercises that include variations of informal communicative strategies, conversational or informal dialogue, direct instruction and more formal focused lessons. In a painstaking process, teachers and students together make an intellectual journey to "capture" each other's interpretive experiences, to connect or reach out according to commonalities. As part of this, the subject of pain or agony is a salient connective tissue in negotiating and negating risks and resistance.

Teaching controversy is not necessarily a contest of opinions but a form of collaborative problem-posing and problem-solving. For example, one of us (Livy Visano) taught a "policing society" course in the early 1990s at the University of Toronto. A large number of the students were police officers, and the subject matter of homophobia created considerable anxiety among them. The first challenge was to try to understand where these students were coming from, and a second was to suspend judgement and work strategically. The problem was not so much that many of the students were white male "straight" police officers, but that they saw no possible connections between their own lives and the lived experiences of others. It was only after we went through considerable time and lengthy discussions—and only after the police officers had connected their own personal, agonized exclusions, both idiosyncratic and patterned, with the experiences of gays, bisexuals and lesbians—that we saw signs of appreciation, let alone tolerance.

A genuine engagement in important issues and a commitment to collaborative learning can overcome a crass consumption or a flat rejection of controversial topics. By shifting the focus of education from the values of discipline to the values of collaboration, teachers and students can experience at least the beginnings of a change in attitude. In the case of the policing class discussion, many students were obviously apprehensive about an upcoming mid-term in-class test. To allay their anxieties Visano asked them, in a discussion, to come up with their own questions—issues they thought it would be good to raise in a test, given the course content. In this case their immediate concern about grades and tests led to a dialogue on police-gay community relations, which generated further themes for investigation. Students identified disturbing situations of "gay bashing," of homophobia as a systemic problem, and they ventured to connect these issues with other exclusionary practices directed at other communities and identities. Consistent with what Brunner (1999) identifies as the importance of the composition, we all decided that since the discussion of gay rights stimulated so much dialogue, it should be further pursued in an essay-type exam question.

This kind of collaboration promotes a learning partnership, which eschews predetermined topics in favour of a pedagogy in which teachers and students cooperatively determine content and performance standards (Gross 1997: 40). This particular exercise sustained inquiry by encouraging divergent thinking. Students were provided with opportunities to exercise choice and recognize consequences, to ask powerful and critical questions. The experience revealed that teachers can make a difference in communicating ideas not only through what we teach, but by how we interact with students.

a) Trust and Trustworthiness

The most important component of student-teacher relationships is trust. For teachers it means having a certain faith or confidence in the reliability of their students. It means being trustworthy, or in other words deserving of trust—being reliable and dependable themselves. For students, trust means having confidence in their teacher's professional competence. Students trust that teachers have the skills that will help them to learn effectively.

The art of instilling trust, though, is usually not emphasized in teaching, aside from vague professional conduct guidelines and institutional protocols. Teachers are often ill-prepared for interpersonal challenges. Regardless of the degrees of competence (from the very mediocre to the very effective) and regardless of the nature of the subject matter (from the most mainstream or orthodox to the most controversial), teachers are required to confront a number of problems in fostering trust, uncompromising honesty and a sense of responsibility.

To ensure trust, teachers ought not to detach themselves from the consequences of their presentations. It behooves teachers not only to engage in controversial issues, but also to be sensitive to the manner in which topics are discussed. Dealing with painful or sensitive personal issues ultimately places an extraordinary burden on these trusting relationships. Trust has to be built slowly and cannot be taken for granted. According to students to whom we have spoken, trust is cultivated by empathy, respect and a positive rapport. They have also noted that, given the authority positions of teachers, it is the teachers who are responsible for establishing and maintaining trust in a learning environment. The maintenance of trust is contingent upon satisfactory teacher-student experiences in continuing encounters inside and outside the classroom.

For teachers, the building of trust requires a personal investment in a) true collaboration; b) self-reflection and an appreciation of teaching as a privilege; and c) a respect not just for the subject matter but also for students, colleagues and the wider community. Both personal experiences and external factors influence the structure or "fit" of teacher-student relationships. One aspect of trust is the granting of validity to the students' voices. By attending to the diverse local knowledges of students, teachers can secure a measure of reciprocity. This approach includes a methodology of genuine feedback that allows teachers and students to work together in interpretive activities. Consequently, teachers listen to and make sense of students' stories and tests, although recognizing that those responses are only part of the whole picture. The teacher-student relationship becomes the vehicle for transforming students' subjective experiences and for arriving at an understanding of a controversial issue. Both teachers and students incorporate and set aside as much as possible their respective ideas, beliefs and feelings in developing an interpretive connection.

Credibility is an essential element in trust. Why should students trust and believe their teachers' interpretations? The credentials or titles of authority figures do not in themselves enhance credibility. Rather, much credibility rests on how well the teacher understands the students' subjective categories for ordering their experiences. Do teachers take the time to explain how they enter, remain in and leave controversial situations? How does the teacher communicate the essence of controversial subjects? How do students gain an appreciation of the complexities of learning to deal with controversial topics? Student curiosity will range far beyond the topic discussed in the classroom to include attempts to understand how the teacher communicates the topic. Students appear eager to learn or unlearn "by example," which is a practice essential to any mentoring role and one that recognizes the need for collaboration in developing trust.

Reciprocal or mutual trust facilitates the dismantling of communicative barriers that lead to contempt, criticism, defensiveness and stonewalling. Teachers sometimes throw up cultural barriers in the pathway of student understanding. Difficult or obscure or perhaps even overly tidy concepts such as consumerist ideology, or fragmented and yet binding binaries (opinion/knowledge, rational/emotional, individualism/collectivity, theory/practice), can, if introduced casually or abruptly and not, for instance, carefully explained as part of everyday direct experience, yield tensions if not boredom, frustration and intolerance. This is particularly the case when university teachers have to confront the alienating effects of mass education in the form of large classes of anywhere from fifty to five hundred students. Institutionalized anonymity inhibits the development of trust.

b) Roles and Experience

The role assumed by the teacher helps to condition the rapport gained and subsequent information collected about a controversial topic. "Role-taking" is a complex interaction. For one thing, it requires adopting positions that are comfortable for both interactants. Teachers must respond to their subject matter by "creating and maintaining a series of viable roles and identities" (Manning 1972: 244). The movement involved goes back and forth between the world of teacher and student and the particular academic discipline. Paley (1997: i) notes:

> Promoting empathy would be a major undertaking for any classroom, but the teachers ... go further. They believe that perceiving the feelings, thoughts, and motives of another person is the first step in building a bridge. What must follow is the discovery, day by day, of how to move—in both directions—across that bridge.

Irrespective of the shifting between roles, of withdrawing and returning periodically to the margins, students are moved by the teacher's experiences with the subject, and those experiences, in turn, shape the discovery and presentation of ideas. Teaching requires that we shuttle back and forth between positions that are often polarized, leaving space for spontaneity and ungluing the fixed image of student and teacher in order to rearticulate a dynamic, uncertain teacher/learner as dialogic *bricoleur*, or handyperson (Brunner 1999).

Roles are related to experience: ideas about controversy are generally framed within a set of clear, consistent and logical guiding notions based on empirical referents. The desire to teach and learn about controversial topics invites a commitment to knowledge generated from experience. But learning also includes knowledge outside the experience of teachers and students—that is, "other codes of experiences as well as other discourses in time and place" (Giroux 1988a: 104).

In Giroux's (1988a: 100) words, knowledge "never speaks for itself, but rather is constantly mediated through the ideological and cultural experiences that students bring to the classroom." Experience is important only if it is authentic. Regardless of the experience—research or lived—students will respect the teaching of socially sensitive material if the teachers base their presentations on a variety of flexible approaches. Triangulation (Denzin 1978), the examination of single empirical events from the vantage point of different methods and viewpoints, provides one way of doing this. This approach encourages the flexible use of a variety of convergent methods, ranging from media and guest speakers to research and life stories. As well, in exploring the relationship of the teacher to her or his learning environment, the use of case histories can enhance the credibility of teachers. As Heyl (1979: 3) notes, a case history is the best available method for illuminating changes—both subjective and situational. The teacher's own life story (decisions, feelings and rationalizations) vis-à-vis the topic represents the continuities and dynamics of a commitment to teaching controversy. Retrospective accounts render the teacher more accessible and trustworthy. Students will link the teacher's sense of self-worth with the ability to communicate connectiveness.

During these cross-cultural challenges, both the teacher and student alike have the need to be affirmed. Both teachers and students respectively need to know how they approach their work and how they relate to each other. This emphasis on mutual interests and intellectual attraction between both parties is fundamental. Ideally, this cooperative demeanour induces perceived similarity, trust, open communication, flexibility and concern for each other.

Teaching the "Politics of Recognition"
by Livy Visano

In teaching controversy, teachers have to prove their trustworthiness again and again. Given the course material, they will not find it easy to avoid showing bias. For example, a York University colleague of mine who knew I had been doing work on prostitution asked me to give a guest lecture on that subject to his undergraduate class. He encouraged me to bring along some of my research participants, and I did: three prostitutes joined me in giving the presentation, which dealt with the misogyny, social injustices and pain experienced by sex trade workers.

Several male students, missing the point of the presentation, interrupted the talk to ask about fees and services. Rather than dismiss this query as inappropriate, if not insensitive, I thought it was essential to determine what informed their curiosity. Why would they assign so much priority to costs (for the client) and benefits derived (services performed)—that is, to market conditions or consumerist interests? When one of the sex trade workers asked why the fees were so important, the student retorted that it was a "male thing." The worker, appreciating the candor, tried to engage these male students by exploring the logic of their own questions. She suggested that this "male thing" was also a cultural "thing" reflecting the dominant values of society, which in turn condemn women who refuse to conform to traditional patriarchal patterns of work. This dialogue became a focal point for the breakdown of authoritarian control over students, allowing instead for active decentralized participation by students in the learning process.

Something similar happened a couple of years earlier when I was invited to give a talk on prostitution to graduate students and faculty at the University of Toronto. As part of my discussion on how the dominant culture treats sex trade workers, I tried to establish the point that all of us, as a society, were implicated in designating prostitutes as deviant. A graduate student and a faculty member objected to the implications of this argument, and the subsequent debate captured the contemporary tensions that characterize the conceptions of crime, culture and women—which in turn brought out tensions related to the intersections among various forms of domination and oppression. Based on the idea that subject positions are not fixed, static or unitary, I believed it would be more fruitful to inquire into how we shape and are shaped by our social locations and life experiences.

Given that notions of value become encoded in what we call a "language of experience," we reflected on personal responses to what is valued and devalued and what is named and unnamed. A nuanced discussion of unrecognized subject positions that incorporate gender inequality emerged as we interrogated traditional notions of privilege that condemned the prostitute's body as a site of specific and generic processes of feminist reproductions. But it was the discussion of recent deaths of prostitutes and subsequent vigils in Toronto's parks that served most strongly to raise personal issues for the students, and myself. I had been at a vigil for a slain prostitute the night before the talk, and it became clear that, while no one from the class had been there (despite their professed academic support for the plight of prostitutes), the immediacy of the issue, and the chance to take part in something public like a vigil, increased their level of interest in learning more about the lived realities of sex trade workers.

The "politics of recognition," a consistent theme of controversial topics, is a method of teaching that must be extended to the student as well. In the classroom the teacher must become the guide on the side, not a sage on the stage (Reitz 1998). By guiding students with study questions for reading assignments and by organizing small-group work and discussion opportunities, teachers facilitate collaborative learning. Reitz (1998) argues that class assignments should take the form of study/action projects or study/service projects, which combine research and in-class learning with the prospects of engaging in effective civic work, community action and community development.

Praxis is an ideologically informed action-based orientation to knowledge or truth claims. Praxis essentially meets the methodological demands of progressive teaching by encouraging the teacher to grasp a first-hand knowledge about the controversy in question. A connection to, or at least familiarity with, alternative social realities enables the teacher to capture more fully the experience of controversy—the pains of confrontation, the consequences, the processes and so on. The nature of the teacher's experience communicates and thereby breathes meaning into controversial topics. Thus, the idea of experiential and intellectual integration refers to the relational, positional and provisional functions of interpretation. This integration serves to validate and repudiate multiple discourses and their expressions of reality construction in divergent social arrangements. In this regard, we can speak of standpoint epistemologies—attitudinal knowledges with their corresponding ideologies—myths, symbols, metaphors (Arrigo 1998).

Fieldwork with Youth: A Methodology
by Livy Visano

In teaching controversy, we have found that students' most frequent concern is the issue of trust in the research. Trust is related to familiarity. Given that students are required to research topics that are often foreign and challenging, they frequently ask: What does one have to do to secure trust? How does one research controversy—that is, research the subject of controversy or research issues that are controversial? How can one study inequality from a privileged position? Drawing on my fieldwork on youth, including research on prostitutes, street transients, police informers and drug dealers (Visano 1987, 1990a, 1990b, 1996, 1998b), I can provide a brief overview of the methods I used to secure trust among various research participants.

In that work, gaining access and maintaining rapport with so-called "deviant" youth involved building trust—and proving trustworthiness was something that had to be done over and over again. Not just our details of their lives and statements—"the facts"—but also our interpretations and conclusions had to be as accurate as humanly possible, and the best way of ensuring this was to maintain close and constant contacts with key informants and the youth. Researchers also have to resolve fundamental issues that centre on ethics, including honesty and acting responsibly. In my case this meant not divulging confidential information that could cause injury to the reputations of the people being studied. Likewise, the researcher's entrance, presence and departure can disrupt the long-term functioning of the social group, especially if the research findings contribute to increased crackdowns by the police or end up building public hysteria against the subjects.

To safeguard my ethical position, both professional and personal, I encouraged youths, individually or collectively, to read my notes. I also promised strict confidentiality, which is always an important ethical question for researchers. The obligation to protect identities becomes heightened when you engage with research subjects who are woefully disadvantaged in the larger society. The sociological practice of using pseudonyms to protect the identity of all actors is a necessity. (Pseudonyms are preferable to less personal case or file numbers.) For the same reason we avoid giving detailed descriptions of the actors, as well as facts and information on specific identifiable locations.

The other important concern is to be sensitive to, and open about, how the research findings will be subsequently used. Again, this is a matter of trust. We told the subjects (youth, in this case) that the details observed would be widely read and published. Some "street kids" would "test" our assurances of confidentiality directly by asking what other actors had said and done. Regardless of the requests, our pledges of anonymity and confidentiality were never negotiable.

Despite these issues—and other problems, such as the danger, from the subjects' point of view, that the police could request our research data—we had a perhaps surprising level of cooperation. According to the participants, my own background played a part in establishing rapport. I had previously done volunteer work with agencies in the area and had established trust in preliminary field work. I had in fact spent some time (about seven months) "living on the street." I also always presented my projects as collaborative ventures, with participants consenting to be involved only after hearing a full explanation of the work. The youth involved would also tend to "check me" out by "asking around." I had to assure them that my research was not connected with the police, and that I wouldn't be producing any evidence that would allow authorities to trace their personal backgrounds and identities. I had to be careful not to show any signs of being judgemental or of trying in any way to "correct" their behaviour—neither of which was part of my project— and gradually they would drop their protective masks.

The most important thing, perhaps, was to consistently maintain the protection of identities. We would conduct interviews carefully so that details about identities and activities could not be overheard by anyone else in the immediate vicinity. In this regard, one significant methodological issue had to do with the relative fears of participants. Interestingly, all the youths involved in the study felt free to divulge extensive details of their early and current relations with the police. In addition, many of them actually insisted that I take notes in their presence or that they write out a record of their experiences. Given their wariness of the police, though, they refused to do taped interviews; they expressed fear that the police would break into my office or apartment and steal the tapes. They wanted to protect themselves from the possibility of being identified and abused by the police.

YOUTH AND MARGINAL LABOUR: THE PEDAGOGICAL SETTING

How, then, is this discussion of trust related to a critical pedagogical analysis of youth? For one thing, critical pedagogy resists a rigid inventory of steps. Instead, the techniques used encourage a more flexible accommodation between theory and methods—a flexibility consistent with the demands of the discipline and the methodological requirements of observation.

In his article "Monday Morning Fever: Critical Literacy and the Generative Theme of Work," Ira Shor (1987) applies Freire's pedagogy to the industrialized "First World." He notes that in this society, "Domination by mass culture ... has left the population either marginally literate, or uncritically literate, and politically underdeveloped" (105). If one of the goals of education, then, is to improve critical thinking—at base "a means to develop literacy and consciousness" (106)—we can begin to do so by examining daily life experiences, including work.

In the classroom, Shor explains, the teacher might begin by asking students to write a composition on the topic "What is the worst job you have ever had?" For students who had not been employed, he asks "for an account of what they considered the worst job around, one they would hate to wind up doing." A second step is what he calls "composite theme development" (113), in which he asks students to examine the idea of "worst jobs" more carefully, considering what the worst jobs have in common and what makes them different. In so doing, "the task of abstracting features of an experience around an organizing principle initiates the class into critical reflection on an ordinary subject." As they read various "worst job reports" students build a more general, conceptual and critical understanding of "marginal labour," linking it, for example, to "low pay, no power to make decisions, little responsibility, routine and repetitive tasks, no creativity or independence, etc." (114).

Shor's example can help us to analyze work systemically, in ways that students can identify with, and to do this here we draw on the issue of youth and marginal labour, in particular "squeegeeing": a controversial urban issue that easily links to students' own work experiences. Our discussion of squeegeeing represents our "codification" of a specific type of marginal work. Adopting Wallerstein's (1987: 37–38) use of "codes" as a framework for reading this case study, we use a series of questions to facilitate discussion:

1. What do you see happening on the streets?
2. How would you define the problem (assuming you see one)?
3. Can you describe similar experiences?
4. If you see what is happening as a problem, *why* is it so?
5. What might be done about the problem?

By using what Wallerstein (1987: 37) calls an "inductive questioning strategy"—moving from the most familiar to more generic concepts—students "ground their discussion in personal experience, integrate the experience into a broader social context, and together evolve alternatives." This exercise "depersonalizes" marginal work experiences while also addressing them more generally. What we teach is related to "how" we teach. The content of marginality, which is central to critical pedagogy, becomes an exercise in codification, and, again, the process is about "problem-posing, not problem solving" (40). By posing problems, teachers learn to draw out meaning, as well as information, from our students.

While this pedagogical approach may not make work less alienating, the "squeegee kids" codification, in the context of problem-posing, should make critical thinking "less remote" (Shor 1987: 121). As Shor maintains, the "problematic study of work" offers a means of engaging students "in an extraordinary re-perception of something very ordinary." The goal may be to hone literacy skills and consciousness in relation to the content theme, but the approach "also validates students psychologically, because the exercise is based in their experience" (120–21).

STREET LIFE AND YOUTH: A CRITICALLY RESPONSIVE ALTERNATIVE

The social organization of teaching consists of a wide spectrum of events and configurations that vary according to circumstances and other factors. For the teacher, getting connected to, staying connected to disconnecting from or reconnecting to a controversial topic are all related and yet analytically distinct levels of work. A career taxonomy of teaching stages can provide a framework for assessing the contingencies that shape the teacher's identity, interactions and social contexts. As a sensitizing tool, the concept of a teacher's "career" (Becker 1963) incorporates objective and subjective elements. The objective features include aspects of social structure—the teacher's affiliations, resources and skills. The subjective contingencies consist of the teacher's ideology, motivations and self-concept. Consequently, structural and experiential factors contribute to the social construction of the teaching enterprise.

Any teaching project can be framed within a set of clear, consistent and logical guiding notions, which are pivotal in shaping an otherwise amorphous mass of observations and experiences. When teachers address controversial issues, both the inner and outer perspectives of human agency become crucial elements in the exercise. The inner perspective emphasizes the ability of actors to know themselves and to understand others through "sympathetic introspection" and "imaginative reconstructions" of "definitions of situations" (Filstead 1970: 4).

The Teacher as Researcher

The methodological strategy of teaching blends well with the central concerns of the praxis perspective. A close proximity to the social reality enables the teacher to formulate conceptual categories based on emergent data. Praxis elicits information and draws inferences from objectively presented and subjectively interpreted behaviour. The intent, therefore, is to capture the experience of actors in their symbolic and behavioural worlds by penetrating their "everyday worlds" (Corrigan 1979; Ben-Ari

1987). Becker and Geer (1970: 133) define this strategy as "a method in which the observer participates in the daily life of the people under study, either openly in the role of a researcher or covertly in some disguised form, observing things, listening to what is said, and questioning people, over some length of time."

As a general methodology, praxis displays an "omnibus quality" by incorporating an array of exercises that can include variations of informal communicative strategies (such as an appreciation of gestures, demeanour, or tone), direct participation, conversational or informal dialogue, and formal focused presentations (fixed item inquiries). This flexibility facilitates a more direct and comprehensive presentation. Moreover, praxis invites teachers to be more responsive to changing situations and more open to pursuing issues and leads in greater detail (Bennett 1981: 249).

Teaching and research are, then, interrelated activities. The classroom becomes an extended ethnography, wherein there is room for engaging in "bottom-up" analyses that assign ontological priority to the "lived" experience, to the conditions of the immediate present, and to the contexts created by teachers and students that are in some cases mediated by shared ideologies.

A Case Study in Codification: Squeegeeing as Marginal Street Work

Squeegeeing, a recent phenomenon in many inner cities of metropolitan areas, is the job of cleaning car windows. Armed with their squeegees and buckets, street youth perform a type of service by standing at street corners, waiting for traffic to stop for red lights at main intersections, approaching vehicles and, if the response is positive, washing car windows for a fee. This sale or commercial transaction is between the motorists and the kids. "Squeegee kids"—or "kidz," as the youths themselves sometimes style it—is the term given to individuals engaged in this practice. Other terms used to describe these kids are "road rodents," "cockroaches," "freaks" and "gutter rats."

Squeegee kids range in age from about ten to thirty but are mainly in their late teens. They flock to the downtown core as a means of survival. Almost exclusively white, but from a variety of socio-economic backgrounds, they tend to have various motives for migrating to the streets of inner cities. For some street kids, "hitting the street" is considered a solution to school and family problems. For others, it is a way of earning extra money needed to survive the increasing unemployment and underemployment of today's market. A small percentage are youths who come from the suburbs to the downtown core to squeegee: they live with their parents, get an allowance and go downtown to squeegee not out of necessity but to make extra spending money. But for most squeegee kids the work is a limited means of subsidizing their living and an alternative to begging or "panhandling." Most squeegee kids are poorly educated and, in the standard sense, unskilled.

The youths who "hit the streets" are seldom unfamiliar with the problems that await them. From their own previous brief weekend excursions and limited information acquired from friends at school, they have built up positive impressions of the excitement of the "street scene." As this site becomes defined as an attractive option, the temptation to be on the street and to abandon abusive, dysfunctional families and school increases. Young boys and girls, for example, tell each other of the weekend excursions to the inner-city streets and "all-nighters" that are part of the lifestyle. They have, then, done at least some informal "research" before making the permanent move to living on the streets, and to some extent they have been drawn in by their exposure to the details about the profitability of street activities and the locations of hostels and missions. These sketches, which provide a positive picture of street life, tend to be both misleading and limited.

Getting connected to this street activity requires a collective effort in which the interests and involvements of others are central. A young person's decision-making process is further influenced by their experiences and the conditions of the street.

i) Living on the Street

For squeegeeing, the work instruments, tools or equipment are relatively simple, consisting of a window cleaner, a cloth and a bucket. The work clothes, demeanour and appearance are interesting and unique. Some of the youth have tattoos, bright orange and red mohawk haircuts and extensive body piercing under their oversized coats and camouflage pants. Others have no hair at all, or it is pushed up underneath a baseball cap or hidden by what they refer to as a "kangaroo" hood. In the late 1990s the average pay for cleaning a windshield was a dollar. The average daily income of squeegee kidz was $40.

The language of the youths' own accounts understates the hardships they encounter during early days on the street. They often gloss over, or blithely ignore, life on the street as a problem. To begin with, apart from exaggerated notions and limited experience, the youths have little information or knowledge about how to survive on the street. Initially newcomers face considerable hardship in trying to fit into the street environment. For the solo or solitary adventurers, this early period is marked by trial and error. Newcomers are not integrated into a web of friendship patterns on the street. Their initial experiences assume a solitary quality. They exist on the border of conventional and "deviant" worlds. They are on, but not of, the street (Visano 1987, 1988, 1990a).

Upon arrival, they do not participate in either the conventional society or in existing street subcultures. Their attitudes and behavioural patterns remain on the fringe. On the one hand, the newcomers have partially relinquished their former cultural traditions. On the other hand, they have not yet won acceptance in the culture into which they drifted. Although they have abandoned familiar associations, they have not carved out a place in their newly found street lifestyle.

During this initial phase on the street, newcomers become impoverished street transients. Despite the advantages of "being free," newcomers soon realize that they are all alone in trying "to make it." In talking about their first few days on the street, they repeatedly single out the difficulties associated with "making it"—in securing even the fundamental amenities of food and shelter. They do have some organizations they can turn to, such as the Covenant House, but these are temporary solutions to an ongoing problem.

In general, age is a liability for these newcomers. They fear the consequences of discovery, because this usually means returning to the family home or being delivered to a group home or training school. Any reliance on welfare workers jeopardizes the likelihood of succeeding on the street, especially since agencies as a matter of course seek to reconcile children with their families. They quickly learn that agencies are also compelled to notify the police of any youths under the age of sixteen. They fear the exposure that presumably follows from divulging information to case workers. Although the welfare system provides for anyone over the age of sixteen, they need an address to be eligible for welfare. In Ontario youths under sixteen are not supported; they are referred to the Children's Aid Society.

Initially, street neophytes may try to find more standard work, but age and other problems restrict the possibilities (Livingstone 1998). If they do apply for a job, they face inordinate odds, given their appearance, lack of experience and limited references. According to Porter (1965: 11), "We make judgements about people's class on the basis of the clothes they wear, the place they live, the church they attend, the kind of jobs they have, or the size of their families. We have an extensive repertoire of class labels." As Rivard adds: "I'm sure that some of them would like to get a job or go back to school, but it's like a vicious circle. Today to get a job you need a certain look. Yes, there are a lot of people who are scared of the way they look. You need to buy clothes for the interview, but you don't have money so you're stuck" (LeBlanc and Rivard 1997).

These youth admit that most job searches are extremely frustrating because of continual rejections. They quickly discover that very few legitimate opportunities exist. After being turned down they become quickly discouraged and abandon further job applications. In discussing their inability to secure employment they seldom focus attention on their limited skills. Instead they provide lengthy explanations that negate work in general. Of the fifty youth studied, ten boys and seven girls had held part-time jobs in restaurants or as casual labourers while living at home or on the street.

They also tend to see work as a restriction on their mobility and subsequently on their "fun" activities. Newcomers say that they did not leave their homes just to embark on yet another constraining commitment. Securing a full-time legitimate job holds little significance for them; indeed, they cast it as an irrelevant concern. Although in need of money, they refuse to be stuck in what they see as meaningless or boring activities, like working in the loading areas of warehouses, washing dishes or sweeping floors in restaurants. They describe these jobs as time-consuming, poorly rewarding and, most importantly, in conflict with adventure. Moreover, even when they come from privileged backgrounds, neither their family nor school experiences have prepared them to function in the legitimate workplace.

Initially, newcomers live a meagre subsistence existence. They learn to rely on their wits to structure and seize upon any opportunity to survive. Living requires them to be constantly on the prowl and ready to score by squeegeeing or simply panhandling. They remain poor even as they squeegee for a living. The term "marginality," then, accurately reflects the general conviction that these children are somehow set apart from society and yet not fully part of street groupings. Their marginality is constituted on the street—a setting that is socially, economically and politically peripheral to the larger urban context. Marginality—the failure, in this case, to be fully implicated in the street scene or in the wider conventional society— becomes the key to identity transformation. Since these boys and girls are not yet well integrated, they render themselves more susceptible to street socialization. Paradoxically, then, the street kid faces the identity problem of developing an ongoing creation of self that is compatible with this newly discovered environment. The paradox of being "on" but not "of" the street does not in itself necessarily cause newcomers to seek out other street kids. But newcomers do justify the development of their street relations accordingly. Early difficulties on the street, especially regarding securing food and shelter, contribute to a lowering of defences and a greater susceptibility to involvements with more seasoned kids who are willing to offer support. Just as the street is perceived as a solution to prior family and school difficulties, street relations are seen as a solution to survival problems for newcomers.

These youth consistently distinguish the early days when they had "just hit the streets" from the later days when they had established a range of street contacts. Early exposure to the streets is a significant prerequisite for initiating street connections that eventually introduce newcomers to squeegeeing as an attractive alternative to their former lives.

Over time the kids' idealized image of street life clashes with their struggle for survival. As contradictions emerge, street kids begin to experience reality shocks. Primarily these shocks consist of discrepancies that follow when they realize that their newly espoused values and newly learned practices in the street setting are dysfunctional. Disengagement is one solution to this career crisis or turning point (Visano 1990a). For instance, as street kids find their activities less rewarding and more alienating, they undergo a restructuring of self. Months on the street, poor nutritional habits, drug abuse, inadequate housing, heavy cigarette smoking, anxieties about the uncertainties of subsistence, and the affliction of sexually transmitted diseases exact a price on their physical and mental health. Typically, after a year on the street kids begin to experience a sense of estrangement and frustration with their nomadic existence. They seldom single out any one factor that would cause them to abandon street life. Rather, they provide a cluster of impressions related to feelings of meaninglessness. Excitement wanes, and romanticized notions of freedom disappear. Identity transformation becomes more manageable when they get support from other people or sources, and often youth abandon the street when they find helpful or viable social alternatives.

ii) Squeegeeing as Controversial "Work"

There has been considerable controversy regarding public complaints against squeegee kids. While these kids were to some extent the victims of government slashing of social safety nets, during his time as Ontario premier Mike Harris was determined to adopt a no tolerance policy, an approach consistent with the North American trend of arresting squeegee kidz. In his "Blueprint for Ontario" (Progressive Conservative Party of Ontario 1999), Harris highlighted an aggressive campaign to crack down on these youths.

For years the police had threatened to crack down on squeegee brigades by charging them with violating a section of the traffic laws that prohibited anyone from stopping a vehicle to sell a service or commodity. Under the police plan, first offenders would be given tickets for $150 under the *Highway Traffic Act*. If the squeegee people persisted, the complaint would be taken to court and a probation order issued, forbidding them from this activity. If that order was violated, offenders could be fined up to $1,000 or imprisoned for up to thirty days (Black and Wilkes 1997: A3). A number of youths were initially ticketed under this police plan.

This penalty remains quite draconian, given their levels of poverty. In response to aggressive police ticketing, the squeegee kidz held a protest on Yonge Street in July 1997. At this protest thirty-six lawyers apparently offered their services (Shariff 1997). Lawyer Edward Sapiano won the first legal challenge to the section in the *Highway Traffic Act* that the police were using to clamp down on squeegees. He noted, "We want to establish that these kids are not violating the law.... It is my legal opinion that they are not doing anything that violates the section in the *Highway Traffic Act* that the cops are using" (Shariff 1997: 5). Likewise, Metro Toronto Councilor Jack Layton notes:

> If the windshield cleaners can sell the public on the notion that they are providing a legitimate service, they might be able to win legal recognition. Squeegees, like hot dog vendors, are going to have to convince the public that they are indeed providing a useful and needed service in a way that's not going to cause problems. If they can convince the public of that, then our politicians may be amenable, and if they cannot, then the politicians will be against them. (Quoted in Shariff 1997)

As squeegee kids descend on motorists stopped at red lights, they are often met with expressions of disdain. Sometimes the motorists appear to be worried about the squeegee people. Comments include: "Oh God! Look!" and "What do they want from me?"—"Do they want to hijack my car?" "Steal my purse?" "Break the window perhaps?" Motorist Chris Day stated, "The squeegee people used to bother me," especially when they would just start cleaning his windows. "But since they've started asking, it doesn't bother me so much." As she pulled away in her van, another driver said, "Let's just say, I never use them" (Black and Wilkes 1997: A3). In a study (MacArthur, McMahon and Visano 1998) outlining the various perceptions of squeegeeing, the researchers noted that respondents typically believed that these street youths were a nuisance and that they were using intimidation tactics to force people into giving them money.

Powerful officials offered various justifications for clamping down on this perceived social "evil." Both Toronto Mayor Mel Lastman and Ontario Premier Harris invoked paternalistic excuses in justifying their moral panic and crusade against the youth workers. Lastman characterized them as "horrible, disgusting individuals ... who spit at cars and bang them and do all kinds of crazy things." According to Lastman, "Women are petrified. Women are scared. Adults are scared." He added, "Women must feel free to walk the streets without fear." Former Ontario Attorney General Jim

Flaherty noted, "Someone in effect extorts money from you and out of fear you give them money" (quoted in Landsberg 1999: A2). Flaherty said, "I would like to live in a province where people can feel free to drive their cars without being intimidated" (quoted in Verma 1999: B1). Montreal Mayor Pierre Bourque also declared war on squeegee cleaners and compared their work locations to "street corners in the Third World" (Verma 1999: B3).

Given this hysteria, it is not surprising that on January 31, 2000, a new law in the province, the *Safe Streets Act*, came into effect. Besides forbidding anyone from asking cars to stop, or approaching already stopped cars and offering to wash windshields for spare change, the law outlaws aggressive panhandling and the disposal of syringes or used condoms in public places. Penalties range from up to $500 for a first offence to $1,000 or six months in jail for repeat offenders. The new law makes it illegal to stop or approach a vehicle with the intent to offer, sell or provide any product or service. When asked about enforcing the law aggressively, Mayor Lastman commented: "You're darned right I am. This has been a long, long wait and I am fed up with squeegies. I'm fed up with people complaining and it's got to stop." (*Globe and Mail* 2000a: A19).

New York provides a comparable example. When Rudolph Giuliani was elected mayor of New York in 1993 he vowed to sweep squeegee people off the streets, saying they filled New Yorkers with "a sense of dread" (Verma 1999: B3). He said that citizens had "a civil right to safety," which was threatened by these street thugs. At the time about 190 squeegee workers patrolled the streets—about the same number that Toronto police estimated to be working their city's streets during the summer of 1999. Giuliani made good his election promise, passing the anti-squeegee baton to his freshly appointed police commissioner, William Bratton. Before the crackdown, squeegee cleaners had simply been charged with interfering in traffic, given a court date and released. Afterwards police began arresting squeegee kids on the spot. They were fingerprinted, checked for outstanding warrants and could be detained for up to eight hours. After two months, their numbers in New York had been reduced by two-thirds. For good measure, the city passed a new law in 1996, banning solicitation of any kind directed at traffic. Unlike their Canadian counterparts, New York squeegee cleaners were mainly middle-aged, Black or Latino with no fixed addresses. The car-window cleaners in Canada are mainly whites in their late teens, and most are homeless.

Citing high-profile shootings in New York, in reference to the police crackdown on squeegee cleaners, Norman Siegel of the American Civil Liberties Union argues that this pernicious approach leads to police abuse: "What's happening in this city is we have a context where the mayor demonizes squeegee guys, and it has created a situation where you have police officers engaging in street justice tactics where the result is the police feel they can violate anyone's civil rights" (Verma 1999: B3). In Canada, the Canadian Civil Liberties Association is also eager to challenge the *Safe Streets Act*. As Association lawyer Alan Borovoy states, "We are very interested in mounting a challenge or intervening in a challenge, especially on the panhandling part, because there are some real problems for freedom of expression" (*Toronto Star* 2000: B1). Lawyer Edward Sapiano concurs: the law is "a very expensive hammer to kill a fly…. They are scheduling hundreds of trials. The government has chosen the most expensive means known to humankind to address a social issue" (*Globe and Mail* 2000b: A14).

Politicians and the media tend to criminalize squeegeeing. Yet this work enables the young poor of the inner city to survive without relying on traditional methods of street survival—the street trade in drugs, sex and stolen merchandise. For example, Corey, a twenty-one-year-old, talks about squeegeeing: "It's relaxed, we don't have someone barking down our throat that the hamburgers are getting burnt, and treating us like we're lucky to have a minimum wage job.… Working at a burger joint, you're not so lucky." He says, with some conviction, "Right now I'm going to school and squeegeeing gives me the money.… I've worked at Wendy's, baked donuts, shoveled chicken shit, pumped gas and sorted carrots for $10 an hour in front of a conveyor belt. Squeegeeing is not the first job where I've been treated like shit, but at least I'm my own boss" (quoted in Kuitenbrouwer 1997: 1). For another youth, squeegeeing became a means of supplementing inadequate income from social assistance: "After I have paid for all of my monthly expenses, I find myself to be approximately $163 in debt. I need the money that I earn through my work as a squeegee kid in order to make up for that $163 that I do not have" (LeBlanc and Rivard 1997: 1).

CRITICAL REFLECTION AND ACTION: DOMINANT STRUCTURES, SOCIAL RELATIONS AND ASKING THE EMBARRASSING QUESTIONS

Squeegeeing, then, is a controversial form of work for youth. For one thing, the system that claims to support capitalism and free enterprise has sought to criminalize squeegeeing. If the welfare system cannot support these kids, and there are few jobs available, what will they do to survive? Go back home to abusive families? Engage in prostitution and other criminal behaviour? The available alternatives seem less than satisfactory. This particular case study can lead to critical reflection on the nature of marginal labour, and it can also invite students and teachers to strategize on solutions to the problem.

For instance, by connecting various instances of marginal labour to the broader social context, we can consider how the particulars contribute to a more general understanding of youth labour. Following two key propositions—"There is no teaching without learning" (Freire 1998: 29) and "To question, to search, and to research are parts of the nature of teaching practice" (133)—we invite critically responsive strategizing on what can be done to address the wider problems of exploitation, marginalization, work and youth alienation. Again adopting Ford's (1994) philosophy that "all positive change starts with one person who cares," we might investigate what traditionally informs our judgements about marginal work. This can in turn lead to various "action" steps. We might look "beneath the surface" of our respective communities to reveal the efforts being made to ameliorate the conditions of youth engaged in marginal labour (Ford 1994: 103–106). This work could involve looking more closely at the views of different community leaders (110–11) as well as the efforts they are making to help youth find more viable work alternatives (119–21). Ultimately these action steps are contingent upon the articulation of individual and communal experiences in contexts open to diverse and dynamic forms of social interaction.

An analysis of the controversy of youth and marginal labour benefits from the adoption of the intrapsychic (self-awareness) and intersubjective (awareness of others) approaches. Out of the exploration of intrapsychic and intersubjective relations emerges a recognition of the roles of "self" and "other," and a subsequent appreciation of issues of domination and submission. By reconceptualizing "togetherness" and "otherness" in terms of intersubjectivity and sense of self, we move away from the isolation of the "self" and the engulfment of the "we" towards a greater social reciprocity that respects differences and commonalities alike.

Essentially, then, teaching controversy is the process of locating or contextualizing our judgement within a broader and deeper unfolding set of influences. Controversy is sometimes mistakenly described as being inherently idiosyncratic, but the particularities can be global, and the comparisons with other sites can facilitate the generation of more generic principles. Teaching controversy recognizes both the internal and external tensions leading towards emancipation for the individual. As always, teaching controversy highlights the importance of intersections of psychology, sociology, cultural studies, history and political economy. In locating the controversy, students and teachers are asked to determine the ultimate goals (understanding), ultimate means (critical thinking), immediate goals (connecting issues) and the immediate means (case studies) of the inquiry. Central to this expectation or performance schema are issues of reform and re-form, responsibility and response ability, structures of domination and processes of intersubjective experiences.

Context and content are central to the generation of an analytical framework for teaching and learning about controversy. The concepts embedded in the case studies of youth and marginal labour, for instance, presented as a contemplative process, indicate a form of imagining: an account of connecting ideas that signify or embody relations between different pedagogic subjects that constitute and are constituted by the dynamics of power and authority relations. Both the meanings of controversy and lived legal experiences are filtered through a series of complementary and seemingly contradictory gestures that reveal and conceal underlying pathologies. Within this context, alternative forms of subjectivity will work to build a much-needed transformation in teaching.

But, as we will see in the next chapter, teaching controversy is both dependent upon, and autonomous of, dominant structures and social relations. The recognition of this interplay creates the possibility of establishing a more complete and therefore more liberating vision of education. We need to work at understanding how the dominant ideological and cultural structures have been produced and continue to be produced by market economies (corporate capital, productivity and growth) and the conditions of managerial chatter (fiscal matters of cost-effective teaching, rationalizing gestures, performance indicators); and analyze how identities are institutionally constructed within and upon a wider interplay of power dynamics (risks and resistance). Given this we can re-evaluate what constitutes a teaching relationship and thus redefine exclusive, normative strategies that govern and manipulate the experiences of teachers and students.

In a convocation address to the University of Toronto in June 2000, Professor Edward Said exhorted graduands to:

> Ask the embarrassing questions that will make you controversial, that one quality so many of us tend to shun like the plague. Controversy is what intellect is all about, since without that sort of energy, and stubborn questioning, and deeply moved humanism, there is really only a sort of death.... Therefore, there can be no standing aside and refusing to enter a controversy just because one isn't an expert or directly involved. As searchers after truth, we must ... raise questions when docility is often required, make trouble when submissiveness is expected, and express dissatisfaction when a sort of lobotomized passivity is aimed at.... I'd be lying if I didn't also warn you that it means trouble, for you and those around you. (Quoted in Siddiqui 2000: A13)

5

Critical Pedagogy as a Response to Structural Obstacles

"To vision is to transform.... come let us share our visions
To create a greater Circle of Interconnectedness."
—Fyre Jean Graveline, *Circle Works*, 1998

An authentic education must be committed to an open inquiry that respects the diverse needs and backgrounds of students. This learning requires that students and teachers recognize the existence of alternative worldviews. It also means understanding the construction of hegemony and, related to that, the silencing of certain voices.

Still, teachers cannot impose their own analysis and conclusions on students—many of whom will not agree, for instance, that equity, social justice and a recognition of the value of diversity are long overdue. As long as students can make their arguments using logic and intelligence they have every right to their conclusions, however much the teacher might disagree. Our approach implicitly rejects any punishing of dissent, which is a misuse of the teacher's power.

How can teaching controversy be an empowering exercise for all students, especially the average white male middle-class students who are asked to question their privileged existence? Are the teachers and students who handle controversial issues asked to undergo a thorough-going political conversion? Are teachers of controversy always expected to respect different perspectives and never silence voices of dissent? These are crucial concerns, and we certainly do not want to adopt a dogmatic, prescriptive position on such questions. The answers to these and other similar questions are related to a broader issue: what are the goals of post-secondary education?

Clearly, controversy does not necessarily amplify threats to the conventional order. Indeed, controversy has always been a catalyst for confronting inertia and a reluctance on the part of both individuals and collectivities when it comes to making, or even considering, structural changes. Typically, people all too frequently examine controversies in isolation, at the "local" level, without inquiring into interrelated "global" trends of exploitation, whether historical (colonialism, misogyny) or contemporary (corporate imperialism, militarism).

Teaching and learning need to be situated within the often neglected structural dynamics and wider relational problems. We need to consider, for example, the impact of prevailing values on teaching and ask whether teaching is contextually determined. We need to consider how teaching fits into a wider social context. For instance, at the more local level, how do the occupational culture, the disciplines and the bureaucratic administrations influence teaching and learning? Within a more global context, what are the influences of "neo-liberalism" and its pervasive mentality of putting the goals of the market economy first above all other factors? The nature of the prevailing social structure and its institutions, and the role of specific socio-economic formations, are keys to the issues raised. In addition to the politics and risks associated with teaching and learning, we must also recognize that much of what we strive to do faces an even greater challenge: the balancing of pedagogical ideals and institutional constraints.

THE IMPACT OF THE DOMINANT CULTURE

Our society's dominant culture values discipline, conformity and respect for authority. These values, perpetuated by long-standing traditional educational practices, pose formidable challenges for critically responsive pedagogical alternatives. Unlike critical pedagogy's emphasis on "the teacher as learner," traditional pedagogy subscribes dangerously to roles that overidentify and wholeheartedly accept "the teaching as authority" mindset. The teacher's status and credentials are enough to establish categorical claims on truth, often doing away with the need for trust development. The teacher's contacts with students are often distant and formal, not allowing for the exploration of certain issues for fear of violating the perceived propriety of a specialized professional role. Binding obligations replete with duties and institutional norms define acceptable means of interactions. Power, privilege and reason prevail in a dominant culture that consistently defies difference.

In this kind of an environment, the teacher enjoys a position of privilege, believing that certain meanings are fixed, despite continuing contacts with new voices (Wertsch 1991: 78; Quiring 1999). Accordingly, the teacher's sacrosanct word commands respect, binding students to a disciplinary structure. To define yourself as a teacher places you in a set of communicative relationships in which the parties to the interaction are required to share a history and parlance that asserts a mutuality of interests. These conditions become political tools in that they can be used to disempower and control outsiders. In this sense, teaching is never neutral. It is encoded with multiple desires and thus multiple ways of knowing. Notions of truth, power and agency are embedded in and embodied by discourses that are biased in favour of the logic and reason that animate the so-called intellectual process.

The teacher/educator is an authority over his/her subject matter—the discipline. In turn the discipline of logic and reason provides a persuasive discourse, communicating exclusively the ideologies that "internalize" a particular voice (Wertsch 1991). Rationality has long been associated with the scientific method, which classifies information according to a particular worldview (Quiring 1999). Logocentrism (an ethnocentric emphasis on a conventional logic) displays a view of the world in which a particular "truth" or "reality" is privileged at the expense of other voices, other perspectives. The tradition of logocentrism, with its powerful set of signifiers, is well prepared to condemn variant epistemologies. The teacher, as authority, claims to speak certain "truths." For Quiring (1999), the rationality inherent in the education system's normative gaze disqualifies other bodies of knowledge that do not fit its view of what is to be described and explained in the world. This sensibility to a particular rationality "is part of the centralizing powers which are linked to the institution and functioning of an organized scientific discourse" (Foucault 1980: 84). This conservative agenda gives short shrift to the importance of making connections to the lives of students who differ culturally, ethnically and socially from the dominant culture (Lee 1999).

Ethnocentric knowledge is understood by the less enlightened in terms of authoritarian elements, utilitarian politics or universal pragmatics. Traditional teaching reflects privilege in its orientation towards "banking" (depositing information) and its adversarial designs cemented to a priori, static and calcified fixations on calculability, predictability, objectivity and control. But privilege can no longer stand in the path of understanding, just as solutions can no longer be left in the hands of the self-interested powerful. Controversy, a fear of the privileged, is not problematic for the marginalized. To the threatened, teaching controversy is subversive because it questions privilege and demonstrates how privilege silences voices from the margin. For Freire (1993: 53), the logic of question and answer is the only logic that generates authentic inquiry. This dialogic process generates the movement towards humanization: "knowledge emerges only through the invention and re-invention in the world, with the world and with each other."

THE INFLUENCE OF THE OCCUPATIONAL CULTURE

The authority of the teacher is also influenced by the "occupational culture," which refers to an organized and recognized constellation of values that are specific to the required activities. First, the academy exerts influence in perpetuating a sense of professionalism replete with standard norms, roles and attitudes. Judged according to Griswold's (1994) normative conceptualization of culture as a historically transmitted pattern of symbolic meanings, teachers communicate, perpetuate and develop "their" knowledge about and attitudes towards, controversy. This means that it is important to know how teachers, as representatives of an occupational culture, make sense of controversy. It is important to consider the inscription of dominant ideologies (narratives) and the "preferred," "oppositional" and "negotiated" teaching styles.

The very structure of the university shapes the neophyte professor's self-image, as well as his or her understanding of situational difficulties. This culture or opportunity structure awaits the arrival of prospective members. The university offers both limitations to and possibilities for effective critically responsive teaching. The self-identities that instructors construct for themselves are congruent with the possible identities that are afforded them within the occupational culture. This culture provides a coherent narrative of identities; it ensures social recognition of these identities and a sense of "we-ness" that stresses the similarities or shared attributes around which group members coalesce.

The emerging collective wisdom serves to guide and validate perspectives and activities. Collective identity is normative in that the attributes and images of teacher identity become fixed. Acculturation—that is, the process of learning new ways and meanings based on collegial involvement—offers a collective solution to actual and perceived occupational strains. These values provide a symbolic framework for the development and maintenance of a collective identity as well as individual self-esteem. The occupational cultures or subcultures provide group standards, behaviour and values that prove to be powerful for the individual actors involved. The collectivities establish hierarchies, membership requirements, informal rules and coping strategies (accommodation and resistance) vis-à-vis the administration. In general, newcomers seek relations that offer them the possibility of solving some of the problems associated with being untenured and unfamiliar with bureaucratic organizational rules. In time, the newcomers build a number of collegial alignments by gravitating towards appropriate service, teaching and research responsibilities.

Despite the long-standing university rhetoric that emphasizes teaching, service and scholarship as being equally significant, the quality of an academic publication record continues to weigh heavily in recruitment and promotion. A critical approach to teaching and learning, however, regards research as an integral dimension of teaching in demonstrating and disseminating knowledge. Herein lies the problem: the social organization of scholarship becomes subjected to enormous cultural manipulations. From the funding of research to the dissemination of ideas in published form, teachers face incredible pressure to engage in performances of legitimation. So-called "objective" frames of reference exist that justify professional practices and protect privilege. On the one hand, according to the culture, teachers are expected to respond to the protocol of journal submissions, cater to marketplace conditions created by the competitive publishing industry, and cope with the stress of professional standing ("publish or perish syndrome"), all often at the expense of teaching. On the other hand, certain provisions reward their research industry, either through lucrative contracts or appointments to government panels and agencies. Accordingly, these exercises of patronage (reciprocal obligations) or of patronizing dissent (cooptation) are culturally accepted and historically rooted phenomena.

What is missing herein is a cultural critique of how corporate interests manipulate by "depoliticizing" and "cooling-out" critical or oppositional research. Financial compensation is not only an integral index signifying the prominence of certain actors, institutes or centres but is also a normative guide of professional standing in the "teaching" culture. Status articulates an investment in a culture that misappropriates a moral language and celebrates possessive individualism, leaving behind only the mirrors and windows of constraining customs through which knowledge is framed. Seldom is there a call for a moratorium on competitiveness, let alone on state and industry-sponsored research centres and studies.

Within this orientation, the culture of corporate interests and collegial complicity have diverted attention away from authentic voices and action. The pedagogies associated with protected professionalism and lucrative consultation have ushered in a new "banking" system. The liberal talk of consent, common sense, citizenship and community also fails to liberate the academy from the disciplinary cadence of corporate capital. After all, pedagogic practices do not exist in a vacuum: economic as well as bureaucratic convenience shape the delivery of "knowledge." Despite the gaze of liberalism with its mimetic gestures of benevolence, the learning process has inherent problems.

To overcome these conditions, we need to relocate ourselves within the wider community of the disaffected. We must more carefully examine to what extent our research is accountable to the discipline, the teaching enterprise, the community of scholars, the community of the studied or the general public. We must more closely consider the implications of teaching informed by "for-profit research." State and corporate-sponsored scholarship and research centres are subject to inherent dangers. Teaching has to respond aggressively to the challenges of capital, to the homogenization of curricula.

In looking at the occupational culture and subcultural explanations of teaching, we must remember that subcultural norms, rules and roles may set conditions, but they do not necessarily determine social action. A subculture is not a neatly articulated response packaged according to shared values and constraints. Rather, a subculture emerges as a social construction fashioned through the characteristic interplay of self-definition, reaction and interaction, that is, a subculture is not only a consequence but a context of ongoing interpretations. A more critical and comprehensive approach to occupational cultures moves beyond fixed, static and self-maintaining systems. Clearly, subcultures are fluid, loose and emerging webs of interaction. Shifting memberships, limited involvements, role discrepancies, norm ambiguities, incomplete rules and change are just as much part of subcultures as stability or cohesively integrated structures. These elements create considerable opportunity for choice and variation. With this in mind, university teachers must recognize the tensions and contradictions underpinning existing, more traditional pedagogies and explore the transcendent possibilities of critical pedagogies. Transcendence refers to the process of moving beyond the established practices of the profession, in particular the fixation on the lesson, discipline and curriculum as a mere moment of administering knowledge.

We would encourage educators to move beyond their traditional cultural roles and expectations, and to situate themselves in the struggle for critically responsive alternatives. One such alternative is to recognize and confront subjects of controversy by addressing the interests of privilege, and to question authority-subject classroom relations that not only defer to privilege but also dismiss as dangerous or futile or simply out of place, any expressed desire or action for social justice.

THE UNIVERSITY AS A SOCIAL INSTITUTION

Bureaucratic Managerialism

University governance has shifted away from the collegial or political end of the spectrum in favour of bureaucratic models (Fisher 2000: 6; Tudiver 1999). As market ideology became dominant in the 1980s, our universities became more corporate in structure and practice, adapting a "market" model of governance. Expanded administrative units took on the role of micro-managing faculty rather than facilitating and supporting research and teaching. Buchbinder (1993: 340) argues that traditional decision-making has been "replaced by a managerial hegemony in which the student and faculty groupings are marginalized and market strategies predominate." Despite the aura of collegiality or the spirit of participatory democracy, an actuarial logic of "the bottom line," guided by enrolment numbers and marketplace language, governs curriculum and planning. Universities and colleges have become "consumer-oriented corporations," dominated not by academics but by administrators and their own mediated "optics" of accountability and excellence. Purpel (1989: 48–49) notes:

> Schools have been captured by the concept of accountability, which has been transformed from a notion that schools need to be responsive and responsible to community concerns to one in which numbers are used to demonstrate that schools have met their minimal requirements.... Obsession with control also gets expressed in school policy.

Within the administration of large North American universities, neither innovation nor strategic thinking are in great demand. Instead, administrative convenience fuels decision-making. A market language steeped in an omniscient neo-liberal vocabulary promotes private market-driven solutions to university financial problems. But what the university needs—what is vital—is not neo-liberal economic and educational rhetoric but transparency in decision-making (Livingstone 1999; Currie and Newson 1998).

Within universities homilies are neatly tailored, as in the case of the administration's talk of the university "community." What emerges from the plethora of talk is the theme that this university community plays an incredibly vital role in shaping education, a critical element in forging new relationships. But the notion of community in these contexts remains situated within an illusory framework that masks any connotations, let alone nuances, of politics and struggle. Within the academic marketplace of rhetoric, jargon and clichés, the concept of community cohesion has become a negotiable commodity, its value conveniently determined by others. The concept of the university as community provides more than ideological legitimacy. It is designed to discipline outside participation, pre-empt criticism and discourage much-needed critical dialogue. The "university community" must not remain an elusive concept that becomes too easily appropriated by entrepreneurs to engineer support for limited initiatives that fail to grapple with central issues such as teaching loads, morale, teaching incentives, working conditions and professional development. As Heck (1999) asks, what are the teaching priorities of central administrations? How committed is the administration to teaching and learning?

Someone who, as often happens, has been both a committed teacher and a high-level administrator will have experienced first-hand the curious interrelationships between the roles. An administrator might find, for example, that basic information-tracking systems that enable effective decision-making about teaching are not in place; or that the activities of teaching, which require incredible time and energy, take time away from the administrative side of things. On the other side, local "administrivial" issues—relatively minor "housekeeping" concerns—can delay a commitment to more strategic, larger priorities. Equally, too, much time can be consumed by the commodification of teaching, by the *in camera* meetings responding to government initiatives, by inventing and assessing target projections and by the delivery of specialized offerings—time taken away from the "bottom-up" community building that can presumably enhance morale, innovation and ultimately enrolments.

Dollars and Sense: The Commodification of Knowledge

The commodification of teaching is not new (Veblen 1965 [1918]; Noble 1977; Atkinson-Grosjean 1998). Commodification means reducing "a person or relationship to an object of economic value, a commodity to be bought and sold in the marketplace" (Czerny, Swift and Clarke 1994: 63). Consequently economic goals and factors dominate social institutions and social life. When defined as a commodity, knowledge tends to be valued in political and economic terms, rather than for its social or cultural significance (Shumar 1997; Atkinson-Grosjean 1998). Atkinson-Grosjean (1998) identifies at least two key problems in the penetration of "market" discourse into the academy: the administration's uncritical and unreflective pursuit of the economic at the expense of the intellectual; and the selective interpretation of market doctrines by university administrations in general, allowing them to attack the " front line" while preserving management. She asks, why would universities—supposed citadels of critical thought—unquestioningly adopt an outmoded and clichéd form of corporate discourse? For Noble (1977), knowledge-based industries pursued a deliberate strategy, beginning with the oil and economic crises of the 1970s, converting university research into corporate intellectual capital. Newson (1994) acknowledges that changes in institutional arrangements and practices evolved to support corporate linkages. Centres of excellence, spin-off companies, and research institutes with special funding arrangements are parasitic on their host institutions (Newson 1994: 147). Federal and provincial governments have encouraged a closer relationship between universities and industry through matching funding policies.

In addition, decades of underfunding—that is, deep cuts in federal payments—are also critical factors. York University president Lorna Marsden notes the dilemma: "The question I'm asked most often is, will there be room for my son or daughter, and will the quality of their education be as good as in the past.... The answer is, I do not know.... Everybody sees the problem quite clearly, they just play the game. It leaves us in a very precarious situation" (Frank 2000: 11). The lack of funding has become a justification for universities to pursue more open partnerships with the private sector as a solution to their respective budget woes. Accordingly, universities are seeking alternative sources of revenue to preserve projects that would otherwise collapse. Universities have also increased their general tuition fees and promoted full-cost recovery programs. Also in evidence are a decline in the number of college and university faculty members, a reduction in research capacity, and reduced spending on infrastructures such as libraries and laboratories (Farr 2000: 24). Essentially, the rising commodification of knowledge and people has become the source of profits as universities actively participate in quasi-educational markets (Fisher 2000: 6; Tudiver 1999).

The Implications of Commodifying Knowledge

The primacy of business interests in the realm of information is dangerous. The world of information is dominated by consumerist values and commercial principles; the sponsor comes to control the means of expression. Information is increasingly treated as a private, rather than a public good, with an associated decline in challenging ideas and reliable information (Farr 2000). Before accepting the money, universities must ask whether the conditions attached would compromise the university's values or erode academic freedom. Donors should not be allowed to set university agenda. Are administrators and members of the board of governors on guard against shaking the wrong hand? For example, the windfall of million-dollar gifts from private donors set off a hiring spree at University of Toronto. The intellectual appeal of funding a research chair that supports study in a designated academic area in perpetuity has struck a chord with private citizens. What, for instance, are the implications of such endowments at the University of Toronto in relation to Bell, CIBC, Noranda, Royal Bank and the Toronto Stock Exchange, to name just a few? There is much reason to suspect that the funding for academic chairs and new programs distorts standards of intellectual integrity.

Regardless of the claims of industry, the encouragement of government and the credulity of university administrators, corporate interests do influence research (Fisher 2000: 6; Tudiver 1999). Private interests use universities and community colleges as sites for the marketing of their particular worldviews as well as promotion of their product names—a marketing that ranges from corporate goods and services to family names on research centres to advertisements in hallways and on washroom walls. The commercialization of universities and the zealous appropriation of a corporate model of management undermine the integrity of the research and researcher as basic and applied research becomes steered by private interests. This commercialization is changing the role of the university from a public service to a more private "for hire" enterprise with a more limited and highly compromised quest for knowledge. The commercial penetration of the university has nothing to do with the important student goal of developing analytical or critical learning tools. The secret agreements with corporate donors undermine issues of accountability and access to university governance. The integrity of the institution, collegial governance and the appreciation of scholarship and teaching become compromised whenever matters take a "for profit" direction. The crass willingness of universities to accept a great deal of money from a company to sell only that company's product on campus can erode public confidence as well as a crucial sense of independence from market strictures. For instance, marketing deals between York University and Pepsi Cola or McGill University and Coca Cola grant these respective beverage corporations exclusive rights over soft drink sales on campus in exchange for an estimated $8 million to $10 million respectively.

DIVIDE AND CONQUER: THE IMPACT OF MARKET ECONOMIES

The scramble for fundraising is ubiquitous and invites a "divide and conquer" mentality. Rather than work towards inter-university campaigns, universities quarrel with each other as they appeal for more money from their respective provinces. Deep divisions within the ranks are inevitable despite their unequivocal agreement that the pie should be bigger. Newer universities, and especially the more progressive, are disadvantaged. The older universities have tradition and more clout with their well-established and respected alumni.

Just as universities are encouraged to engage in competition to secure government and corporate funding, within large universities faculties are also encouraged to compete to secure funding from the central administration. Herein too is the belief that certain faculties deserve more support. This hostile environment dismantles the basic assumptions that undergird intellectual inquiry and advances instead the utility of bureaucratic control and the structural maintenance of inequitable resources. The availability of resources has an impact on teaching and research. This Darwinistic approach does not encourage imaginative solutions as long as parties are busy tripping over each other to curry favour, which in turn does not challenge the encrusted hierarchies of power.

The slogans and logos set in place are congruent with the curricular demands of government and business authorities who seek to shape various intellectual disciplines. The framing of teaching according to artificial criteria contributes to the functional rationality of the modern education system and is in turn "especially conducive to the maintenance of inequitable distributions of power." As Atkinson-Grosjean (1998) argues, the pervasive new market-driven ethos values application over enquiry, research over teaching, and science and technology over all other forms of knowledge, thereby neglecting traditional areas of scholarship that produce ideas rather than outcomes—and therefore potentially undermining the university's wider social role. Knowledge in the corporate university is defined as "intellectual property, a commodity to be bought and sold" (Tudiver 1999: 155), and only knowledge with commercial value is promoted. This commercialization is blatant, demanding and unapologetic.

In liberal arts education, for instance, external factors are having an impact on enrolment trends. In this climate, universities across North America are experiencing an incredible competition for a shrinking pool. Most of the humanities and social science programs have been in decline. Internally, numerous challenges face us as well, including restructuring activities, mergers of departments, pan-university centres or schools, faculty transfers, structural problems with the base budget and privatization. Moreover, we are faced with yet another challenge—not to lose sight of what we as educators represent. Students need both thoughtful and ethical education, as well as specialized skills. In the humanities and social sciences the emphasis is on educating people as cultural and historical beings who inquire into social, political, economic and cultural structures. This kind of education goes far beyond mere "technical know how" to incorporate, at a minimum, a cultural literacy in appreciating the so-called new global economy. Technical skills and critical self-analysis, that is, skills and intellectual acumen, and not just "high-tech fetishes," are both part of a high-quality education. The government, though, continues to see the goal of the university as one that leads to the creation of more technocrats, more flexible consumers and better employees for the global marketplace. According to Chomsky:

> As decision-making is shifted even more into the hands of unaccountable private power, the public must be indoctrinated in the virtues of subordination and discipline, and taught to regard government as an enemy to be feared, not an instrument they might use for public purposes in a democratic community.... An unspoken premise is that the role of government is not to be lessened, but rather shifted, away from public participation and service to public needs, toward private control and service concentrated private power. (Siddiqui 2000: A13)

The basic logic for schooling, therefore, relies on preparing students for a market economy. Underneath this rubric of market logic lies the students' motivation to specialize.

A passive acceptance of the new status quo can no longer be acceptable. Both teachers and administrators need to build and support new programs, promoting programs that attract new cohorts while retaining academic excellence. Universities need diversification of knowledge, critical thinking and a strong foundation in progressive approaches. We need to pull together as a collectivity. In determining what it is that we want to pull together and what it is that fundamentally defines education we will need to grapple with a number of problems: structural (funding, competition among faculties and universities), institutional (cultures of the faculty to which students and faculty members are affiliated, discipline-oriented foci); and interactional (student priorities, staff concerns). Here we hold steadfast to a vision that fosters collaboration, builds effective programs, and creates an inclusive climate for all (staff, students, alumni, faculty). The determination and implementation of principles and values require difficult administrative decisions. Issues such as relevance, enrolments, retention and recruitment are too important to be left solely in the hands of a few administrators, regardless of how well intentioned they are. These issues require universal attention. For instance, how can department chairs become involved in recruitment? How do they think about retention of students? How are decisions made to offer courses (on the bases of pedagogy, requirements of the discipline, historical trends, areas of familiarity and student interests)? We need to do more, much more, as a collectivity. How have we responded to course cancellations, new cohorts of students, changing demographics, interdisciplinary or multidisciplinary foci? Strategic thinking is long overdue. Among other things we need to create more imaginative experiments with a program emphasis, repair enrolments in extant structures, create new structures for allocating resources and enhance student presence.

The priority and hierarchy of principles suggest that a strategic goal is to provide a balanced, accessible and equitable university education for non-traditional students as well. Specifically, a number of operational measures may include "front-end" services for students (counselling, guidance, referrals), a re-examination of program or discipline specialization, and an enhanced enrolment management that effectively balances budgetary with curricular considerations. Formal structures and informal cultures influence governance, which should encourage widespread participation and consultation as well as initiatives from below within interrelated, multitiered and long-term solutions. These solutions include: a) the restoration of confidence: image and imagination; b) institution-building: providing a strong and coherent planning and administrative process; a strong and coherent voice on and off campus; c) enrolments: strategic enrolment management, recruitment, planning and advancement; d) governance and collegiality: active leadership roles in the university; and, e) the maintenance of the university and faculty spirit and curricular strengths. Smaller liberal arts colleges and universities represent an alternative to the bureaucratic models of larger universities. A relatively small institution's autonomy, principles of integrity, strategic planning as an authentic community project, and fundraising guidelines can serve to ensure the preservation of healthy university values.

Again, the future direction is far too serious a subject matter to leave solely in the hands of senior administrators. It is a subject matter that requires significant collaboration and a unity of purpose. This message directly confronts the prevailing raison d'être, the nature of the niche of curricular offerings and the concomitant challenges of innovation. Despite numerous retreats, reports and recommendations, we are still faced with the quintessential question about the university's or college's identity. To advance more inclusive paradigms and taxonomies of thought that go well beyond an ad hoc style of academic administration, we need to seek alternatives informed by progressive thinking and a logic reflective of the both the teachers' and students' interests and ideologies.

Although lip service is paid to teaching and student demands, students are still paying more money to sit in crowded classes in poorly maintained buildings. They have less contact with TAs not to mention professors. They have more multiple choice exams and shorter writing assignments because there aren't enough faculty staff to handle more extensive work

(Frank 2000: 8). The present formula of student loans, interest relief and income tax credits has generated huge debt loads, rising from about $9,000 in 1990 to $28,000 in 2000 (Farr 2000; Fisher 2000; Frank 2000: 9). The reality is that in an era of escalating class sizes and tuition fees, and reduced course offerings and access to professors, students are paying more and getting less.

In contrast to the competing neo-liberal view of skills training, critical pedagogy maintains that education is practical, in that it provides practical knowledge for living life dynamically, critically and creatively. Moreover, a more critical and emancipatory education provides us with roots—n historical consciousness. A critical pedagogy rejects liberal assumptions about education, artificial claims about individual merit and the benefits of competition. Specifically, liberalism, with its emphasis on egoism and self-fulfilment, must be juxtaposed against the history of human inequality (Lakoff 1964: 196). Efforts to privatize, corporatize and commercialize universities with various schemes including advertising and corporate curricula have infiltrated the language, logic and common sense of liberals and progressives who only a few years earlier would have considered privatization unthinkable (Saltman 1998). Understanding the social, economic and political context for current educational debates provides us all with interpretive maps for challenging material and ideological forces that threaten the democratic tradition and hinder the possibility of democratizing all social spheres (Saltman 1998).

THE CONTROVERSY OF RISK AND RESISTANCE

As professors from two different universities, we find ourselves continually asking a series of questions: to what extent have we implemented a set of comprehensive strategies to achieve our mission as educators? To what extent are we achieving our mission—that is, of providing non-traditional, critical approaches? These approaches are vitally important to the diversity of the university. We believe, like many of our predecessors, that learners demand unique pedagogies and curricula. The agenda cannot only be based on the characteristic profiles of our students alone, it also needs to be grounded in sound academic and pedagogical practice. Curricular offerings must be committed to equity, social justice, diversity and balance. Herein lies the gist of the problem. We are continually faced with the challenge of honouring these principles, despite the welter of change within the wider economic order that is shaping the nature of education.

We began writing this book after many months of listening to the concerns of both professors and students. Upon closer scrutiny and with a degree of reflection, we discovered within ourselves a need to share both the strengths and challenges of our pedagogical vision. This vision is one that includes a more meaningful, mutually respective and reciprocal relationship between teachers and students. For some, it is a pedagogical vision that in and of itself is and will be controversial. Woven within the very fabric of this engagement is a process of teaching and learning that is political. It is a counter-hegemonic cultural production that is critically responsive, responsible and action-oriented.

Obviously, no one message can hope to do justice to the enormous breadth and depth of the teaching and learning enterprise. Even to catalogue salient directions is an ambitious enterprise that suffers from the dangers of trying to do too much while accomplishing relatively little. The corpus of existing curricular practices provides an opportunity to revisit contemporary practices, to transcend local and more wide-ranging politics to consider the relatedness of what we do well as teachers and learners, to discuss the new activities we should be considering and how we might face the challenges proffered by this vocation. Our view is based on a review of relevant experiences and documents, various retreats and iterations of the teaching mission. In addition to these texts, we have reviewed the accomplishments of critical pedagogy.

More specially, we addressed questions related to the kinds of issues that are considered "controversial" and to how we might negotiate the resistance that arises from different constituencies in the face of controversy. We considered the importance of responsibility and accountability, in relation to both our students and the "controversial" communities that are tightly connected to the work we do.

In addition to calling for a fundamental change in thinking, critical pedagogy invites a more generalized attitude of risk-taking. Risk is generally defined as a systematic way of dealing with uncertainties, insecurities or hazards. Since all aspects of our lives involve decisions, human beings are risk calculators, and, interestingly, capitalism rewards risk-taking in business. There are, however, greater risks in learning and teaching about controversy.

Controversy as a contested terrain articulates antagonistic or contradictory sets of interrogative possibilities. Critical pedagogy incorporates the dialectic of collaboration and contestation. Regardless of the merits of the arguments, controversial challenges are collisions that often result in scrapes or bruises to personal identity, ego or deeply held perspectives. In oppositional pedagogies, teachers and students are asked to account for their "opinions" and learn from conceptually challenging thoughts. The term transformative intellectual, coined by Henry Giroux (1988a), simply means (for our purposes) that teachers possess the knowledge, skills, values and attitudes to question, understand, interrogate and eventually act as agents of change, working to overcome structural inequities in their places of employment (Giroux 1988b). To educate rather than school is to resist the very base of school value structures; and creating transformative intellectuals means being critical of all forms of schooling (Giroux 1988a). Critical thinking thus intersects with a critical praxis that is understood within the context of the economic, political and cultural (Kanpol and Brady 1998). Shoshana Felman (1987) writes that teaching is as much about resistance as it is about knowledge. Moreover, she maintains that the truly revolutionary insight, which can be discovered from teaching, is that "ignorance itself can teach us something" (Felman 1987: 79).

In the search for alternative ways of seeing social relations, the solution rests with consciousness, knowing ourselves and our location (Jouve 1991: 8). Critical self-consciousness is not an illusion but a series of connections; it is created in "social" relationships that link levels of awareness. An awareness of difference can inspire manoeuvres to remove cultural closures and can facilitate the sharing of interpretations. "Working through privilege" is no facile task, because it is oppositional—defying the defining gaze of legitimate authorities and challenging the unitary, polarizing and totalizing view of traditional cultural models. Enlightened teachers and learners are asked to be courageous, given that their arguments will be easily discarded as rancorously polemical and controversially provocative. As they risk bruising and weather more fully the contradictions of the dominant culture, the marginalized tearcher will succeed in interrogating complex problematic relationships. As part of this dynamic, teachers will have to situate themselves in the debates and struggles that characterize the dominant culture; they will have to firmly ground their perceptions and avoid self-incarceration by empowering themselves.

The dominant paradigm of teaching and learning needs to be replaced by one that imagines the possibilities, through education, of emancipation and empowerment not only of individuals but also of the dominant culture itself. The privileging of any one person or one group over another cannot be tolerated. Yet educators must, to paraphrase Cornel West (1993), realize that these possibilities—of becoming more autonomous, less dependent on dominant cultural values—will not be easy, that sacrifices must be made.

As students and teachers come to terms with their privilege, they will work to understand their privilege by confronting themselves and transforming their approaches to knowledge-seeking. This effort requires character, courage and conviction. It is not simply a matter of the privileged "moving over" and making room, but of exerting genuine pressures from within their communities, pressures that challenge fundamental social inequalities. To experience the particular consequences of privilege, people have to "connect" to themselves, to each other and "those others." Towards this end, students and teachers together need to move towards community action-based, socially transformative initiatives that integrate advocacy and scholarship (Fisher 2000: 6; Tudiver 1999). After all, action-based initiatives are more effective when "the academy" partners with "the community." Thus, beyond situating themselves as participants committed to a particular initiative, teachers and students must be open to coalition-building with the socially disadvantaged, with the economically deprived, with community-based organizations, with feminist and anti-racist action groups, with youth groups, labour unions, and Aboriginal associations. They must also establish open communication networks with the media and civil liberty organizations, and/or progressive political party members.

Critical teaching is strategic teaching. Pedagogy is as much about ethics and re-forming alliances as about content (Brunner 1999). In issues of alliance, negotiation, not harmony, is key. Alliances are sites of struggle on which different meanings and values conflict and retreat, take shape and are reshaped. They are not unified or harmonious cultures. The work of forming new alliances, then, is part of the call for a more humane education. It requires vision and stamina as well as a continuing dialogue. Martin Luther King, Jr., (1963: 20) suggested that the "ultimate measure of a man [woman] is not where he [she] stands in moments of comfort and convenience, but where he [she] stands at times of challenge and controversy." Nowhere does the challenge of shaping social history, fashioning new cultural narratives, and rethinking the nature and purpose of schooling become more urgent than in the struggle to define the civic responsibility of the teacher (McLaren 1989: 240).

In essence, what we offer herein is our vision of a learning process that invites the participation of alternative, traditionally marginalized voices—voices that are regularly silenced. We remain committed to situating ourselves, with open minds, in the debates and struggles that characterize the nature of education. In the words of Freire (1998: 120–21):

> To live in openness towards others and to have an open-ended curiosity toward life and its challenges is essential to educational practice. To live this openness towards others respectfully, and from time to time, when opportune, critically reflect on this openness ought to be an essential part of the adventure of teach-

ing.... The experience of openness as a founding moment of our unfinishedness leads us to the knowledge and awareness of that unfinishedness.... The person who is open to the world or to others inaugurates thus a dialogical relationship with which restlessness, curiosity, and unfinishedness are confirmed as key moments within the ongoing current of history.

Given the dialectical nature of teaching and learning, then, our journey along the path of a critical pedagogy is continuing, and always unfinished.

Appendix
R. v. Warren George

The Honourable Judge Gregory A. Pokele Presiding
Court Information no. 96-0373
Ontario Court of Justice
Provincial Division
February 12, 1998

Warren George stands charged with 3 offences under the Criminal Code of Canada. The allegations are outlined in the informations (read in per Sched. 1 attached). As in all Criminal cases heard in this country, the Crown Attorney, prosecuting these matters on behalf of the State, bears the evidentiary burden of proving all of the essential elements of the offence beyond a reasonable doubt. The accused is cloaked with the presumption of innocence throughout the trial. The accused need not call evidence on his own behalf as there is no burden upon the accused to prove his innocence. Indeed, whether or not the accused chooses to call evidence, the common law and the Charter of Rights enshrines [sic] that the accused cannot be compelled by the State to testify in his own proceeding, in that an accused is not compellable to give evidence that could lead to self-incrimination.

Evidence regarding all 3 offences was lead within one trial proceeding. The Crown called 18 witnesses to testify and some evidence was admitted into the record with the consent of the Defence pursuant to S. 655 C.C.C. The Defence called one witness and the accused and some evidence was filed by way of an admission. Thirty exhibits were filed. Crown and Defence vigorously cross-examined all witnesses and the evidentiary weight and validity of each exhibit was [sic] subject to challenge. Against this evidentiary background, this court must make findings of fact which involve a determination of the credibility of the witnesses and the reliability of their observations and testimony, remembering always the evidentiary burden placed upon the Crown. The ultimate findings of fact must be draped over the 3 charging offences to determine whether there is prima facie evidence to support the allegations. The evidence must also be reviewed to determine whether there are defences available to the accused.

The Court must decide whether the accused possessed the necessary mens rea.

The Court cannot ignore that this is the last of many criminal trials arising out of incidents that took place at or near Ipperwash Provincial Park on September 6, 1995. Within this trial, references were made to testimony given by witnesses and rulings and decisions made by other judges in previous trials. Indeed, defence counsel included two of these decisions in his case book even though they offer little value to this court as precedents. It is *not* the function of this Court, within the adjudication of Criminal charges against Warren George, to justify or reconcile the evidence heard in this proceeding with any evidence or decisions made in any other legal forum at any other time. The evidence in this trial must be considered by the Court within the context of a tightly framed snapshot or tableau, defined not by "common knowledge," rumour, or media depiction, but defined only by the admissible and unique evidence tendered within this trial relating to events in a relatively small location over a very brief period of time. The Court is aware that the mix of witnesses and evidence called in this trial was not duplicated in the other related proceedings, nor were the legal issues. The Court ought not and will not speculate as to what happened beyond the borders of the snapshot, as this is not the function of a Court adjudicating criminal charges.

Returning to the issue of evidentiary reliability and credibility, all of the evidence in this matter has been assessed pursuant to well-established principles in our common law. Reliability issues are related to the quality of the evidence given by the witness, the perspective, points of observation, ability to recall, etc. Credibility issues are more often related to issues about the desire and intention of the witness to convey evidence truthfully and honestly. This Court is directed by the decisions of *R. v. White, R. v. Covert, R. v. McNamara* (1981), 56 CCC (2d) 193 OCA and *R. v. W.(D)* (1991), 63 CCC (3d) 397 (S.C.C.) and all of the evidence has been assessed having regard to these principles.

Background

On September 4, 1995, at the conclusion of the Labor Day holiday weekend, Ipperwash Provincial Park (IP) was illegally entered and occupied by a group of individuals claiming to have historic aboriginal property rights in priority to those of the Government of the Province of Ontario. IP was adjacent to the much larger CFB Ipperwash which had been similarly occupied since May 1993. IP had been operated by the Ministry of Natural Resources (MNR), and in the face of this occupation, the Park Supervisor closed IP and unsuccessfully attempted to determine from the occupiers who might have a leadership role. The OPP cordoned off the park and set up checkpoints outside IP to warn and protect innocent passersby; the fence to the park had been cut, property had been vandalized, and there were concerns about public safety. The OPP were unable to enter into dialogue with the occupiers and no occupier presented in a leadership role. The occupiers lit a large bonfire at the park entrance, picnic tables and police cruisers were the subject of vandalism. The OPP felt that they heard gunfire in the park. Certain occupiers directed extreme profanities to the OPP, brandished weapons such as axes, and made threats.

The occupiers soon decided to occupy public areas outside the confines of IP and this trial has been focused on one particular public area, a sandy parking lot, proximate to privately owned cottages outside the park boundary, at the intersection of East Parkway Dr. and Army Camp Rd.

The Participants

The OPP assembled a Crowd Management Unit (CMU) of 32 officers out of two Emergency Response Teams (ERT). These officers were, for the most part, ordinary OPP patrolmen, drawn from various detachments throughout Southern Ontario, ranging in age from their mid twenties to their late forties. Membership in a ERT involved some annual training in crowd management principles, and the use of related equipment. They would only be called out to assemble when the OPP leadership deemed that a particular situation warranted this particular, and somewhat unusual response. In its most simplistic form, ERT members dressed in helmets, visors, protective gear, carrying shields and batons, would be used to provide a police presence at demonstrations and rallies such as might be found at a Queen's Park demonstration or a strike picket line. An ERT would move people and occupy a location by marching in a human wall of plexiglass, armed with batons; it is apparent that an ERT/CMU was not designed, trained or intended to respond effectively to the type of attack unleashed upon the CMU at IP on September 6, 1995. An ERT is not, by any stretch of the imagination, a military/paramilitary force trained in combat or assault tactics. At IP on September 6, 1995, the CMU was called upon to clear the occupiers from the sandy parking lot and to cede IP to the occupiers.

The Occupiers

Relying upon generalized observations and the evidence of Warren George (WG) and Cecil George (CG), the occupiers were First Nations people, a significant number of whom came from the nearby Kettle Point Reserve. No evidence was heard regarding the degree of organization involved in occupying IP and regarding any organizers or leaders. The MNR and OPP, at different times, attempted and were unable to communicate with any occupiers in a position of authority, and indeed, Cecil George testified that upon his own initiative he assumed the role of peacemaker at the confrontation in the grassy [sic] parking lot. The activities of the occupiers were not peaceful, respectful and dignified. There was vandalism to vehicles and other personal property, weapons were brandished, threats were made to police officers, citizens made complaints to the police. Ultimately, at about 11:30 p.m. some 15 to 20 occupiers came into contact with the CMU at the sandy parking lot, in circumstances outlined in evidence.

The Confrontation

At about 10:45 p.m. the CMU was deployed towards the sandy parking lot in a multi-tiered formation of contact units and arrest teams. The primary goal of the CMU was to clear the parking lot, not enter IP, and cede IP to the occupiers; if the occupiers withdrew peacefully no one would have been arrested or detained. It was dark and the only illumination came from the large bonfire inside IP and moonlight. As the CMU advanced, occupiers outside the park boundary lit up the CMU with portable halogen-type lights and with headlights from vehicles parked inside the park. This backlit the occupiers and negatively affected the vision of the CMU members as their visors and shields generated glare. The CMU occupied the sandy parking lot without resistance and all occupiers appeared to have withdrawn and entered the park. The CMU, having achieved its purpose, and having no intention of entering IP, pulled back. Regretfully and tragically for all parties, this was not the end of it.

Cecil George, Warren George and other occupiers then commenced a course of conduct which was extremely dangerous, violent and assaultive. Adapting a principle known at civil law, these activities constituted the "proximate cause" of all violence, and injuries which occurred that night, and the death of a man. One can only speculate how a more principled, reasoned, enunciated protest or demonstration by the occupiers might have assisted them in achieving their goals. One cannot help but wonder whether an organized well-spoken leadership, having advanced a statement of principles justifying the occupation, might have moved public opinion to the side of the occupiers and accomplished some positive goal without bloodshed. Instead, despite the fact that the CMU had not used firearms, had not injured anyone while clearing the sandy parking lot, had not entered IP, and had withdrawn back from the park fence, the CMU was stoned and attacked by the occupiers. From within IP, several occupiers began to hurl rocks, paving stones and firebrands with potential lethal force at the CMU. Many occupiers then exited the park, entered the sandy parking lot, and armed with poles, baseball bats and similar items attacked the CMU. Cecil George, who testified in this proceeding, was part of this group; he apparently confronted the CMU and spoke out loudly concerning the occupation and OPP presence; while he would categorize himself as a peacemaker, the facts fail to support this and he escalated the conflict by assaulting OPP Sgt. Wade Lacroix with a pole. CG was driven to the ground by a baton blow, arrested, struggled, subdued and taken rearward to a police van. All the while, the CMU were subjected to a hail of rocks and firebrands. Several officers came under attack from armed occupiers. Warren George, by his admission, threw paving stones at the police. The CMU punched out at occupiers and eventually withdrew up a road, out of the sandy parking lot. Moments later, a school bus was driven out of the park and up the road at the CMU. Within the close confines of this location, many members of the CMU were in danger of death and serious injury. Seconds later, Warren George exited the park, driving a large Chrysler automobile, and followed the path of the bus up the road. When it reached the area where the CMU were recovering from evading the bus, George's vehicle veered into several officers at the roadside, causing injury. Warren George admitted that he was the operator of this vehicle.

Defence Theory

There are many aspects to the defence theory, some interrelated. These theories are dependent upon making certain findings of fact.
1. The arrest of Cecil Bernard George was not lawful, and therefore the police were acting without lawful authority. The OPP ought not to have been in the parking lot, and had no lawful authority to encounter the occupiers for purposes of moving them back into IP.
2. The force used in the arrest of Cecil Bernard George was excessive and impermissible and constituted an unlawful and illegal act.
3. Under the common law and the Criminal Code, Warren George was entitled to the defence of "justification," particularly, he was justified in driving a motor vehicle at the CMU in those unique circumstances because it was necessary to save Cecil George from being beaten while being arrested for no lawful cause.
4. Regarding ct. 3 of the information, using a motor vehicle to commit an assault with a weapon, a conviction cannot stand since the accused did not "intentionally" strike P.C. Cloes with his motor vehicle.
5. Regarding the allegations of "Criminal negligence," a conviction cannot stand since the accused did not demonstrate the "wanton and reckless disregard" required to convict (per *R.* v. *Tutton*) since the

accused had a reasonable belief that Cecil George was in great physical danger.

6. That s.27, 30, 37 CCC authorize the use of reasonable force to prevent the commission of a criminal offence, a breach of peace, an assault.

7. The accused need not "prove" beyond a reasonable doubt, any of the defences raised. He must merely "raise" a reasonable doubt.

Prosecution Theory

1. The cumulative progression of violent acts by Warren George demonstrates that he was intent upon assaulting the CMU, and he now is trying to justify his behaviour under the guise of "righting the wrongs" inflicted upon Cecil George.

2. The erratic driving of the accused, under current case law, constitutes dangerous driving and criminal negligence as defined by existing legal interpretation.

3. The defence of "justification" is not available to the accused. The CMU was acting lawfully to establish a police presence in a troublesome situation where there were concerns about vandalism and gunfire. The accused's own testimony fell short of establishing that what he had observed would justify his intervention.

4. S. 27, 30, and 37 CCC are not validly available in these circumstances. The accused used more force than was reasonably necessary. S. 37 was inapplicable due to the absence of the necessary relationship between Warren and Cecil George. Even if Cecil George had been assaulted by the police, it was over by the time Warren George engaged in criminal driving conduct.

FINDINGS OF FACT/ASSESSING CREDIBILITY AND RELIABILITY

[...]

A. Warren George

He was the owner of the Chrysler motor vehicle which was driven by him into the CMU. After working all day in London, he went to IP to join the assembled multitude of occupiers. At about 11 p.m. he realized the police were marching towards the sandy parking lot. He began to gather rocks in case the police were coming to take him to jail. He was present at IP that night because the "government" had desecrated a burial ground and "they" had stolen our land. He stated that the CMU advanced within 10 to 15 feet from the fence to IP and *stopped*. He said that "we" began to throw rocks and he participated; his rationale for this was that he felt the "police would try to murder us." He said that "people" (plural) tried to talk to the police but they wouldn't listen. To this point in the testimony of Warren George, I find his evidence to be incredible, hyperbolic, illogical and unworthy of belief. His comments about "murder" are unfounded and illogical as he advanced no foundation for such beliefs which would hold up to objective analysis. A relatively insignificant amount of force had been used by the CMU to clear the parking lot, merely the noise of batons rattling on shields. No firearms were drawn by the police. No one had been struck. Yet, the accused's first action was to gather paving stones so he might use them against the police if people were arrested. He saw occupiers armed with baseball bats and poles and later these were used against the police. Under cross examination he admitted that he was not going to let the police push him back and not resist, nor would he let the police "take him." His evidence supports the Crown theory that the accused was engaging in an escalating course of violent conduct which culminated in criminal driving behavior minutes later. Furthermore, absolutely no one evidence supported WG's testimony regarding "people" (plural) attempting to speak to the police. Cecil George did address the police but I find the circumstances of this communication more consistent with bravado and antagonism than an attempt to defuse a confrontation.

The accused does not testify that Cecil George had anything (a pole?) in his hands. It is clear from evidence of Cecil George and Sgt. Wade Lacroix that he did. This goes to the accused's power of observation.

The accused said that Cecil George went out to speak to the police and shortly thereafter the CMU engaged in "shield chatter." His response was to jump the fence and start gathering rocks. He saw CG dragged by the police, clubbed by batons and kicked. WG responded by throwing rocks to get the police away from CG.

WG said that when he saw the bus go for the gate, he ran to his car. His intention was to "Help Slippery, maybe force the police away and get him into the car." He followed 25 feet behind the bus, both moving at 15 mph. He was going to go past the bus and look for CG.

Under cross-examination, the evidence of the accused unraveled and the net effect was that the accused left the Court with the following impressions, as supported by summaries of the evidence:

1. The testimony of WG, for the most part was unreliable and cannot be believed.
- contradicted by the evidence of police officers on many of the material points and by CG on some of the collateral issues.

2. There was an attempt to portray the police generally as assaultive, violent, unreasonable. This evidence was exaggerated, unsubstantiated and unsupported. The accused appeared to be projecting his beliefs and behaviors upon the police.

    *   felt the police would try to murder us
    *   people tried to talk to them (police) but they wouldn't listen
    *   I ducked down (below the dashboard) to avoid being shot
    *   we felt the police were trespassing
    *   expected that anyone arrested by the police would resist. The police would not let them go and might even shoot them.

3. WG demonstrated that he was intent upon ignoring and violating the law, and was prepared to resist, obstruct and confront any attempts by the police to enforce compliance with the law. *This was his intention even before CG was arrested.* The evidence of the accused supported the Crown's theory that the accused's driving behavior was the culmination of a series of escalating, violent and assaultive behaviors.

    *   he knew the occupation of IP was without consent of the MNR
    *   he anticipated a problem with the MNR and police as a result of the occupation
    *   he was aware that a police scanner was being used, and that some occupiers were arming themselves with baseball bats and metal poles (note: it was the testimony of Sgt. Lacroix that his shield was shattered by a blow from a steel pole and it circumstantially appears this was CG). Lookouts awarded [sic] of the approach of CMU.
    *   was not going to let the police push us back and not resist
    *   was not letting the police take me
    *   threw sticks and rocks because they were trying to *intimidate us* (not because we feared/were being touched by police)
    *   he did not expect a gunfight because the police were using shields and batons, but did expect a rock and stick fight (his expectation not generated by the police)

4. WG had a vast array of excuses, beliefs, and justifications for his conduct in occupying IP, confronting, resisting and stoning police officers and driving his vehicle out of IP into the CMU officers. Upon review, these were unrealistic, illogical and unfounded.

    *   the government had desecrated a burial ground and had stolen our lands
    *   the police were trespassing
    *   I threw rocks because I felt the police would try and murder us

- I threw rocks because I felt the police were trying to *intimidate us*
- the police might shoot anyone who was arrested
- it is highly unlikely that WG and the driver of the school bus, without communicating would independently be struck with the idea that CG could only be rescued from the hands of the police by using a motor vehicle, in the fashion of a tank or armoured car, and would then independently drive down East Parkway Dr. only seconds apart
- if WG were truly looking for CG, his driving behavior, 25 feet behind the school bus, would afford limited visibility for such a search. Having regard to the darkness and location, there is a lack of reality to the contention that this was the purpose of WG's driving.

5. WG really did not see an extensive struggle between CG and CMU which would afford him the defence of justification or under s. 27, 30, 37 CCC. His evidence in this regard was a retrospective reconstruction of events.

- his observation that CG was being kicked, beaten and dragged (3 separate elements) were made in a "quick glimpse" as CG was being dragged to the van. He did not see CG being carried to the van by police officers, a fact which is accepted by the court.
- later concedes he saw one punch, one quick kick in his glimpse, showing the earlier testimony was an exaggeration
- later stated that at the police van, it "looked like" CG was being beaten but was unable to provide any detail as to how his observations showed that anything more than a struggle took place at the van
- in a later statement to SIU he told the police that part of the reason he drove out of IP was to "keep the police away from the women and children."

6. By his own evidence, his driving behaviour was sufficiently negligent and dangerous to warrant conviction on the charges of criminal negligence and dangerous driving. He clearly appreciated the risk of injury to any police officer in that area when he drove his car onto East Parkway Drive.

7. WG's evidence is not accepted that he swerved into the police involuntarily and only as a result of ducking down and swerving "to avoid being shot." His own evidence shows a lack of logic in this position. Why would he be shot if he was not endangering anyone, as he testified; wouldn't the pointing of the gun be consistent with a demonstration of potential force if the driver did not stop? WG stated that he

did not stop because he did not want to be a target, yet he was driving so slowly that he braked within 5 feet.

B. Cecil Bernard "Slippery" George

This resident is a 43 year old resident of Kettle Point. On September 6, 1995, he was aware of the occupation of IP by other people and decided to visit and speak with some relatives. The police presence in the area was obvious: cruisers on the highway, police vans, police checkpoints. At dusk, he went home to get walkie-talkies for the occupiers to facilitate communications. Upon leaving IP he saw more cruisers and police and *was told by the police to leave the area.* He returned to IP after dark with walkie-talkies, batteries and a police scanner. Near IP, he saw an obvious build-up of police, cruisers with flashing lights and entered the park by an overland route. He warned the occupiers of his observations and distributed the walkie-talkies and scanner. He took up a forward observation period about 1000 feet from the park, towards the police and saw the advancing CMU.

From this point onwards in his testimony, CG casts himself in the role of a peacemaker, a conciliator, someone who was trying to negotiate a non-violent resolution to this impending conflict, and someone who was viciously assaulted and beaten despite his immediate submission to police force. The evidentiary value of this evidence to the defence rests in the establishment of the defence of justification and s. 27, 30, 37 CCC as raised by WG. Buttressing this position is the evidence of the injuries suffered by CG, through his testimony and some police witnesses, the medical report filed, and the exhibit containing photos of his injuries.

The Crown cross-examined CG and attempted to portray CG as someone who did not attempt to defuse this volatile situation, but rather was aligned with the occupiers and was prepared to be in the vanguard of the assault against the CMU, shouting inflammatory, non-conciliatory, words of incitement. The Crown further argues that any injuries suffered by CG occurred as a result of his refusal to submit to a lawful arrest and his repeated resistance to arrest.

I accept the Crown's argument and reject the evidence of the accused.

There is little logic in CG's position that he was a peacemaker and that he approached the police with words of moderation. He was a short term visitor to IP and did not indicate that he had any authority to speak for the occupiers. If he was a peacemaker, why did he not speak to the occupiers *first* about withdrawing, attempting to dialogue? After all, the occupiers were gathering stones, armed with poles and clubs, and readying for violence. If he were a peacemaker, why would he have provided communication devices and a scanner to the occupiers, traveling overland to avoid the police in making his delivery? This is consistent with aiding and abetting the occupiers in any act of resistance or obstruction to the police. And more obviously, if CG was concerned about violence, the risk of harm to the occupiers, women and children, why did he not stop at one of the checkpoints and identify himself as an individual with relatives inside IP, a band councillor at Kettle Point, a man who might have status among the occupiers, and someone who could attempt to interface and open communications between the police and the occupiers? CG did not do this because this was not his intention and his words betray him.

CG testified that he approached the police before they reached the sandy parking lot and told them, "Put your guns away. Deal with me like a man." If he said this, and I doubt it, the police were not brandishing guns, only batons. Why did CG choose to deal with CMU in the middle of a roadway, in the face of advancing CMU rather than by offering intervention to the police at one of the checkpoints. Clearly, there was a different audience for CG on the roadway.

He testified that he said "something about the land" before the CMU rushed across the sandy parking lot. He also recalls speaking about being "of the seventh generation." Some prosecution witnesses recall a spokesperson (and only one person doing so) saying words to the effect "Officers you can kill us here as you killed our grandfathers. You fight with guns. We fight with courage," "Our forefathers died for this property and we are prepared to die also. Go back with the Pilgrims." The direction of defence cross-examination was intended to show that the speaker of these words was CG, a "leader" who was "picked off" by the CMU as part of a crowd management tactic. I find the speaker *was* CG, and I find these words were spoken to promote resistance, and to demonstrate a readiness to resort to violence. These were not words of peace, mediation or negotiation.

CG admits that in the sandy parking lot, he was armed with a stick and in the face of the CMU advance, he raised his stick to defend himself and others behind him and then swung the stick and struck a police shield, accompanied by the sound of cracking glass. It is clear that CG struck the first blow, that he had seen no one struck or harmed by the CMU, that he had re-entered the parking lot after the CMU had cleared the area, that the CMU were being stoned. In fact, rather than staying inside IP, where the CMU chose not to enter, he went out to confront the CMU, armed with a stick, shouting words of resistance and violence, *and would have this Court believe he was acting in self-defence!* I find that CG has colored his evidence to evade the truly violent and assaultive nature of his activities and I prefer the evidence of Sgt. Wade Lacroix in this regard. I find that CG in fact used a metal pole against Lacroix as part of an attack; CG delivered a blow that actually smashed the plexiglass shield, deflected off a helmet, and off his shoulder. Lacroix felled this assaulter, CG, with a baton blow to the hip area.

The next area of importance in CG's evidence deals with his arrest, apprehension and transportation to the police van, and the use of excessive force by the police. There are sub-issues such as whether CG was informed of the reason for his arrest.

Upon all of the evidence, it is clear that the police had lawful grounds to arrest CG for assaultive behavior. He attacked Sgt. Lacroix with a pole, using potentially lethal force. Lacroix's response with the baton was appropriate. With respect to being advised of the reason for the arrest, I must prefer the police evidence. CG, clearly lost consciousness and was batonned into submission by the police. His evidence that he was not advised of the reason for his arrest, cannot be determinative of this issue.

Then, even if WG had been in a position to witness excessive force, an issue I have decided in the negative, was excessive force used? Exhibit 9 contains 17 photographs depicting blunt force injury to CG all delivered by the police. CG had cuts and swelling to his face, a laceration to the back of his head and his lip, and had been rendered unconscious. CG admits that after "cracking the shield," he went down and covered his face with his hands, that "shadows" approached (the arrest team?) and he swung at them to try and get away. He recalls being kicked and losing consciousness. He recalls "coming to" and being on his hands and knees, and then being clubbed on the back of his head. He recalls finally saying "I give up" twice, and then being kicked in the stomach, and then kicked in the face and losing consciousness. The prosecution theory is that CG continued to resist arrest and refused to submit.

It is difficult to accept CG's version of the events as being determinative of this issue, as I have already made negative findings about his credibility on so many crucial issues, and throughout his testimony he has negatively skewed his evidence of police activity and has attempted to portray his behavior in an unrealistically favorable light. This Court does not labour under any illusions that the average policeman in this province, CMU member or otherwise, is possessed by any significant special skills in hand to hand combat which enables them to decommission a violent raging citizen. Long gone are the days when patrolmen were hired "big and strong" to discharge one of the primary duties in policing, dealing with inebriated citizens. The modern policeman and now policewoman are physically smaller, but better educated. We now need officers who have the education and intelligence to operate sophisticated computers, equipment, voluminous paper work, deal with complex evidentiary issues, deal with complex social and cultural issues, understand complex legal issues such as the Charter of Rights. When faced with force and a threat to their individual safety, police officers should and must use the tools available to them, be it batons, restraints, pepper spray, tear gas, and a full array of firearms in order to protect themselves while acting as police. The police are entitled to use the force necessary to dominate the situation and should always err on the side of personal safety. When a citizen is arrested, our society and the CCC demands [sic] a full and immediate submission to police authority. In CG's own words, after he was batonned by Sgt. Lacroix, he swung out at the police.

Reviewing Lacroix's evidence, after CG was felled, the CMU was under a barrage of rocks and firebrands, and several officers had been engaged by occupiers swinging bats and poles. Lacroix wanted to disengage to a position of safety. Sgt. Hebblethwaite saw CG on the ground struggling as several policemen tried to handcuff him ... this difficulty clearly was due to CG's failure to submit to arrest; Hebblethwaite felt the police were in danger and ordered them to remove CG first (to safety) and cuff him later. This evidence was confirmed by P.C. Wade Jacklin. When he approached the group attempting to handcuff CG, CG was still thrashing and kicking. CG had stood in the vanguard and wanted to be defiant and confrontational. He assaulted a police officer with a pipe, possibly metal, with a potentially lethal blow, and he did not immediately submit to the police and permit himself to be handcuffed. The police were blinded by spotlights and were being stoned, presenting a situation of great danger to the police. Until such time as he did submit, or lapse into unconsciousness, the police were entitled to use dominating force. I cannot make a finding whether any significant force was applied once CG became unconscious. I cannot make a finding that CG was subjected to excessive and unreasonable force while being arrested and restrained.

C. Prosecution Evidence

In coming to my decision in these matters, the prosecution evidence was analyzed before the defence evidence. Even though I have rejected the more material portions of the defence evidence, the principles enunciated in *R. v. W.(D.)* still must be adhered to.

Overall, the defence exposed many inconsistencies and inaccuracies in the evidence of the various prosecution witnesses, and many contradictions. For the most part, all police witnesses were subjected to vigorous and intense cross-examination concerning every detail of every possible observation related to the incident. Much of this evidence was not material to the issues at hand. Most of the inconsistencies, inaccuracies and contradictions occurred in areas of evidence which were collateral and remote to the main issues. When a witness does not demonstrate an encyclopedic and photographic memory for collateral detail, it does not mean that his memory of vital and material evidence should be rejected. When witnesses have offered different evidence concerning the same item, it can be the result of different perspectives, different opportunities to observe, different stressors. The police witnesses were called upon to recount an incident that took place over a few minutes, in a situation of great stress, where they were under potentially lethal attack, accompanied by concerns about the occupiers having access to firearms. Most of the police witnesses had already worked a shift commencing at 7 a.m. that day. At the sandy parking lot, the combination of bright lights playing on plexiglass shields and visors, created such glare that they were only able to see in silhouette. Dust was raised. Their visors made hearing difficult. The court heard little evidence as to whether any of these witnesses had/have ever seen this location in daylight. When the bus and car roared down East Parkway Drive, these witnesses were compelled to leap and jump for their safety, only to find themselves without clear escape routes and trapped against fences and brambles. Several officers stated that they felt their death was imminent. Over and above this, there was great consistency with respect to the material and important elements of the prosecution case.

It is not relevant to the determination of this case to comment upon many of the issues raised by the defence during cross-examination. The facts are simple. Thirty-two OPP officers formed into a CMU were ordered to occupy the sandy parking lot, and were ordered not to enter IP. They cleared the parking lot without any harm being done to anyone, and after determining that the occupiers were now inside IP, they withdrew. Then the occupiers began to stone the CMU with bats and poles. There was no reason known to man which would justify the violence as directed to the CMU. Few policemen had the opportunity to observe what was happening to Cecil George. The withdrawal back up East Parkway Drive became bottlenecked. A bus was driven out of IP towards the CMU, putting many police in imminent danger of being struck. The police had a real reason to have feared death or serious injury. The accused, driving a large motor vehicle, followed the bus and then veered off the road into a group of CMU members who were off the edge of the road. One of the officers suffered bodily harm. The accused was shot at by the CMU when it appeared that after having reversed, he was going to drive back at the group. The driving was patently dangerous and criminally negligent. The nature of his driving was confirmed by repetition from the various witnesses called as part of the prosecution case.

Having rejected the evidentiary foundation for the defences under s. 27, 30 and 37 CCC, the court has received no evidence by way of explanation which might ameliorate the criminal nature of the driving. The court has not accepted the accused's evidence that he did not intend to drive into the police officers. His blunt actions confirmed his intent. In all material matters the prosecution witnesses were not shaken regarding any of the material issues of fact raised by the prosecution. I have reviewed all relevant case law and find that the evidence in this matter warrants conviction pursuant to the principles enunciated in *R. v. Tutton, R. v. Rajic, R. v. Hundal.*

Warren George is found guilty on counts 1, 2, 3. Pursuant to the judgment in *Kienapple*, I will enter a conditional stay on ct. 3, the dangerous driving.

Postscript

On April 3, 1998, Judge Pokele passed sentence. On the charge of "Criminal Negligence Causing Bodily Harm"—s. 221 CCC, Warren George was sentenced to serve six months in jail. On the charge of "Assault with a Weapon"—s .267 (1)(a) CCC, he was sentenced to serve six months concurrent with the previously mentioned sentence. On the charge of "Operating a Motor Vehicle in a Manner Dangerous to the Public Causing Bodily Harm"—s. 2 49 (3) CCC, the judge ordered a conditional stay. The trial decision was appealed to the Ontario Court of Appeal [see *R. v. George* (2000), 49 O.R. (3d) 144, 145 C.C.C. (3d) 405 (C.A.)]. The appeal of the conviction and sentence was dismissed. The application for leave to appeal the Ontario Court of Appeal decision to the Supreme Court of Canada was dismissed on January 25, 2001.

About the Cover

Boozhoo, my given name is Ashley Aleta Kewayosh. I am an Anishinabequay from Bkejwanong First Nation. I am a student at Brescia University College, affiliated with the University of Western Ontario. I am currently working towards both an Undergraduate Degree in Sociology and a Certificate in Palliative Care and Thanatology. In the future I hope to teach in my home community.

I would like to describe to you how I created this book cover. Controversy does not always wear a friendly smile, nevertheless our classroom was a place for opinions to be voiced in a positive way. We learned through many complicated, and at times emotional discussions, about diversity and how to respect each other's differences. Through experiencing each other's ways of thinking and expressing, we were able to appreciate the importance of teaching controversy.

In our classroom, I saw opposing forces, each one vital to the function of learning. All these forces, although very different, came together in a beautiful, accepting way. I thought about how these opposing forces in life balance Creation and bring wholeness to all things. The sacred bond between male and female. Sacred fire and life giving water. The balance of the four directions. This book cover is the bringing together of all of those images I had. On the left, I depicted our Grandmother Moon and the beautiful water she cares for. On the right is her equal counterpart, our Grandfather Sun, who lights the day as she does the night. In the bottom right there is our Grandfather Fire doing his work in the world. I decided to add a rainbow as a societal symbol of diversity. The four sacred directions in the center, each offer their own gift to Creation. With this balance we are made whole.

About the Contributors

CLAUDIO DURAN is an Associate Professor in the Department of Social Science, Atkinson Faculty of Liberal and Professional Studies, York University. His main research and teaching interest is related to ideology, propaganda and mass media. He has been conducting research on the Chilean press since 1972, covering the period 1954–1994. His publications include *El Mercurio: Ideologia y Propaganda, 1954–1994, Vol.1* (1995). Currently, Professor Duran is working on the second volume of the study: *El Mercurio: Ideology and Propaganda 1954–2000*. Claudio Duran received the honour of CASE Canadian Professor of the Year in 1993.

JOHN ELIJAH, a father of five, and a husband, is of the Oneida Nation. John is a strong believer in his natural Iroquoian ways. While separated from his natural ways as a young person, John has come to value and appreciate these natural methods and philosophies over the years.

John is "natural helper" in the social field. He spends much of his time devising healing strategies and educational programs for understanding "the Self." He shares his knowledge, wisdom, beliefs and abilities with all people with whom he comes into contact. John has received various certifications, including his *Native Counselling Training Certificate*. He continues to this day to enlighten and stimulate others with his experiences and reciprocal guidance for motivation and inner peace.

URSULA ELIJAH, a mother of two, and a wife, is of the Cree Nation. She has spent much of her career in the social field. She herself, is a residential school descendant and spends much of her time sharing her skills, experiences and natural abilities with others.

Ursula is naturally talented at developing "self-help" educational programs and literature. She received her BA from the University of Western Ontario (Brescia University College) and continues to learn about the trials, tribulations and life lessons of others. She is also a "natural helper", giving support, help, guidance and encouragement to those who seek to find personal direction.

JULIE GEORGE is an Ojibway Indian from Kettle and Stoney Point First Nation. She graduated from Brescia University College in June 2001 and is currently a graduate student in Sociology at the University of Western Ontario. She has specific interests in Sociology related to inequality and social justice issues, and has written at length about the extent to which traditional justice systems and processes of education in Canada have been targets of assimilationist policies.

About the Authors

LISA JAKUBOWSKI is an Associate Professor in the Department of Sociology at Brescia University College, where she teaches courses in the Sociology of Law, Sociology of Education, Individual and Society, and Community Development. Her research is concentrated in Action-Oriented, Critical Pedagogy and Sociology of Law (with a focus on Immigration and Refugee Issues). Her publications include: *Immigration and the Legalization of Racism* (1997) as well as several articles and book chapters.

LIVY VISANO is an Associate Professor of Sociology in the School of Social Sciences at the Atkinson Faculty of Liberal and Professional Studies, York University, specializing in law, culture, and inequality, with a focus on critical criminology, critical legal studies, cultural studies and youth. His current research centres around: the Differential Impact of the Media on Delinquency; Inequalities in Everyday Life: Gender, Race and Class; and, Law, Culture, Youth and Cyber-Prostitution. His publications include: *Crime and Culture* (1998), *This Idle Trade* (1987), several co-authored edited books, and a number journal articles and book chapters. He has been a recipient of a number of Teaching and Publication Awards, including: the OCUFA Teaching Award for Outstanding Contributions to University Teaching and the Dean's Award (Faculty of Arts) for Outstanding Contributions in Teaching, York University.

References

Anderson, A. 1992. "Policing Native People: Native Militancy and Canadian Militarism." In V. Satzewich, (ed.), *Deconstructing a Nation: Immigration, Multiculturalism and Racism in 90's Canada*. Halifax: Fernwood.

Anyon, J. 1980. "Social Class and the Hidden Curriculum of Work." *Journal of Education* 49,3: 381–86.

Apple, M. 1986. *Teachers and Texts*. New York: Routledge & Kegan Paul.

Arnold, R., B. Burke, C. James, D. Martin and B. Thomas. 1991. *Educating for a Change*. Toronto: Between the Lines and Doris Marshall Institute for Education and Action.

Arrigo B. 1998. "Marxist Criminology and Lacanian Psychoanalysis: Outline for a General Constitutive Theory of Crime." In J. Ross, (ed.), *Cutting the Edge: Current Perspectives in Radical/Criminology and Criminal Justice*. New York: Praeger.

Atkinson-Grosjean, J. 1998. "Illusions of Excellence and the Selling of the University: A Micro-Study." *Electronic Journal of Sociology* 3,3.

Barnaby, J. 1992. "Culture and Sovereignty." In D. Engelstad and J. Bird, (eds.), *Nation to Nation: Aboriginal Sovereignty and the Future of Canada*. Concord, ON: House of Anansi Press.

Barak, G. 1998. "Time for an Integrated Critical Criminology." In J. Ross, (ed.), *Cutting the Edge: Current Perspectives in Radical/Critical Criminology and Criminal Justice*. New York: Praeger.

Barresi, J., and T. Juckes. 1997. "Personology and the Narrative Interpretation of Lives." *Journal of Personality* 65: 693–719.

Battaile, G., and C. Silet, eds. 1980. *The Pretend Indians: Images of Native Americans in the Movies*. Dubuque: Iowa State University Press.

Becker, H. 1963. *Outsiders*. New York: Free Press.

Becker, H., and B. Geer. 1970. "Participant Observation and Interviewing: A Comparison." In W. Filstead, (ed.), *Qualitative Methodology*. Chicago: Rand McNally.

Ben-Ari, E. 1987. "Pygmies and Villages, Ritual or Play? On the Place of Contrasting Modes of Metacommunication in Social System." *Symbolic Interaction* 10,2 (Fall): 187–208.

Bennett, J. 1981. *Oral History and Delinquency: The Rhetoric of Criminology*. Chicago: University of Chicago Press.

Black, D., and J. Wilkes. 1997. "Now the Police Squeeze Squeegee People: Plan to Get Them off the Street Corners." *Toronto Star*. June 11: A3.

Bogardus, E. 1925a. "Social Distance and Its Origins." *Journal of Applied Sociology* 9: 299–308.

_____. 1925b. "Measuring Social Distances." *Journal of Applied Sociology* 9: 299–308.

Bohmer, S., and J. Briggs. 1991. "Teaching Privileged Students about Gender, Race, and Class Oppression." *Teaching Sociology* 19,2 (April): 154–63.

Bourdieu, P., and J.C. Passeron. 1977. *Reproduction in Education, Society and Culture*. London: Sage.

Bowles, S., and H. Gintis. 1976. *Schooling in Capitalist America*. New York: Basic Books.

Boyer, E. 1990. *Scholarship Reconsidered: Priorities of the Professorate*. Princeton, NJ: The Carnegie Foundation for the Advancement of Teaching.

Brah, A. 1992. "Difference, Diversity, and Differentiation." In J. Donald and A. Rattansi, (eds.), *Race, Culture and Difference*. London: Sage.

Brookfield, S. 1987. *Developing Critical Thinkers: Challenging Adults to Explore Alternative Ways of Thinking and Acting*. San Francisco: Jossey-Bass.

_____. 1990. *The Skillful Teacher: On Technique, Trust, and Responsiveness in the Classroom*. San Francisco: Jossey-Bass.

_____. 1995. *Becoming a Critically Reflective Teacher*. San Francisco: Jossey-Bass.

Brookfield, S., and S. Preskill. 1999. *Discussion as a Way of Teaching: Tools and Techniques for Democratic Classrooms*. San Francisco: Jossey-Bass.

Bruner, J. 1990. Acts of Meaning. Cambridge, MA: Harvard University Press.

Brunner, D. 1999. "Performance, Reflexivity, and Critical Teaching." *The Journal of Critical Pedagogy* 3,1 (November).

Buchbinder, H. 1993. "The Market-Oriented University and the Changing Role of Knowledge." *Higher Education* 26: 331–47.

Carr, D. 1986. *Time, Narrative and History*. Bloomington: Indiana University Press.

Cartier, J. 1924. *Voyages of Jacques Cartier: Published from the Originals with Translations, Notes and Appendices*. Publication of the Public Archives of Canada, no. 11. A.P. Biggar, Chief Archivist for Canada in Europe. Ottawa: F.A. Acland.

Champlain, S. de. 1971. *Samuel de Champlain: Voyages to New France. (Being a Narrative of the Many Remarkable Things That Happened in the West Indies in the Years 1599–1601, with an Account of the Manners and Customs of the Savages of Canada and a Description of That Country in the Year 1603)*. Trans. M. Macklem. Ottawa: Oberon Press.

Clarke, R., and C. Cavanagh, with F. Cristall. 1997. "Introduction." In dian marino *Wild Garden: Art, Education and the Culture of Resistance*. Toronto: Between the Lines.

Cohen, L. 1995. "Facilitating the Critique of Racism and Classism: An Experiential Model for Euro-American Middle-Class Students." *Teaching Sociology* 23,2 (April): 87–93.

Corrigan, P. 1979. *Schooling the Smash Street Kids*. London: Macmillan Press.

Currie, J., and J. Newson, eds. 1998. *Universities and Globalization: Critical Perspectives*. Thousand Oaks, CA: Sage.

Czerny, M., J. Swift, and R. Clarke. 1994. *Getting Started.* Toronto: Between The Lines.

Denis, C. 1997. *We Are Not You: First Nations and Canadian Modernity.* Peterborough, ON: Broadview Press.

Dennett, D.C. 1992. "The Self as a Center of Narrative Gravity." In F. Kessel, P. Cole and D. Johnson, (eds.), *Self and Consciousness: Multiple Perspectives.* Hillsdale, NJ: Erlbaum.

Denzin, N. 1978. *Sociological Methods: A Sourcebook.* New York: McGraw-Hill.

Dewey, J. 1916. *Democracy and Education.* New York: Macmillan.

_____. 1938. *Experience and Education.* New York: Collier Books.

Dickason, O. 1992. *Canada's First Nations: A History of Founding Peoples from Earliest Times.* Toronto: Oxford University Press.

Downey, D., and R. Torrecilha. 1994. "Sociology of Race and Ethnicity: Strategies for Comparative Multicultural Courses." *Teaching Sociology* 22,3 (July): 237–47.

Drake, J. 1976. *Teaching Critical Thinking.* Chicago: Interstate Publishers.

Ennis, R.H. 1962. "A Concept of Critical Thinking." *Harvard Educational Review* 32,1: 81–111.

Ericson, R. 1975. *Criminal Reactions: The Labelling Perspective.* West Mead: Saxon House.

Everett, K. 1998. "Understanding Social Inequality through Service Learning." *Teaching Sociology* 26,4 (October): 299–309.

Farr, M. 2000. "Brave New BA." *University Affairs* (March).

Feagin, J.R., and M.P. Sikes. 1994. *Living with Racism: The Black Middle Class Experience.* Boston: Beacon Press.

Felman, S. 1987. *Jacques Lacan and the Adventure of Insight.* Cambridge, MA: Harvard University Press.

Ferber, E. 1926. *Show Boat.* New York: Doubleday.

Filstead, W. 1970. *Qualitative Methodology.* Chicago: Rand McNally.

Fisher, D. 2000. "Commercialization Threatens the University Mission." *CAUT Bulletin*, January: 6.

Fleras, A., and J. Lock Kunz. 2001. *Media and Minorities: Representing Diversity in Multicultural Canada.* Toronto: Thompson Educational Publishing.

Ford, C.W. 1994. *We Can All Get Along: 50 Steps You Can Take to Help End Racism at Home, at Work, in Your Community.* New York: Dell.

Foucault, M. 1980. *Power/Knowledge: Selected Interviews and Other Writings 1972–1977*, C. Gordon (ed.). New York: Pantheon Books.

Fox, N. 1995. "Intertextuality and the Writing of Social Research." *Electronic Journal of Sociology.*

Frank. T. 2000. "Death by a Thousand Cuts." *University Affairs*, February: 8.

Frankenberg, R. 1993. *White Women, Race Matters: The Social Construction of Whiteness.* Minneapolis: University of Minnesota Press.

Freire, P. 1970. *Pedagogy of the Oppressed.* New York: Herder and Herder.

_____. 1985. *The Politics of Education: Culture, Power and Liberation.* South Hadley, MA: Bergin and Garvey Publishers.

_____. 1993. *A Critical Encounter*. London and New York: Routledge.

_____. 1995. *Pedagogy of Hope: Reliving Pedagogy of the Oppressed*. New York: Continuum Publishing Company.

_____. 1998. *Pedagogy of Freedom: Ethics, Democracy and Civil Courage*. New York: Rowman and Littlefield Publishers.

Friar, R., and N. Friar. 1972. *The Only Good Indian*. New York: Drama Book Specialists.

Frideres, J.S. 1998. *Aboriginal People in Canada: Contemporary Conflicts*. 5th ed. Scarborough, ON: Prentice-Hall.

Gaianguest, K. 1998. "Radical Pedagogy Is Social Change in Action: Response to 'Practicing Radical Pedagogy: Balancing Ideals with Institutional Constraints.'" *Teaching Sociology* 26,2 (April): 123–26.

George, R.C. 1999. "The Marginalization of Aboriginal People: Conflict Theory and the Policy of Assimilation." Prepared for Professor Larry Chartrand, University of Ottawa.

Gimenez, M. 1998. "The Radical Pedagogy Mystique: A View from the Trenches. Response to 'Practising Radical Pedagogy: Balancing Ideals with Institutional Constraints.'" *Teaching Sociology* 26,2 (April): 116–20.

Giroux, H. 1981. *Ideology, Culture and the Process of Schooling*. Philadelphia, Temple University Press.

_____. 1988a. *Schooling and the Struggle for Public Life: Critical Pedagogy in the Modern Age*. Minneapolis: University of Minnesota.

_____. 1988b. *Teachers as Intellectuals: A Critical Pedagogy for Practical Learning*. Westport, CT: Bergin and Garvey Publishers.

_____. 1993. *Living Dangerously: Multiculturalism and the Politics of Difference*. New York: Peter Lang Publishing.

_____. 1995. "Teaching in the Age of Political Correctness." *The Educational Forum* (Kappa Delta Pi) 59 (Winter): 130–39.

_____. 1996. *Fugitive Cultures: Race, Violence and Youth*. New York: Routledge.

_____. 1997. *Pedagogy and the Politics of Hope: Theory, Culture and Schooling*. Boulder, CO: Westview Press.

Giroux, H., and P. McLaren. 1994. *Between Borders: Pedagogy and the Politics of Cultural Studies*. New York: Routledge.

Giroux, H., and R. Simon. 1988. "Schooling, Popular Culture and a Project of Possibility." *Journal of Education* 170,1.

Globe and Mail, The. 2000a. "Critics, Panhandlers Plan Next Move as Province's Squeegee Law Takes Effect." Feb. 1: A19.

_____. 2000b. "Squeegee Kids Reeling from Police Campaign." April 21: A14.

Goff, C. 1997. *Criminal Justice in Canada*. Scarborough, ON: International Thomson.

Goffman, E. 1952. "On Cooling the Mark Out: Some Aspects of Adaptation to Failure." *Psychiatry: Journal for the Study of Interpersonal Processes* 15,4: 451–63.

Gramsci, A. 1971. *Prison Notebooks: Selections*. Trans. Q. Hoare and G. Smith. New York: International Publishers.

Graveline, F.J. 1998. *Circleworks: Transforming Eurocentric Consciousness*. Halifax: Fernwood.

Griswold, W. 1994. *Cultures and Societies in a Changing World*. Thousand Oaks, CA: Pine Forge Press.

Gross, P. 1997. *Joint Curriculum Design: Facilitating Learner Ownership and Active Participation in Secondary Classrooms*. Mahwah, NJ: Lawrence Erlbaum Associates.

Gunder Frank, A. 1967. *Capitalism and the Underdevelopment of Latin America*. New York: Monthly Review Press.

Hallett, G.L. 1984. *Logic for the Labyrinth: A Guide to Critical Thinking*. Washington, DC: University Press of America.

Heck, M. 1999. "Educators as Human Rights Leaders: A Paradigm of Praxis." *The Journal of Critical Pedagogy* 2,21 (April).

Henry, F., C. Tator, W. Mattis and T. Rees. 2000. *The Colour of Democracy: Racism in Canadian Society*. 2nd ed. Toronto: Harcourt Brace and Company, Canada.

Henslin, J.M., L.K. Henslin and S.D. Keiser. 1976. "Schooling for Social Stability: Education in Corporate America." In J.M. Henslin and L.T. Reynolds, (eds.), *Social Problems in American Society*. 2nd ed. Boston: Holbrook Press.

Hermans, H., H. Kempen and R. van Loon. 1992. "The Dialogical Self: Beyond Individualism and Rationalism." *American Psychologist* 47: 23–33.

Heyl, B. 1979. *The Madam as Entrepreneur: Career Management in House Prostitution*. New Brunswick, NJ: Transaction Books.

hooks, b. 1990. *Yearning: Race, Gender, and Cultural Politics*. Toronto: Between the Lines.

_____. 1994. *Teaching to Transgress: Education as the Practice of Freedom*. New York: Routledge.

Howell, P. 1998a. "Smoke Signals: An Engrossing Tale." *Toronto Star*, July 3: C6.

_____. 1998b. "Movie Entirely Made by Indians Has Fun Rebelling against Hollywood." *Toronto Star*, July 3: C1, C6.

Hullfish, H.G., and P.G. Smith. 1961. *Reflective Thinking: The Method of Education*. Westport, CT: Greenwood Press.

Hutchings, P., and A. Wutzdorff. 1988. "Experiential Learning across the Curriculum: Assumptions and Principles." In P. Hutchings and A. Wutzdorff, (eds.), *Knowing and Doing: Learning through Experience*. San Francisco: Jossey-Bass.

Jacoby, R., and N. Glauberman, eds. 1995. *The Bell Curve Debate: History, Documents, Opinions*. Toronto: Random House.

Jakubowski, L.M. 1992. "'Schooling' and the 'Naturalization' of Racial Injustice." *Journal of Human Justice* 1,1 (Autumn): 71–88.

_____. 2001. "Teaching Uncomfortable Topics: An Action-Oriented Strategy for Addressing Racism and Related Forms of Difference." *Teaching Sociology* 29,1 (January): 62–79.

James, W. 1950 [1890]. *Principles of Psychology*. Vol. 1. New York: Dover.

Jouve, N.W. 1991. *White Woman Speaks with Forked Tongue: Criticism as Autobiography*. London: Routledge.

Kanpol, B. 1994. *Critical Pedagogy: An Introduction.* Westport, CT: Bergin and Garvey Publishers.

Kanpol, B., and J. Brady. 1998. "Teacher Education and the Multicultural Dilemma: A Critical Thinking Response." *The Journal of Critical Pedagogy* 1,2 (April).

King, M.L. Jr. 1947. *The Purpose of Education.* Atlanta: PD Maroon Tiger.

_____. 1963. *The Strength to Love.* New York: Harper and Row.

Kirby, S., and K. McKenna. 1989. *Experience, Research and Social Change: Methods from the Margins.* Toronto: Garamond Press.

Kirkpatrick, F. 1986. *Community: A Trinity of Models.* Washington, DC: Georgetown University Press.

Kitchener, K.S. 1986. "The Reflective Judgment Model: Characteristics, Evidence and Measurement." In R.A. Mines and K.S. Kitchener, (eds.), *Adult Cognitive Development: Methods and Models.* New York: Praeger.

Klinck, C., and R. Watters. 1966. *Canadian Anthology.* Toronto: Gage.

Knockwood, I. 1992. *Out of the Depths: The Experiences of Mi'kmaw Children at the Indian Residential School at Shubenacadie.* Lockeport, NS: Roseway.

Kozol, J. 1991. *Savage Inequalities.* New York: Crown.

Kuitenbrouwer, P. 1997. "Listen to the Squeegee People." <www.eye.net/eye/issue/issue_02.2797/news-view/kuit.html>.

Lakoff, S. 1964. *Equality in Political Philosophy.* Cambridge, MA: Harvard University Press.

Landsberg, M. 1999. "Squeegie Kid Terror Is Just a Whitewash." *Toronto Star,* Oct. 31: A2.

La Roque, E. 1975. *Defeathering the Indian.* Agincourt, ON: Canadian Book Society.

Lazerson, M., J. Block McLaughlin, B. McPherson and S.K. Bailey. 1985. *An Education of Value: The Purposes and Practices of Schools.* Cambridge: Cambridge University Press.

LeBlanc, S., and I. Rivard. 1997. "Spotlight: In Defence of Squeegee Kids." <www.spotlight/aug06/squeegee.shtml>.

Lee, J. 1999. "'Standards of Excellence' in Democratic Classrooms: A Description and Critique of Three Philosophical Approaches with a Model for Linking Theory to Practice." *The Journal of Critical Pedagogy* 3,1 (November).

Lewin, E., and A. Lewin. 1988. *The Random House Thesaurus of Slang.* New York: Random House.

Lines, R. 1992. "Dare to Struggle." In K. McCormick and L.A. Visano, (eds.), *Canadian Penology.* Toronto: Canadian Scholars' Press.

Livingstone, D.W. 1998. *The Education-Jobs Gap: Underemployment or Economic Democracy.* Boulder, CO: Westview Press (draft).

_____. 1999. "Universities at the Crossroads." *CAUT Bulletin* (April).

Long, D. 1998. "A Radical Teacher's Dilemma: Response to 'Practising Radical Pedagogy: Balancing Ideals with Institutional Constraints.'" *Teaching Sociology* 26,2 (April): 112–15.

Lorber, J. 1994. *Paradoxes of Gender.* New Haven, CT: Yale University Press.

Lowe, J., and M. Reisch. 1998. "Bringing the Community into the Classroom: Applying Experiences of Social Work Education to Service Learning Courses in Sociology." *Teaching Sociology* 26,4 (October): 292–98.

Lucal, B. 1996. "Oppression *and* Privilege: Towards a Relational Conceptualization of Race." *Teaching Sociology* 24,3 (July): 245–55.

Lusk, A., and A. Weinberg. 1994. "Discussing Controversial Topics in the Classroom: Creating a Context for Learning." *Teaching Sociology* 22,4 (October): 301–308.

MacArthur, C., S. McMahon and L. Visano. 1998. "A Culture and Control at the Crossroads: A Case Study of Local Squeegee Kids as Subversive Subjects." In S. McMahon, (ed.), *Women, Crime and Culture*. Toronto: Centre for Police Studies.

Macedo, D. 1997. "An Anti-Method Pedagogy: A Freirian Perspective." In P. Freire, (ed.), *Mentoring the Mentor: A Critical Dialogue with Paulo Freire*. New York: Peter Lang Publishing.

MacIntyre, A. 1981. *After Virtue: A Study in Moral Theory*. Notre Dame, IN: University of Notre Dame Press.

Manning, P. 1972. "Observing the Police: Deviants, Respectables and the Law." In J. Douglas, (ed.), *Research on Deviance*. New York: Random House.

Marchant, G., and I. Newman. 1994. "Faculty Activities and Rewards: Views from Educational Administrators in the USA." *Assessment and Evaluation in Higher Education* 19,2: 145–52.

Marcroft, M. 1990. "The Politics of the Classroom: Toward an Oppositional Pedagogy." *New Directions for Teaching and Learning* 44 (Winter): 61–71.

marino, dian. 1997. *Wild Garden: Art, Education and the Culture of Resistance*. Toronto: Between the Lines.

Marullo, S. 1998. "Bringing Home Diversity: A Service-Learning Approach to Teaching Race and Ethnic Relations." *Teaching Sociology* 26,4 (October): 259–75.

Martinez, T. 1994. "Popular Music in the Classroom: Teaching Race, Class and Gender with Popular Culture." *Teaching Sociology* 22,3 (July): 266–69.

Marx, K. 1956. *Selected Writings in Sociology and Social Philosophy*, ed. T. Bottomore. London: Watts and Company.

Mason, M. 1997. *Development and Disorder: A History of the Third World since 1945*. Toronto: Between the Lines.

Matza, D. 1969. *Becoming Deviant*. Englewood Cliffs, NJ: Prentice-Hall.

McAdams, D.P. 1990. "Unity and Purpose in Human Lives: The Emergence of Identity as a Life Story." In A.I. Rabin, R.A. Zucker, R.A. Emmons and S. Frank, (eds.), *Studying Persons and Lives*. New York: Springer Publishing Co.

McCammon, L. 1999. "Introducing Social Stratification and Inequality: An Active Learning Technique." *Teaching Sociology* 27,1 (January): 44–54.

McIntosh, P. 1995. "White Privilege and Male Privilege: A Personal Account of Coming to See Correspondences through Work in Women's Studies." In M., Anderson and P. Hill Collins, (eds.), *Race, Class and Gender: An Anthology*. Belmont, CA: Wadsworth Publishing.

McLaren, P. 1989. *Life in Schools: An Introduction to Critical Pedagogy in the Foundations of Education*. Toronto: Irwin.

_____. 1994. *Life in Schools*. New York: Longman.

McLaren, P., and T. Tadeu da Silva. 1993. "Decentering Pedagogy: Critical Literacy, Resistance and the Politics of Memory." In P. McLaren and P. Leonard, (eds.), *Paulo Freire: A Critical Encounter*. New York: Routledge.

Menzies, C.R. 1999. "First Nations, Inequality and the Legacy of Colonialism." In J. Curtis, E. Grabb and N. Guppy, (eds.), *Social Inequality in Canada: Patterns, Problems, and Policies*. 3rd ed. Scarborough, ON: Prentice-Hall, Allyn and Bacon Canada.

Meyers, C. 1986. *Teaching Students to Think Critically: A Guide for Faculty in All Disciplines*. San Francisco: Jossey-Bass.

Myers-Lipton, S. 1998. "Effect of a Comprehensive Service-Learning Program on College Students' Civic Responsibility." *Teaching Sociology* 26,4 (October): 276–91.

Miles, R., and A. Phizacklea. 1984. *White Man's Country: Racism in British Politics*. London: Pluto Press.

Miller, H. 1997. "White Man, Red Man, Justice Not Served." *Turtle Island News*, July 9: 5.

Mills, C.W. 1978 [1959]. *The Sociological Imagination*. New York: Oxford University Press.

Monture-Angus, P. 1995. *Thunder in My Soul: A Mohawk Woman Speaks*. Halifax: Fernwood.

Mooney, L.A., and B. Edwards. 2001. "Experiential Learning in Sociology: Service Learning and Other Community-Based Learning Initiatives." *Teaching Sociology* 29,2 (April): 181–94.

Morrissey, M. 1992. "Exploring Social Distance in Race and Ethnic Relations Courses." *Teaching Sociology* 20,2 (April): 121–24.

Morse, B. 1990. *Indian Tribal Courts in the United States: A Model for Canada*. Saskatoon: University of Saskatchewan Native Law Centre.

Moulder, F.V. 1997. "Teaching about Race and Ethnicity: A Message of Despair or a Message of Hope?" *Teaching Sociology* 25,2 (April): 120–27.

Murray, S. 1984. *Social Theory, Homosexual Realities*. New York: Gai Saker.

Murray, C., and R. Herrnstein. 1994. *The Bell Curve: Intelligence and Class Structure in America*. New York: Free Press.

Newson, J. 1994. "Subordinating Democracy: The Effects of Fiscal Retrenchment and University-Business Partnerships on Knowledge Creation and Knowledge Dissemination in Universities." *Higher Education* 27: 141–61.

Nietzsche, F. 1973 [1887]. *Genealogy of Morals*. New York: Vintage.

Noble, D. 1977. *America by Design*. New York: Alfred A. Knopf.

Noddings, N., and C. Witherell, eds. 1991. *Stories Lives Tell: Narrative and Dialogue in Education*. New York: Teachers College Press.

Norman, R., and S. Sayers. 1980. *Hegal, Marx and the Dialectic: A Debate*. Atlantic Highlands, NJ: Humanities Press.

O'Neill, T. 1985. *Censorship: Opposing Views*. St. Paul, MN.: Greenhaven Press.

Paley, V.G. 1997. "Foreword." In M. Fleming et al., (eds.), *Starting Small: Teaching Tolerance in Preschool and the Early Grades*. Atlanta: Southern Poverty Law Center.

Parilla, P., and G. Hesser. 1998. "Internships and the Sociological Perspective: Applying Principles of Experiential Learning." *Teaching Sociology* 26,4 (October): 310–29.

Parker-Gwin, R., and J.B. Mabry. 1998. "Service-Learning as Pedagogy and Civic Education: Comparing Outcomes for Three Models." *Teaching Sociology* 26,4 (October): 276–91.

Pearson, G. 1979. *The Deviant Imagination*. London: Macmillan.

Pence, D.J., and J.A. Fields. 1999. "Teaching about Race and Ethnicity: Trying to Uncover White Privilege for a White Audience." *Teaching Sociology* 27,2 (April): 150–58.

Pepinsky, H., and R. Quinney. 1991. *Criminology as Peacekeeping*. Bloomington: Indiana University Press.

Petruzzi, A. 1998. "Hermeneutic Disclosure as Freedom: John Dewey and Paulo Freire on the Non-Representational Nature of Education." *The Journal of Critical Pedagogy* 2,1 (November).

Progressive Conservative Party of Ontario. 1999. *Ontario PC Blueprint: Mike Harris Plan to Keep Ontario on the Right Track*. Toronto: Ontario P.C. Party, April.

Pokele, G.A. (Presiding Judge). 1998. *R. v. Warren George*. Court Information no.96-0373. Ontario Court of Justice, Provincial Division, Feb. 12.

Porter, J. 1965. *The Vertical Mosaic: An Analysis of Social Class and Power in Canada*. Toronto: University of Toronto Press.

Price, J.A. 1973. "The Stereotyping of North American Indians in Motion Pictures." *Ethnohistory* 5: 153–71.

Purpel, D. 1989. *The Moral and Spiritual Crisis in Education*. Westport, CT: Bergin and Garvey Publishers.

Quinney, R. 1991. *Journey to a Far Place: Autobiographical Reflections*. Philadelphia: Temple University Press.

Quiring, D. 1999. "Accept Our Differences: 'Internalized' Racism and the Culture of Power in Schools." *The Journal of Critical Pedagogy* 2,2 (April).

Reimer, E. 1972. *School Is Dead: Alternatives in Education*. New York: Anchor Books.

Reitz, C. 1998. "Elements of EduAction: Critical Pedagogy and the Community College." *The Journal of Critical Pedagogy* 1,2 (April).

Ritzer, G. 1992. *Classical Sociological Theory*. 2nd ed. Toronto: McGraw-Hill.

Rochon, M., and P. Lepage. 1991. *Oka-Kanehsatake—Summer 1990: A Collective Shock*. Quebec: Commission des droits de la Personne du Québec, April.

Rose, G. 1996. "As If the Mirror Had Bled: Masculine Dwelling, Masculinist Theory and Feminist Masquerade." In N. Duncan, (ed.), *Body Spaces: Destabilizing Geographies of Gender and Sexuality*. London: Routledge.

Rose, S., R.C. Lewontin and L. Kamin. 1984. *Not in Our Genes: Biology, Ideology and Human Nature*. New York: Pantheon Books.

Ross, R. 1996. *Returning to the Teachings: Exploring Aboriginal Justice*. Toronto: Penguin Books.

_____. 1992. *Dancing with a Ghost: Exploring Indian Reality*. Markham, ON: Reed Books Canada.

Roth, R. 1985. "Learning about Gender through Writing: Student Journals in the Undergraduate Classroom." *Teaching Sociology* 12,3 (April): 325–38.

Ruggiero, V.R. 1975. *Beyond Feelings: A Guide to Critical Thinking*. Palo Alto, CA: Mayfield Publications.

Rundblad, G. 1998. "Addressing Social Problems, Focusing on Solutions: The Community Exploration Project." *Teaching Sociology* 26,4 (October): 330–40.

Rushton, P. 1989. "Evolutionary Biology and Heritable Traits (with Reference to Oriental-White-Black Differences)." Paper Presented at the American Association for the Advancement of Science Meeting, San Francisco, Jan. 19.

Safire, W., ed. 1992. *Lend Me Your Ears: Great Speeches in History*. New York: W.W. Norton.

Saltman, K. 1998. "Why Doesn't This Feel Political?" *The Journal of Critical Pedagogy* 2,1 (November).

Scriven, M. 1976. *Reasoning*. New York: McGraw-Hill.

Shariff, A. 1997. "Squeegee Kids' Squeeze Play." <www.Now.com/issues/16/45/News/Feature.html>.

Shawana, C. 1998. "'You Can Always See the Stars Brighter When It Is Dark'— An Exploration of Justice From a First Nations' Perspective." Unpublished paper.

Shor, I. 1987. "Monday Morning Fever: Critical Literacy and the Generative Theme of Work." In I. Shor, (ed.), *Freire for the Classroom: A Sourcebook for Liberatory Teaching*. Portsmouth, NH: Boyton/Cook Publishers.

_____. 1992. *Empowering Education: Critical Teaching for Social Change*. Chicago: University of Chicago Press.

Sociology On-Line. 2000. *The Dialectic*. May 29th. <www.sociologyonline.f9.co.uk/marxism1.htm.>

Shumar, Wesley (1997). *College for Sale: A Critique of the Commodification of Higher Education*. Washington, DC: Falmer Press.

Siddiqui, H. 2000. "Chomsky and Said Stir the Soul." *Toronto Star*, June 18: A13.

Silvera, M. 1989. *Silenced*. Toronto: Sister Vision—Black Women and Women of Colour Press.

Sleeter, C.E. 1993. "How White Teachers Construct Race." In C. McCarthy and W. Crichlow, (eds.), *Race, Identity and Representation in Education*. New York: Routledge.

Solorzano, D. 1989. "Teaching and Social Change: Reflecting on a Freirian Approach to the College Classroom." *Teaching Sociology* 17,2 (April): 218–25.

Sternberg, R.J. 1985. "Teaching Critical Thinking, Part 1: Are We Making Critical Mistakes?" *Phi Delta Kappan* 67,3: 194–98.

Stevens, S. 1997. "Native People within the Judicial System." In A.P. Morrison, (ed.), *Justice for Natives: Searching for Common Ground.* Montreal: McGill-Queen's University Press.

Stice, J., ed. 1987. *Developing Critical Thinking and Problem-Solving Abilities—New Directions for Teaching and Learning.* No. 30. San Francisco: Jossey-Bass.

Sweet, S. 1998a. "Practising Radical Pedagogy: Balancing Ideals with Institutional Constraints." *Teaching Sociology* 26,2 (April): 100–11.

_____. 1998b. "Reassessing Radical Pedagogy" *Teaching Sociology* 26,2 (April): 127–29.

Toronto Star. 2000. "Squeegee Law Faces Challenge." Feb. 1: B1.

Tripp, D. 1993. *Critical Incidents in Teaching: Developing Professional Judgement.* London: Routledge.

Trotman, A. 1993. "African-Caribbean Perspectives of Worldview: C.L.R. James Explores the Authentic Voice." Ph.D. dissertation, Department of Sociology, York University, Toronto.

Tudiver, N. 1999. *Universities for Sale: Resisting Corporate Control over Canadian Higher Education.* Toronto: James Lorimer.

Veblen, T. 1965 [1918]. *The Higher Learning in America: A Memorandum on the Conduct of Universities by Business Men.* New York: Kelley, Reprints of Economic Classics, by arrangement with the Viking Press.

Verma, S. 1999. "Squeegee Kids in Your Face." *Toronto Star*, Sept. 18: B1, B3.

Visano, L. 1983. "Tramps, Tricks and Trouble: Street Transients and Their Controls." In T. Fleming and L. Visano, (eds.), *Deviant Designations: Crime, Law and Deviance in Canada.* Toronto: Butterworths.

_____. 1987. *This Idle Trade.* Concord, ON: Vita Sana Books.

_____. 1988. "Generic and Generative Dimensions of Interactionism: Towards the Unfolding of Critical Dimensions." *International Journal of Comparative Sociology* 29,3–4: 230–43.

_____. 1990a. "The Socialization of Street Kids." In P.A. Adler, P. Adler, and N. Mandell, (eds.), *Sociological Studies of Child Development*, vol. 3. CT: JAI Press.

_____. 1990b. "Crime as a Commodity: Police Use of Informers." *Journal of Human Justice* 2,1 (Autumn): 105–14.

_____. 1992. "Becoming a Hustler." In T. Fleming, (ed.), *Youth Injustice.* Toronto: Canadian Scholars' Press.

_____. 1994. "The Italo-Canadian as the Other: Criminalizing Communities and Communities of Crime." Unpublished paper, Elia Chair in Italian Canadian Studies, Columbus Centre, Toronto, April 13.

_____. 1996. "War on Drugs: From the Politics of Punishment to the Prospects of Peacekeeping." *Addictions: An International Research Journal* 1 (Fall): 81–95.

_____. 1998a. *Crime and Culture.* Toronto: Canadian Scholars' Press.

_____. 1998b. "Profane Paradoxes of Performative Pleasures: Prostitution as a Punitive Practice." In S. McMahon, (ed.), *Women, Crime and Culture.* Toronto: Centre for Police Studies.

Walczak, D., and M. Reuter. 1994. "Using Popular Music to Teach Sociology: An

Evaluation by Students." *Teaching Sociology* 22,3 (July): 266–69.

Wallerstein, N. 1987. "Problem-Posing Education: Freire's Method of Transformation." In I. Shor, (ed.), *Freire in the Classroom: A Sourcebook for Liberatory Teaching.* Portsmouth, NH: Boyton/Cook Publishers.

Webster's New World Dictionary. 1974. Toronto: Nelson, Foster & Scott.

Weber, M. 1969. *Max Weber on Law in Economy and Society.* Cambridge, MA: Harvard University Press.

Wertsch, J.V. 1991. *Voices of the Mind: A Sociocultural Approach to Mediated Action.* Cambridge, MA: Harvard University Press.

West, C. 1993. *Race Matters.* Boston: Beacon Press.

Williams, R. 1977. *Marxism and Literature.* London: Oxford University Press.

Willis, P. 1977. *Learning to Labour: How Working Class Kids Get Working Class Jobs.* London: Gower Press.

Wink, J. 2000. *Critical Pedagogy: Notes from the Real World.* 2nd ed. New York: Addison-Wesley Longman.

Wotherspoon, T., and V. Satzewich. 1993. *First Nations: Race, Class and Gender Relations.* Scarborough, ON: Nelson Canada.

Yeo, F. 1997. *Urban Education, Multiculturalism and Teacher Education.* New York: Garland Publishing.

York, G. 1989. *The Dispossessed: Life and Death in Native Canada.* Toronto: Lester and Orpen Dennys.

York, G., and L. Pindera. 1991. *People of the Pines: The Warriors and the Legacy of Oka.* Toronto: Little, Brown and Company.

York University, Office of the President. 2000. "Announcement." <www.yorku.ca/president/whatsnew/McClelland%20and%20Stewart%20Donation.htm>. June 27.

Young, R.E., ed. 1980. *Fostering Critical Thinking—New Directions for Teaching and Learning.* No. 3. San Francisco: Jossey-Bass.

Young, M.F.D., ed. 1971. *Knowledge and Control.* London: Collier-Macmillan.

Ziegler, M., F. Weizmann, N. Wiener and D. Wiesenthal. 1991. "Phillipe [sic] Rushton and the Growing Acceptance of 'Race-Science.'" In O. McKague, (ed.), *Racism in Canada.* Saskatoon, SK: Fifth House.

INDEX

Action,
  and comfort levels, 45, 60
  educating towards, 41-46, 146
  Moulder's experience with, 60-61
  as a phase of education, 38, 40
  as a phase of problem-posing, 59, 60
  against racism in the criminal justice system, 97
  recommendations of Clyde W. Ford, 60
  strategies, 45
  and youth doing marginal labour, 127-28
"Action-oriented pedagogy," 14
Active learning, 38
Activism and learning, 27
African Americans, 108
African Canadians, 42-44, 46, 49, 108
Anishinabequay, 163
Anti-racism education, 47-51, 68
Asian Canadians, 46, 49
Assembly of First Nations, 95
Assessment of students, 29, 46.
  Also see Grading
Authenticity, 15, 37
  as generated by question and answer, 132
Blacks. *See* African Canadians
Brookfield, S., 10, 34, 35, 37, 51-55, 57
Canada-Cuba Friendshipment

Caravan, 19-20, 22
Canadian Alliance in Solidarity with the Native Peoples (CASNP), 79, 105
Carmichael, Stokely, 108
Cayuga, 87
Chippewa, 105
Chomsky, Noam, 141
"Circle," First Nations talking, 61, 67
  adaptation of, 68-69, 73, 97
Class, 6, 23, 41, 46, 51
  as shown in films, 42
  and hegemony, 30, 31
Class sizes, 3, 143
Coast Salish, 91
"Codes,"
  of First Nations people, 61-73
  Wallerstein's definition of, 59
Codification, 41, 43, 59
  definition of, 39
  of marginal work, 118, 120
"Community-based learning," 38, 40
"Community-building" pedagogy, 69
"Concept-oriented" approach, 40
Controversy, 163
  as a catalyst for structural change, 130
  as feared by the privileged, 132
  as inherent, 3, 5, 129
  as interrelated with global trends, 130-31

Technologically enhanced
learning, 3
Tracking, 31
"Transformative" pedagogy, 33,
38, 144-45
Triangulation, 114
Trust,
and CIQs
and learning, 2, 17, 18
and research participants, 116-
17
and student evaluations, 55
between students and teachers,
111-14
"Underdevelopment," 32
Universities,
commercialization of, 136, 139-
41, 143
and constraints on teachers, 26-
29, 113, 131, 133
and corporate interests, 137-41,
143
as discouraging critical dialogue,
136
needs of, 141-42
and public funding, 138-40
as social institutions, 135-39
and teaching, 131, 133-35
Verstehen, 14
"Voice," 22. *Also see* "First voice"
Wallerstein, Nina, 39, 41, 42, 45,
57, 59, 60, 118
Weber, Max, 14
Wet'suwet'en, 83
Whites,
expression of anger by, 92. *Also
see* Students, anger of
elites among, 96
female, 23
male, 47-48, 58-59, 110

and privilege, 58, 108
as having no race, 57-58
young, 49
Also see European Canadians
WI CHI HI TOOK, 68
WIICH KE YIG (Friends Who
Walk with Us), 79
Women, 22, 23, 42
Youth, 106, 116-17, 119-28
and marginal labour, 117, 118,
120-29